AN EXISTENTIAL APPROACH TO HUMAN DEVELOPMENT

AN EXISTENTIAL APPROACH TO HUMAN DEVELOPMENT

PHILOSOPHICAL AND THERAPEUTIC PERSPECTIVES

MARTIN ADAMS

macmillan education
palgrave

First published 2018 by
PALGRAVE

Palgrave in the UK is an imprint of Springer Nature Limited, registered in England, company number 785998, of 4 Crinan Street, London, N1 9XW.

Palgrave® is a registered trademark in the United States, the United Kingdom, Europe and other countries.

ISBN 978–1–137–50473–9

This book is printed on paper suitable for recycling and made from fully managed and sustained forest sources. Logging, pulping and manufacturing processes are expected to conform to the environmental regulations of the country of origin.

A catalogue record for this book is available from the British Library.

A catalog record for this book is available from the Library of Congress.

For Willow and Robyn,
who are just beginning to
discover the mystery and
excitement of existence.

Banquo: If you can look into the seeds of time,
And say which grain will grow and which will not,
Speak then to me, who neither beg nor fear
Your favours nor your hate.
Macbeth 1: 3
William Shakespeare

CONTENTS

ACKNOWLEDGEMENTS

In one sense this book is the product of everyone I have ever met, everything I have ever done and also of the many people I have not met and things I have not done. They all played their part and all were valuable.

Having said that the contribution of some particular individuals needs to be acknowledged.

I would like to thank Emmy van Deurzen for having the faith in the project of an existential approach to human development at all by giving me the space to develop and teach the course which eventually gave rise to this book.

I would like to thank Barbara Karban and Prunella Gee for their particular insights into the project.

I would also like to thank the students and trainees at the New School of Psychotherapy and Counselling, and elsewhere, for contributing to this book in their different ways. They have always asked the best questions. This is how knowledge develops.

I would also like to thank all my past and present clients and supervisees whose wisdom and courage have taught me more than they could ever have imagined.

I would also like to thank Peter Hooper and his editorial staff at Palgrave for making the whole process so painless.

Last but not least, I need to thank Penny for tolerating the many occasions my attention was distracted by writing, rewriting, organising and reorganising this book.

You are all in your different ways present in these pages.

INTRODUCTION

In a frequently paraphrased passage, the Danish philosopher Søren Kierkegaard wrote that,

> It is perfectly true, as philosophers say, that life must be understood backwards. But they forget the other proposition, that it must be lived forwards. And if one thinks over that proposition it becomes more and more evident that life can never really be understood in time because at no particular moment can I find the necessary resting place from which to understand it.
>
> Kierkegaard (1996: 161)

One of the philosophers he was referring to was Arthur Schopenhauer who said, 'The first forty years of life furnish the text, while the remaining thirty supply the commentary; and that without the commentary we are unable to understand aright the true sense and coherence of the text, together with the moral it contains and all the subtle application of which it admits' (2004: 94).

That these two writers are talking about human development is obvious, but what human development is, is less obvious. Questions like these follow from the insights of Kierkegaard and Schopenhauer, *What is it that develops, from what to what and how does it happen?* and *What do we mean when we use the word 'develop'?* and *How do I write the story of my life; my autobiography?* These are questions that will recur in the pages that follow.

At a point that turned out to be about halfway through the writing of this book it felt like not only that I'd been writing it forever but also that it would never be finished. That some of this introduction was written after I had finished is an example of the truth of Kierkegaard's words.

Another question that recurred was *Why am I writing this book, and not another, or no book at all?* Depending on when I asked it I gave a different answer. One answer is because the subject has been given far less attention by existential psychotherapists than the existential philosophers gave it. But although interesting, this answer does not go far enough; there are personal reasons. I am writing it because I have always been intrigued by time and the mystery of the space between birth and death. What it means to make and then lose a life.

I can mark the beginning of my formal interest in this as the time I decided to do a psychology degree. Like many people, then and since, I was naïve in that I thought I would find out something about how both myself and other people 'worked'. I didn't know and I wanted to know. If I found out, I thought, I would be able to live better and life would be easier. Psychology seemed a good place to start. The alternative, formal art training, didn't at that time hold the same promise, but in hindsight could possibly have been more fruitful. Instead I learnt a great deal about statistics and the inappropriateness of natural science for looking at the nature of human beings and in hindsight I am glad I did as I would never have done it by choice.

Instead of psychology, I spent my time reading fiction and philosophy. Fiction in particular seemed to me to contain the most truth about the everyday struggles of life, or as I later came to term it, the human striving for meaning and purpose in an indifferent universe. They were also better written than the psychology textbooks. The task of the novelist, the philosopher and also the therapist is to facilitate reacquaintance with something both known and unknowable: life. This is the reason why Sartre, Camus, Beauvoir and others wrote novels and plays. Camus particularly felt that fiction was a legitimate form of philosophy; he said, 'People can only think in images. If you want to be a philosopher, write novels' (1996: 10). Theory and philosophy are abstract and say what something is about; fiction says what it is like. A review of the ways fiction represents human development is outside the scope of this book, but in the meantime readers can start with Mendelson (2007) and Weinstein (2003, 2011).

R.D. Laing was my introduction to phenomenology, existentialism and psychotherapy, and in this sense I started writing this book fifty years ago. Actually, I started writing it long before that, when I first started to wonder about the kind of world I was born into and what its possibilities could be. That was when I started to write my autobiography, although I wouldn't have called it that then. Life was just beginning, and unlike now, over fifty years later, death was little more than a theoretical possibility.

But most of all I learnt from experience. When starting this book I was reminded of Laing's words in *The Politics of Experience*. He begins it like this,

> Few books today are forgivable. Black on the canvas, silence on the screen, an empty white sheet of paper, are perhaps feasible. [...] The requirement of the present, the failure of the past is the same: to provide a thoroughly self-conscious and self-critical account of man. [...] Even facts become fictions without adequate ways of seeing 'the facts'. We do not need theories so much as the experience that is the source of the theory.
>
> (1967: 11–15)

He means, What can be said? By what authority do we say anything? These too are points I will return to.

At various times the subject of this book has been met by my colleagues with either scepticism or enthusiasm but rarely indifference, and I have come to regard it as a research project. It is an attempt to clarify, to understand something that seemed to me to be unclear, undeveloped (there's that word again) or misunderstood. As it is a research project it has a central question that is, *What are the characteristics of an existential phenomenological model of human development?*

Every research project has to make clear what kind of evidence it will value. When I say this is a research project I am talking phenomenologically, and by this I mean that it is my research project. It is my book and I take full responsibility for everything in it. Not in a narcissistic or grandiose way, but phenomenologically and existentially. The views represented here can only be the views I have gained as a result of my life experiences. How could it be any other way? But I am not talking about simple subjectivity here; I am talking about, as Martin Heidegger would put it, my experiences as a being-in-the-world.

When making sense of anything, we always select some features and deselect others. An artist draws in order that they can see, and the more they see, the more they become aware not just of what they are looking at, but also of themselves as interpreters. When I draw a landscape, for example, I have to decide how to represent, or rather, how to re-present the hills and the trees. This point is illustrated by the following story (quoted in Hare 2002). Alfred Munnings – a painter in the classical tradition, the artistic equivalent of the natural scientific tradition – commenting on the work of Picasso said, 'Picasso cannot paint a tree.' To which Picasso is alleged to have replied, 'He's right, I can't paint a tree. But I can paint the feeling you have when you look at a tree.'

There is a link between Picasso and the tree that makes the tree in the painting simultaneously personal and universal. Munnings' tree can only ever be particular. We can never be separate from the objects we perceive and Picasso knew this. In fact the emergence of photography in the mid-nineteenth century allowed artists to get closer to the objects as well as closer to themselves as perceiving beings. Attending, concentrating, helps us to see. But attending is not easy, especially these days, as Matthew Crawford (2016) reminds us. The success of an artist can be measured in the way something singular and intensely personal, for example Picasso's *Guernica*, can become at the same time profoundly universal. At this point it can be said to contain phenomenological and existential truth rather than either objective or subjective truth. This kind of understanding is not gained by reading the explanation in the catalogue. It has to be experienced, by attending to it, opening to it and experiencing what it has to say, by truly seeing it. This is also the kind of truth Mark Rothko was aiming at (Rothko 1987). But there is a paradox here, as Picasso also said, 'We all know that art is not truth. Art is a lie that makes us realize truth' (Fry 1966: 165). This sort of truth is based on experience. It is also dynamic and is dependent on context.

As Laing said, consistency in how we find things out and what sort of evidence we value is important for effective living and in philosophy this is called epistemology. Epistemologically the research method used to investigate a subject will always produce findings in accordance with the assumptions of the research method. It is therefore important that the assumptions of the research method match what is being researched. Although natural science can give us a lot of interesting and useful facts about the material world its assumptions are derived from the qualities of the material world, not the human world. Natural science takes a positivist position. Human beings do not share the qualities of the material world because we have freedom of choice and respond differently depending on context.

Social constructionism (e.g. Burman 2008) has enabled us to understand something of how our understandings are embedded in and defined by our social and cultural contexts, but they confine their critiques to the social and cultural arenas and because they do not acknowledge either the psychological or the ontological dimensions of experience, the individual can get lost. I will therefore not be taking a relativist social constructionist position. Instead I will be taking a position of ontological constructivism; acknowledging firstly that there is a world that exists independently of our perceptions, theories and constructions, and that this world is not just a social world – its parameters are those of existence; and secondly that we construct our understanding of this world from our own experience of it. Implicit in this is that there is no possibility of attaining a single, correct understanding of the world, what Hilary Putnam (1999) describes as a 'God's eye view' that is independent of any particular viewpoint. A simpler way of saying all this is that, yes, we are all subject to a world of constraint, randomness and chance – we can call these the givens of existence – but the ways that we strive for meaning and purpose throughout our lives is down to the ways we understand these givens at every particular moment of our lives.

A few words are necessary about the nature and structure of the book. Some books are writers' books in which the writer does most of the work and then presents it. Other books are readers' books in which the reader is required to fill in the empty spaces, pursue their own paths of enquiry and even to argue with what is being said. Readers' books are those that open up rather than narrow down the field of speculation. One specific area in which this book can be a readers' book is in the area of psychotherapeutic case illustrations and exercises. Although I have given some general pointers, the number of topics that can be used for such illustrations is simply too great and too variable for each one to be illustrated in any meaningful way in a book of this size. I have therefore decided not to include any, preferring to leave it up to readers to apply the ideas to their own lives and to their therapeutic experience.

It is also not just intended for those well versed in the existential literature. In order to make it accessible I have endeavoured to write with a minimum of technical jargon and when I do use it, I explain it and it is because the ideas cannot be referred to in any other way and their provenance needs to be acknowledged.

Also I have come to prefer the phrase 'life cycle', rather than the more conventional 'life span', or 'life course', because it contextualises life within all past and all future, within both human time and eternal time. It is a human conceit to see all life on earth in terms of the span of one current human life. All life on earth is interdependent.

The book is divided into three parts. In Part I, I introduce and contextualise human development existentially and phenomenologically.

In Part II I review the life and work of six major existential philosophers, Søren Kierkegaard, Friedrich Nietzsche, Martin Heidegger, Jean-Paul Sartre, Maurice Merleau-Ponty and Simone de Beauvoir, with respect to their references to human development and to psychotherapy. I will also be talking about their lives, not just because it is interesting, but because how we live, think, feel and develop are inextricably linked. We know this from both clinical and personal experience.

But in reviewing their work, some problems arise. They all wrote in different ways, with different specialist terms, from different vantage points and for different purposes, and they also used different literary genres to develop their ideas. Also, the time span between the birth of Kierkegaard (1813) – one year before Stephenson's first steam locomotive – and the death of Beauvoir (1986) – two years after the first Apple computer – is long: 173 years; and these reasons make it hard to compare like with like without abstracting and potentially losing much of what is valuable from each. Although they all referred to human development, their contribution has not previously been summarised in the way I am doing here and I believe there is a value in stating clearly what each have said and let them speak for themselves.

Nevertheless some common experiential themes recur throughout their work and in Part III I reflect on the implications these have for therapeutic practice.

In common with usual conventions, unless the sense demands otherwise, I will be using masculine and feminine pronouns to refer to people as a whole. I have also tried to use the distancing third person (he, she, one, they, people, etc.) only when unavoidable, preferring to keep the issues more experience-near.

But more than this, as the central axis around which this book revolves is one of age, the dominant voice will be the adult voice, because I am adult and also because the readership will be adult. This means that I will be using the first person (I, we) when referring to adult experience. In contrast, when talking about infancy and childhood, I will be using the third person.

A dilemma arises though when talking about what I could call the final two or three decades of the expected life cycle. Although I am in this period myself there is no guarantee that the readership will be. The question then arises about whether I should use the more experience-near first person, knowing that many readers will not be a part of this collective 'we', or the more distancing third person which would suggest that it was someone other than me writing. If I was to do the latter, though, I would be complicit in the familiar marginalisation of this section of the population, as 'they', as 'others'. With the priority of making the text easy to read and understand I have hopefully steered a course between the two, acknowledging both when necessary.

PART I

1

A Short History of Human Development

The questions addressed by human development are the questions that human beings have asked themselves ever since they were able to reflect on their existence. They are,

Who am I?

How shall I live?

What happens after I die?

The way an individual responds to these questions goes towards answering the overarching question, *What is the story of my life?*

All the world's cultures and religions have stories, we could call them myths, about how humans came to be, what their life task is and what happens after death.

It is worth considering here what is meant by myth. Armstrong (2006) notes that myths are ways of making existence comprehensible and meaningful in human terms and that they can be thought of as overdetermined, or thick narratives, which explain the fundamental dilemmas of life.

They are ways of thinking about experiences that cannot easily or perhaps ever be put into language. They are not meant to be objectively true, but rather have a temporary sense of truth that resonates with experience. Their purpose is to make life seem coherent and understandable. They are living stories, readers' stories, and in this sense they are forms of theory in the sense that they fulfil the three criteria that a theory needs to have: to make sense of the past, to inform present understanding and to have some predictive power. They are about what really matters to all human beings; they are about issues of birth, life and death. Myths, as ways of making sense of experience, have narrative truth; history on the other hand aspires to having objective scientific truth.

Since myths are products of constant human interpretation it would be more accurate to refer to them not with the familiar noun, i.e. 'myth', since this gives them a status that does match their true nature, but with the more unfamiliar verb, 'to myth', since this emphasises not only the human action involved in making sense of life but also that they can change. Myths are not things separate from us that we have; they are stories we make up that help us to live with meaning and purpose. They are parts of our autobiography. In an analogous way, life, and self, can be changed into 'living', which is familiar, and 'selving' which is not. We make myths that try to answer our existential questions about the dilemmas and paradoxes of life.

Human development in mythology

The earliest known surviving written story is the Assyrian epic of Gilgamesh, written and recorded anonymously and in poetic form by different authors about 4,000 years ago. In examining the human desire for eternal life of some sort, it is about one person's path through life to wisdom. It charts how in our struggle against the inevitability of death and the desire to leave something behind us, we come to be formed by our choices and values as much as our successes and failures.

That there are so many variations on the Greek myths is testament to the idea that myths are used to understand experience and each one was an alternative understanding. The Greek myths used a metaphorical language that all Greeks were familiar with and all eras, our own included, produce stories cast in the preoccupations of the time and place.

One of the greatest writers of the Roman period, Ovid, wrote and recorded stories about the intensity, passion and ambiguity of love and the capriciousness of the gods of chance, and his timeless stories about the continuity of change have been a source of inspiration for writers through the ages from Shakespeare to Bob Dylan.

It seems to be a human tendency to anthropomorphise both the givens of existence and also the human qualities. The ancient Greeks had many different myths about the beginning of the world and by extension the beginning of each individual person's world, and the Gods who were immortal, embodied these. One such myth is that at the dawn of creation. Out of Chaos, the formless void, came Gaia, earth; Tartarus, the space under the earth; and Eros, desire.

In another, Chronos, individual time, age, became distinguished from Aion, eternal time. The latter is usually translated into aeon, and taken to refer to a very long time, when being eternal, it is unmeasurable. Only age can be measured; eternal time cannot be measured. The cyclical nature of eternal time – creation and destruction, birth and death – is represented in many cultures as well as the ancient Greeks by the ouroboros, a serpent eating its own tail.

Another way the life cycle is represented in Greek mythology is in the myth of the Moirai. The Romans knew them as the Parcae. The Moirai – the three Fates, Clotho, Lachesis and Atropos – were above both the gods and men, and controlled the life of every mortal. Using the then familiar metaphor of spinning, Clotho was called upon in the ninth month of pregnancy to give a skein of wool to Lachesis who spun and measured the length of the thread of life – the length of each person's life – and when their time was up Atropos chose the manner of each person's death and she cut their thread of life with her shears. A more contemporary version of Atropos is the Grim Reaper.

Another representation of the life cycle is the better known Oedipus myth, and it is represented by the riddle that the Sphinx, who terrorises Thebes, poses to Oedipus, a man who is trying to find out his origins and what his purpose in life is. The riddle is, 'What being, with only one voice, has sometimes two feet, sometimes three, sometimes four, and is weakest when it has the most?' (Graves 1960: 10)

As we know, the answer that Oedipus gets, fresh from murdering the person he later discovers is his father Laius, is mankind and the Sphinx, who represents the arresting of development and therefore of time, dies as a result of its riddle being solved and Oedipus is feted as the saviour of Thebes. The plot, as told by Sophocles (1947), who lived to be ninety years old, does not mention the riddle or the solution, and unfolds in a series of flashbacks, which is just the way insight occurs: after the event, in hindsight. As Kierkegaard said, life is lived forwards but understood backwards.

While there were powers over which even the Gods had no influence, we should not get the idea that Oedipus' fate was unavoidable once it had been announced by the oracle at Delphi; this would destroy his tragic dignity as a person who brought his misfortune upon himself by his human frailty. His is the familiar story of a good person coming to a bad end by an error of judgement. Oedipus might have said, as most of us have said at one time or another, *it seemed like a good idea at the time*. The omnipresence of tragedy tests our faith, and this is a tension that is with us throughout life.

In Oedipus' case, his demand for and subsequent acquisition of knowledge about his past gave him both power and an enormous responsibility. The tragic and universal element of the story is that the idea of the future can only be grasped by an understanding of our connectedness to the past. When Nietzsche writes in *The Birth of Tragedy* (1993) about life being tragic he means it in the sense that life is perpetually poised between form and order on the one hand, and formlessness and chaos on the other. Life is tragic because it is about persevering against the forces of formlessness in the full knowledge that we will sooner or later return to formlessness.

The medieval period

The Middle Ages in Europe was a time when numerical systems were used to bring order to many different areas of human understanding. One was Gothic architecture. Another was human development and there were many different schemes that divided life into three, four, five, six, seven, ten or twelve parts or phases, both linear and circular, of varying sophistication and complexity, but their portrayal all followed the same pattern (Sears 1986). Because verbal literacy was not widespread and printing did not emerge until the late medieval period the schemes were invariably represented visually. Art and sculpture were the mass media of the day. All the schemes covered the time from birth and infancy to decline and death, and each age was represented by the figure of a man, rarely a woman, who revealed his 'age' through his physical appearance and actions, illustrated by the symbolism of the time. This visual language would have been understood by all who saw them. Many of the schemes were a combination of a number of different cultural influences and Christianity was only one of these influences. Although post-dating the medieval era, Nicholas Poussin's (1636) painting *A Dance to the Music of Time* is one such. It is also the inspiration for Anthony Powell's sequence of novels of the same name.

Although best known for *The Divine Comedy*, one such system is referred to by Dante Alighieri (1265–1321). In the *Convivio* (1308) he talks about the life cycle in the language of Hippocrates: the four humours, and also the metaphor of the cycle of the year representing a single life. The life cycle is spilt into four parts; the seasons, up to age seventy. In this he borrowed from Psalm 90: 10. The first period (0–25) he calls adolescence, and it corresponds to spring and is hot and moist. The next (25–45) is adulthood. This is maturity and corresponds to summer and is hot and dry. This is followed by old age (45–70), which corresponds to autumn and is cold and dry. The final period is senility (70–death) and corresponds to winter and is cold and wet. Dante's final part is what we now call the third and fourth ages (Laslett 1989; Higgs and Gilliard 2015). The peak age for Dante then is the middle of maturity, about thirty-five, which incidentally is also the age when the main character in *The Divine Comedy*, also called Dante, enters his own crisis of meaning, wondering what the story of his life will turn out to be. It is ultimately from Dante that we get the contemporary idea of the mid-life crisis. Significantly he also describes a period of eight months prior to these four, which corresponds to gestation in the womb. Something also interesting about this is his idea of the length of the life cycle, about eighty years. He arrived at this for two reasons: firstly, it was that it was the age Plato was alleged to have died at, and secondly, it was the age that Christ would have lived to had he not been crucified. It is a contemporary misconception that it is only recently that people have lived into and beyond the seventh decade (Thane 2005). The average longevity in previous eras may well have been much lower than now but this was primarily because of high infant mortality. People were more familiar with death; it happened to all ages, not just the old. That it was not that unusual that people lived into old age is shown by the painting and literature of the time. Perhaps it is the nature of the people of every era to rewrite history with themselves as special and different and in some way not just more than everything that came before but also the most that could ever be.

The idea of a post-infancy childhood is also relatively recent. For example, until the end of biological dependence in the medieval period, people were distinguished only by their physical ability to work. At age seven a boy was expected to look after the village geese, at eight the pigs, and at nine he helped with the oxen, and so on (Hagen 2001: 24). Ariès (1962) agrees that children were given no special attention, affection or care by older members of the family or community.

Shakespeare

Shakespeare (1564–1616) makes a number of references to the life cycle but he is best known for his often quoted Seven Ages of Man from *As You Like It*. While to contemporary readers these ages may have some resonance even from 500 or so years away, it is important to contextualise this classification for it gives a particular spin to the life cycle. This is emphasised by the start of Jacques' speech which is,

> *All the world's a stage,*
>
> *And all the men and women merely players;*
>
> *They have their exits and their entrances,*
>
> *And one man in his time plays many parts,* (2: VII)

This suggests determinism and that 'the script of our lives has been written and the parts are all fixed' (Neiman 2014: 212). While the ideas would certainly have been current, we must be careful not to see the speech as Shakespeare's own view, or as fact, or as representing mainstream sixteenth-century English thinking about human development. This is because the speech is spoken by Jacques whose description of his own melancholy throughout the play is so extreme that no one else takes him seriously. An alternative view is put earlier on in the play by the older servant Adam, who describes his own ageing as, 'a lusty winter,

Frosty, but kindly' (2: III) and this provides a counterbalance to Jacques' view of ageing as 'second childishness and mere oblivion, Sans teeth/ sans eyes, sans taste, sans everything.'

Whereas Jacques is speaking from the position of relative youth not knowing how to use the time remaining to him, and anxious about his own death, Adam is speaking from other end of life and of knowing how to use time well. Nevertheless Jacques' view often matches how the life cycle is represented in our current era. It is certainly a way to make sense of the inevitability of ageing, but not the only way, as is shown by some of Shakespeare's other older characters like Falstaff, Lear, Prospero and Shylock. Shakespeare wanted us to ask questions, not to give us answers. He wrote for readers.

Slightly prior to but known to Shakespeare and anticipating the Enlightenment was the philosopher Michel de Montaigne (1533–1592). In his essay *Of the Education of Children* (1580), he notes both the importance and the difficulty of educating children. In words that contemporary policy makers could do well to acknowledge, he said that 'we often take very great pains, and consume a good part of our time in training up children to things, for which, by their natural constitution, they are totally unfit'.

And turning the tables on the question of who is teaching whom, he says, anticipating Kierkegaard, that 'They begin to teach us to live when we have almost done living.'

The Enlightenment

What became known as the Enlightenment was a philosophical movement that dominated Europe in the eighteenth century with different national emphases. For example, in France it became associated with individual liberty, scientific empiricism and with the questioning of religious authority. One of the Enlightenment philosopher Jean-Jacques Rousseau's best-known works is *Emile, or On Education* (1979) and in it he considered the physical, emotional and social development of the child for perhaps the first time in European history and in direct contrast to the prevailing orthodoxy; it was not popular with the French government of the day, who had it burnt.

Rousseau split what we now call the period between birth and early adulthood into five 'Ages'. The first (0–12) was the Age of Nature, and emphasised the value of the development of the physical senses and free play. The second (12–15) was the Age of Reason and was characterised by the disciplined application of physical abilities gained earlier. The third (15–20) was the Age of Force, Energy and Vitality of Life and was when formal, but child-centred education should begin and sexuality be discovered. The fourth (20–25) was the Age of Wisdom in which the person began to understand the meaning of complex human emotions, relationships and citizenship. The fifth (25–death) was the Age of Maturity and would follow on naturally if the needs of the previous four Ages were addressed.

William Blake came from a tradition of radical dissent and had a complex relationship with the Enlightenment but he shared Rousseau's view of childhood. Whereas children were previously thought about as deficient adults who needed to be taught the ways of the world, Blake repositioned the child as openness and innocence and constrained by adulthood and adult institutions.

Although the Enlightenment marked a change in attitude that acknowledged the existence of children and childhood, for example in the establishment of Foundling Hospitals in eighteenth-century Europe, and in Wordsworth's 1807 poem that contained the line 'The child is father of the man' (1994: 91, l.7) change was gradual and it was not until 1870 that the UK Education Act brought in compulsory education for children between five and ten.

Modernism

In the nineteenth century, science, and its application in technology and industrialisation, was seen as offering a brighter future. It was also in the nineteenth century that psychology was born as a discipline separate from both philosophy and religion and the route it took to do this was to ally itself to the new sciences. Nietzsche, for one, felt that the emphasis that the Enlightenment put on reason, on the notion of scientific objectivity, devalued the authority of human experience. But neither philosophers like Nietzsche and Kierkegaard nor psychologists like William James could stop this cultural and ideological turn towards positivism. Psychology then became established as the natural scientific study of behaviour and it was not for another 100 years or so that its horizon was widened to include reported experience as in the cognitive turn in the 1970s and the development of phenomenological research methods later on. It is with the birth of scientific psychology that we see the start of the separate discipline of human development, which invariably meant child development, and in this way there was a turning away from considering the whole of life to a concentration on childhood.

Taking the philosophical lead from the Enlightenment, in the late nineteenth century Freud placed enormous importance on childhood and gave almost no importance to any other part of life. Jung took the opposite view. And in line with the dominant thinking of the age, psychoanalysis cast its assertions in mechanistic and positivist terms. It thought of the mind in terms of hydraulics and of energy passing from one part of the mind to another and that dysfunction, neurosis, lack of development, was due to blockages in the passage of energy. While there is some evidence that Freud was using these terms metaphorically, the model persists to the present day and reached its extreme in Wilhelm Reich's literal understanding of the psychic economy model.

In terms of other psychotherapy theories and the way they thought about human development through the life cycle, behaviourism and learning theory on the one hand had little to say and was in any case establishing its natural scientific credentials. The humanistic tradition on the other hand, perhaps in opposition to the concentration psychoanalysis gave to childhood, concentrated on adulthood and although Abraham Maslow (1962) and Charlotte Bühler (Bühler and Massarik 1968) referred developmentally to the whole of life, their ideas have had little influence on the world of psychotherapy but have led to the work of Gould (1979) and Baumeister (1992).

Natural science and stage theory

Any investigation, and psychotherapy is an investigation, needs an appropriate research method that will produce reliable findings. Although this is familiar enough to researchers, something not often acknowledged in psychotherapy is that all theories are based on theories of how to make theories. Most therapeutic perspectives – the existential perspective is the exception – do not make it at all clear how they derived the ideas that constitute their theories.

Natural science assumes the independence of the observer from the observed and it works very well with inanimate objects, but does not work well with people, because we are never independent from each other. The prototype natural science question is, *Why ...?*, and it hopes to explain, to find causation and objective truths, and is seen in the various stage theories which have had and continue to have considerable influence in psychotherapy theory and practice. These theories conceptualise life as consisting of fixed chronologically derived stages, phases or periods and change is from one to another, rather like going up a ladder with the rungs as invariant stages. A person progresses from a simple and immature level of behaviour towards more and more complex levels. Looking at all the stage theories together it is not easy to get a consensus of the principles of human development. They can be superficially distinguished by the number of stages they have. Some have two (Freud 1911; Klein 1946), some three (Fairbairn 1952; Grotstein and Rinsley 1994), some four (Winnicott 1991), some five (Freud 1923; Maslow 1962), some seven (Jung 1934), some eight (Erikson 1950; Marcia 1980); or more (Sheehy

1976; Levinson 1980 and 1996). Bowlby (1969, 1988) does not talk so much about stages as of critical periods. Some (Jung 1934; Fairbairn 1952; Grotstein and Rinsley 1994) have stages with transitions between the stages.

But the number of stages is the least interesting difference. What is more important is not that they have stages at all or that few consider the whole of life, but that they all claim to have discovered fixed rules of human development.

In his critique of Descartes, the philosopher Gilbert Ryle (1949) says that a category error is when a quality of one group of constructs is attributed erroneously to another group of constructs. Using natural science to investigate human qualities leads to the category error of mechanistic qualities of causation being attributed to human beings. This process is also called reification (Laing 1965, 1971; Rycroft 1972) and because of this, stage theories can only deal with the structural dimensions of development and not the existential dimensions (Silverman 1979).

The historical psychologist Jan van den Berg (1961) pointed out that before the modernist era, discontinuity, leaps and accidents were accepted as being more descriptive of the life cycle and furthermore that stage theory in general is an artefact of economics and the socio-political dominance of natural science.

In his phenomenological critique of stage theory, Briod (1989) says that what happens when natural science looks at human development is that the textured world of lived time and space is cut up into its so-called constituent parts and then reconstituted to what it 'really' is.

Both Fourcher (1981) and Kagan (1984) suggest that with respect to developmental theory a large amount of incompatible assertions have arisen which are themselves untrustworthy because the founding principles are flawed.

Although written over thirty years ago and being echoed in more recent years by narrative writers like McAdams (1993) and Sugarman (2001, 2012), and by no means being solitary voices, these critiques have had comparatively little effect on the way human development is thought about in psychotherapy theory and practice.

The cultural dominance of natural science and positivism has led, as van den Berg (1961) says, to the assumptions of natural science becoming embedded not only in the theories but in the cultural discourse about human development. Stages are taken as human fact when they are an artefact of the research method and cultural assumptions. Although some elements of stage theories undoubtedly have some resonance with everyday experience, they are unable to account for the very qualities that are most distinctive of human life: the ability to choose, to hope and to love and the need to live with meaning and purpose.

In psychology and psychotherapy the debate about human development has been dominated by three principles (Keenan and Evans 2009):

1. Continuity versus discontinuity. The question here is, *Do we develop gradually, or do we develop in steps, or stages?* Stage theories have been most influential but whether they are read literally or metaphorically the critical feature is that the order is fixed and that passage through them is one way only.
2. Stability versus change. The question here is, *When we develop, in what sense do we become different from the way we were?* This question is tied into the debate about the importance of early experience with the consequent idea that we can become as if 'stuck' at an earlier time, or stage, and hence not change.
3. Nature versus nurture. The question here is, *What has the greatest influence on us and our development; what we are born with, or what happens to us?* While the current answer is that they are in continuous and reciprocal interaction, it does not stop either nature or nurture having their adherents. It is still a live debate. Those theories that emphasise nature are essentialist theories in that they propose that our personality is fixed and while being psychological, they are nevertheless biological because they enable distinct chronological periods to be identified and defined. Those theories that emphasise nurture focus on the influence of the environment in the way human characteristics are created and then made into tradition. Neither nature- nor nurture-based theories are able to accommodate human freedom and choice. Also in their different ways they both give primacy to the authority of the experience of the observer rather than the observed.

Alternatives to this debate are Baltes' (1987) life span theory and Cohler's (1982) life narrative theory that conceptualise human development in terms of processes rather than essences, and say that development:

- is lifelong;
- is multidimensional and multidirectional. Multidimensional, because it cannot be described by an increase or a decrease in a single criterion. And multidirectional because there is no single normal path that can be taken. Different pathways can appear to lead to the same place, and vice versa;
- is situated in context and history. Not only is human development different in different eras and cultures, but it is not possible to understand

an individual without understanding their personal biography as well as their social and cultural context.

These suggest that chronological age is at best a gross oversimplification and at worst a distraction, and by focusing on life processes rather than chronology, they have contributed to the idea that the person is actively engaged in a process of self-determination rather than passively moving through fixed stages independent of context.

2

Thinking Phenomenologically and Existentially about Human Development

Phenomenology

Previously referred to by Kant and Hegel, in the early years of the twentieth century Edmund Husserl developed phenomenology into a way of researching into the nature of experience, of consciousness. As such, it investigates human qualities and is therefore a more appropriate research method for the human sciences. Natural science can only talk about a life as viewed from without, whereas phenomenology can talk about a life as lived from within. Literally, phenomenology means the study of how things appear to consciousness. But these appearances are not simple or obvious; they are complex and ambiguous, and our assumptions, our theories about them, influence how we interpret them. Phenomenology acknowledges the impossibility of separating the objective and the subjective and instead tries to find the relationship between them.

Everybody creates his or her own precursors and one of Husserl's was Franz Brentano. From Brentano he took the idea of intentionality, that when we are conscious we are always conscious of something in particular. Our consciousness is like a light we shine on the world we are a part of, and that we are always making sense of the phenomena, the elements of experience, that we apprehend. We are never simply observers; we are always participant observers. Heidegger later incorporated this into his idea of being-in-the-world.

In contrast to natural science, the prototypical phenomenological question is, *What is it like that ...?* and the answer leads to description rather than explanation. In eliciting successive descriptions and resisting asking *Why?*, the phenomenologist stays experience-near. We know this as the common injunction *describe don't explain* and phenomenology aims to arrive at an understanding of individual human experience not by explaining it with a number of fixed laws but by opening out the richness and mystery of life by successive description a bit like the way an artist works, but more systematic.

Husserl called our tendency to see the things we want to see our *natural way of seeing* and he is using the word 'natural' to mean 'usual' rather than 'most basic'. An element of this is that we see the world as being separate from our experience of it, as in natural science, rather than seeing it as something that we are a part of and that we create. Phenomenology is a way to reduce the effect of this natural attitude and see things as if for the first time, assumption-free. It is a way we can become more aware of the assumptions we make about ourselves and the world and also understand the self that is created in the process of relating to the world. This process is called reflexivity and our capacity for self-awareness is a product of our reflexivity.

These assumptions are like filters that distort and determine how we see the world. We sometimes get a glimpse of this when we go to somewhere new and notice it with a more heightened sense of awareness than at home, where we are surrounded by familiar objects. Children can do this more easily than adults – to them everything is new. They are not so weighed down by their assumptions about how things are, or how they wish them to be.

Our worldview, as Husserl called it, is the sum total of our assumptions about the world and the more we become aware of it the more we understand that ours is only one vantage point among many.

The primary question of phenomenology is therefore,

> *How can I understand anything without first understanding that which does the understanding?*

Phenomenology is the basis of the practice of existential therapy and by being phenomenological, the existential therapist endeavours to be aware of their assumptions about what the client is saying and aims just to attend and be curious about what it all means.

Every phenomenological investigation begins with and is sustained by attention and by attending to our own attending, by being reflexive, we become aware of the assumptions we are making about what we are attending to. Because phenomenology is systematic it has characteristic actions and interventions that have been formalised into the skills of existential therapy and these need to be applied carefully and systematically if the results are to be reliable (Deurzen and Adams 2016).

Phenomenology and human development

Looking phenomenologically at the life cycle immediately presents us with a problem. This is that we are perpetually situated in a context, a situation, from which we view and construct the world. We always look at it from a particular place. This raises Kierkegaard's question, paraphrased as *What is the best way to describe a life?* From what vantage point? The point of view of the other, looking forward, looking back, in the present ... or what?

Most writing on the life cycle, and most other subjects, is by adults simply because they have the biological and economic power to do so. Existential and phenomenological writers are no exception. This gives an adult middle-aged and usually male-centred view to existence and the life cycle. Looking at the life cycle from an adult point of view gives rise to the notion of three parts of life that are seen as being separate from each other only because of where they are viewed from.

Childhood is viewed as having happened – how it was. With respect to childhood, or anything in the past, the way we remember our childhood is always as a remembering adult. Young people often say that older people do not understand them. But those older have had the experience of being young, although they may forget its impact on them, while those younger are yet to have the experience of being older.

Adulthood is viewed as presently happening. It is hard to make any judgement about its significance or banality. We usually only find out later. Sometimes much later. Sometimes never. There is no perspective or way of looking at it based on distance in time to see how it is.

Old age is usually viewed from the point of view of an adulthood that has no direct experience of it, only imaginative and inferred. It is not immediate, nor is it reconstructed. We do not know anything about the part of life to come, because we have not been there, but we have to project ourselves into it. We can never understand the experience of someone older than ourselves in the same way that we can potentially understand the experience of someone younger. Old people are not like us, they are other, and this is translated into everyday ageism because it is associated with death. Ageism as a term is relatively recent, being coined first by Robert Butler in 1969. But being associated with death at least in the eyes of the young, means that it has an existential dimension. A recent study (RSPH: 2018) suggest that it is the most commonly experienced form of prejudice and discrimination in the UK and Europe and also the form most likely to go unchallenged.

With respect to the difference between a child's and an adult's experience, Briod (1989: 117) notes that we must not assume that there is no difference, merely that such things are likely to have a strong cultural and epistemological overlay. The lived experience of the child cannot be deduced either by subtraction – the child is lesser than the adult – or by equation – the child is the same as the adult.

Phenomenologically therefore, our experience of the life cycle depends on where we are in it and this point relates to the meaning of the term development. As Kierkegaard said, development only ever comes into focus in hindsight and identifying development is essentially a historical enquiry that reconstructs the present in terms of the past, but it is a history which has an artificial endpoint: now. Whenever we narrate our life story, if only to ourselves, we are always telling it with the end of the story already known. Today always forms a temporary end for all our stories because we can never know what will happen next. The same sequence seen from yesterday, or tomorrow, six months ago or in six months' time will have a different meaning. It will be a different story and a different life. A different development.

Rather than asking the question, *How do people develop?*, which has obvious natural science echoes, or even *What is it like to develop?*, which is unanswerable because of the disjunction between the experience-near *What is it like?* and the experience-distant *to develop*, we should be asking questions like

What is it like to be me, now?

or

What is it like to look at my life in both directions, now?

The complexity of this is something that Simone de Beauvoir was only too aware of. She said that while one disadvantage of the novel form is that it failed to represent the superfluous elements of everyday life before they assume shape (if they ever do) as significant events, a diary, on the other hand, can incorporate these elements although if published would need to be cut to keep the reader's interest, leading to the charge of using hindsight to adjust the past to fit the present (1979: 453).

What all this is adding up to is that the meaning of lived experience and the reality of that experience can never be captured in a single type of writing. Beauvoir's solution was to use the novel to represent the meaning of lived experience, and the autobiography to represent the facticity and contingency of that experience. In her case, her novels and autobiographies can be read in parallel.

The language of human development

Language is a double-edged sword: it can help us to think but it can also stop or divert our thinking. It is never neutral or objective; it always represents a particular point of view and the words we use to refer to development are instructive because of their resonances and the nature of their category errors. There are words borrowed from biology like instinct, maturing, flowering, ripening, development, growth and evolving. It will be remembered, for example, that after apples ripen they go rotten. These cannot help but give us a biological spin to our understandings.

During the nineteenth century the dominant technology led to the mind being thought of in mechanistic, hydraulic terms. People talked, and still talk, of running out of steam, letting it out and releasing pent up emotion. Implicit in these is another hydraulic metaphor, that of a blockage. Much twentieth-century psychotherapy draws on the hydraulic metaphor, believing catharsis to be central to the notion of cure. It is interesting to note that the word catharsis is associated with tragedy in ancient Greek drama and refers to the emotional reaction when a character realises that a sequence of events is the consequence of human frailty rather than of divine intervention.

From twentieth-century technology there are words like making, transforming, changing, building and changing gear, usually associated with the idea of the self as fixed. The most obvious flaw in this is that to get more output from a machine you just run it for longer or faster. If you run humans for longer, output goes down because humans need time for reflection. This is one of the purposes of psychotherapy: to provide a time for reflection for people who have been treating themselves like machines.

There is now much talk of the brain as an information processor, of memories being stored in the brain, of retrieving or recovering memory as if the brain was a hard drive. And of the need to be re- or deprogrammed. Although recovered memory therapy has long been discredited (Brandon et al. 1997) some contemporary theoretical perspectives are based on this model which is only a updating of the nineteenth-century Gestalt psychology visual image model because it still assumes that there is a true image of the event recorded that just has to be recovered.

The contemporary enthusiasm for neuroscience is similar in that it sees the brain as a complex biological machine that runs algorithms on sets of data (Crawford 2010b). While the findings are interesting it tells us no more about origin of human choice, autonomy, meaning, responsibility and ethics than we knew before. Such language also distracts us from the project of trying to stay close to experience in order to understand the nature of being and the mysteries of embodied existence (Tallis 2011).

In contrast, contemporary narrative researchers see memory as being reconstructed differently each time it is remembered. In this case it is more accurate to talk about memories as being re-membered, put back together again in a different way. There is no correct memory to be found. This constitutes a resilient phenomenological challenge to developmental theory derived from natural science (Singer 2004; Fivush 2013).

All these metaphors, like considering memory as unchanging and stored, or the self as something which is true or constant, or the unconscious as a place with contents, or the past as having gone, are category errors and only make it superficially easier to think about life cycle events. This ease is at a cost of the loss of our sense of being co-constituted responsible reflective beings.

Because of their resonances, none are consistent with phenomenology. None are true to experience. Phenomenologically, life is dynamically co-constituted, continuing, in flux, constantly changing, constantly uncertain. Life is change. Briod (1989: 19) suggests that a word that is more consistent with a phenomenological perspective is 'opening'. This corresponds with Heidegger's terms dis-closing, and dis-covering and his preoccupation with the fundamental principle that we are always in and of the world and we are constantly opening (and closing) to experience depending on circumstance.

Principles of existential philosophy

Philosophy is fundamentally an enquiry into personal meaning and everything we do has a philosophical basis; assumptions about the nature of truth, reality and the origin of human meaning underlie our every action.

The existential perspective's field of vision reaches beyond the individual to consider the wider philosophical context of the human condition. As such, rather than thinking about function and dysfunction, it prefers to think in terms of a person's ability to meet the challenges that life inevitably presents. Sartre (1973a) described existentialism as a practical discipline that concerned itself with everyday human issues.

Warnock (1970) says that there are three basic principles that all existentialists share. The first is that 'existence comes essence' (Sartre 1973a: 26). This means that the fact that we are – what existentialists call our existence – is more basic than what we are – what existentialists call our essence. Existentially, we are 'thrown' into our lives (Heidegger 1962). This means that certain facts of our existence, like our genetic make-up, family circumstances, gender, race, culture, as well as the fact that we are born in the first place, are imposed upon us without any choice. Human beings have no pre-established purpose or nature, nor anything that we have to be or ought to be. The unsolvable dilemma of our birth is its utter randomness, *Why this egg and why this sperm? Why me? Why here? Why now?* The only answer is, *Why not?*

Beauvoir (1977: 9) put it like this: 'Tossed into the world, I have been subjected to its laws and its contingencies, ruled by wills other than my own, by circumstances and by history.' An everyday example of this is that we are given our names by others and they locate us in time, place and relationship. Even though many other people may have the same name, our task is to own the name we have been given and make it personal and particular to us in whatever way we choose. A way to dislocate someone is to give them another name against their will, or substitute it for a number. We are also thrown out of our lives in the sense that we do not know when we will die.

On our path through life from birth to death, we start with something we are given which is neither ours nor requested; our individual existence, and our life task is to make it into something which is personal and owned ... only to lose it when we die. Existentialists like Sartre and Camus described this as absurd and the most basic challenge of life is to find a way to live with this absurdity and discover ways of being that get us what we decide we need, bearing in mind that what we need changes as we go through life. The way I do this becomes the story of my life; the way I story my life.

Our awareness of our thrownness leads to the second principle: personal responsibility (Warnock 1970: 12). What we come to think of as our essence, our self, is therefore a matter of interpretation and choice and is the result of the way we meet the biological givens of our personal existence – nature – and the way we are treated – nurture. Existentialists prefer to use the phrase sense-of-self and the hyphens are important because they reinforce the primacy of experience, and that there is no fixed self as such to live up to as it is a natural science positivist notion. When Sartre (2003: 129) wrote that 'To be free is to be condemned to be free', he meant that we have responsibility for our lives whether we like it or not. The only choice we do not have is not to choose. Only when we take responsibility for our own choices can we truly learn about the consequences of our actions, our own authority and hence the meaning of our lives, and this is how we find out about the world, by engaging with it, not simply by observing it. Our autonomy is this fundamental; we are born into it. We always know this – even the most hard-line determinists look when they cross the road. The legal right to freedom of speech, having been fought for, still leaves us with the existential question of finding something to say that we believe in every minute of every day ... and the need to take responsibility for what happens next. Not having the legal right to freedom of speech only changes the context of our freedom. One of the consequences of internet technology and social media is the rise in the number of anonymous or pseudonymous postings. These enable people not to be accountable for what they say – to have freedom without responsibility – and its cost is plain to see. This brings in the idea of guilt. Existential guilt is different from everyday guilt which is when we do something we should not have done. It is also different from neurotic guilt when we imagine we have done something wrong because we have learnt to be afraid of our own freedom. Existential guilt is when we realise we have lied to ourselves about our situation and denied our freedom. Sartre called it bad faith. It is present when we pretend that something is true when we know it is not, or deny that something is true when we know it is or do not act when we know we should, or we pretend there is nothing we can do when there is.

The example most often quoted is that of the waiter who by overacting his role becomes a 'waiter-thing' (Sartre 2003: 82). But this misses out the crucial fact that because the waiter is simply in role as a waiter, he is not necessarily in bad faith because his purpose as waiter is not to escape from his freedom, it is to do a job. He is no more in bad faith that an actor is in bad faith for playing Macbeth. However, if the actor was to carry on playing Macbeth after the end of the play, in his everyday life, this would be a different matter. The same applies to psychotherapists. We are all, always, in some sort of social role that can be used to evade freedom, and therefore there is always a danger that we may be in bad faith.

We are obviously not free to be anything we like; we are constrained by circumstance and context – what existentialists call facticity – but our stance to this is ours and ours alone. We only see ourselves as fixed because it evokes too much anxiety – existential anxiety – to acknowledge that we are the product of our choices and actions. When we understand this, we can choose whether to be the active creator of our own life, or the passive recipient of a life. Heidegger (1962) uses the word authenticity to describe this process. Authenticity is not normative and the clue to its meaning is in the first four letters, 'auth', because it refers to the degree to which thrownness, absurdity, can be owned and we can accept our existential responsibility to be the author of our own lives. Inauthenticity then is the denial of this authorship. To live life, rather than be lived by life. Because this responsibility is hard to accept we tend to evade and deny it, we close down our possibilities imagining that our life will become easier and simpler and in a sense it does, except that it also becomes narrower and less flexible, more fixed. But like the tides or the relationship between day and night, there is a continuous ebb and flow between the two poles of authenticity and inauthenticity such that they are better considered as a single concept.

The third principle is about how the theory is arrived at. The relationship between phenomenology and existentialism is complex in that some existential philosophers, like Kierkegaard and Nietzsche, being nineteenth-century writers, are existentialists without being phenomenologists, or perhaps they were phenomenologists before their time, and there are others like Merleau-Ponty who was rather more of a phenomenologist than an existentialist. But the general principle is that existentialism is the body of knowledge that arises when the research method of phenomenology is applied to the study of existence as a whole.

Existentially, experience has two interlocking dimensions. Heidegger called these the ontic and ontological. The ontic dimension refers to everyday personal lived experience, and the ontological refers to the universal dimension of existence. Every experience is simultaneously personal, singular – ontic – at the same time as being universal – ontological.

The practice of existential psychotherapy is based on phenomenology and in this way there is an intimate and ethical connection between theory and practice. By being phenomenological, we allow existential issues and concerns to come to light.

More recently, existential and phenomenological ideas have begun to be a major influence within all major therapeutic perspectives (Cooper and McLeod 2010; Cooper 2015) because of the growing realisation that the epistemological basis of existentialism, phenomenology, is more appropriate for the human sciences.

Defining human development existentially and phenomenologically

Human development has not been covered well by the existential-phenomenological therapeutic tradition (Cohn 1998; Adams 2006, 2013b, 2014) and some accounts (Knowles 1986; Becker 1992) transpose existential and phenomenological ideas onto stage theory. This is curious because with the exception of Heidegger, whose project was ontological and who had little personal or professional interest in biography, Kierkegaard, Nietzsche, Sartre, Beauvoir and Merleau-Ponty all wrote extensively about it. Sartre and Beauvoir were both passionately interested in human biography and Beauvoir considered both gender and old age developmentally and philosophically. In spite of this, partly perhaps because of Heidegger's influence in the development of existential-phenomenological therapy it has been under-represented in existential-phenomenological texts.

Another reason is perhaps that within psychotherapy as a whole, the most dominant voice on human development has been psychoanalysis and in a move to distance themselves from psychoanalysis, existential psychotherapists have reactively turned away from thinking developmentally.

Although, like all of us, a product of his time, R.D. Laing also had the ability to anticipate future trends and in *The Divided Self* he says this about human development:

> Biological birth is a definitive act whereby the infant organism is precipitated into the world [...] Under usual circumstances, the physical birth of a new living organism into the world inaugurates rapidly ongoing processes whereby [...] the infant feels real and alive and has a sense of being an entity

> with continuity in time and a location in space. In short, physical birth and biological aliveness are followed by the baby becoming existentially born as real and alive. Usually this development is taken for granted.
>
> (1965: 41)

And in this he echoes Martin Buber who says,

> Every child that is coming into being rests in [...] the undivided primal world that precedes form. From her [...] we are separated and enter into personal life. But this separation does not occur suddenly and catastrophically like the separation from the bodily mother; time is granted to the child to exchange a spiritual connexion for the natural connexion with the world. But he does not possess it yet, he must make it into a reality by seeing and hearing and touching and shaping it.
>
> (1958: 41)

Laing spends the rest of his book, and others, talking about what happens when it is not taken for granted. In this statement, which echoes his own reading of Kierkegaard and Sartre (Heidegger's *Being and Time* was not translated until 1962 although Laing knew Heidegger's translator John MacQuarrie well), he says that physical birth is the starting point for a process of opening to the world, which nevertheless is capable of being interrupted, that leads to a relatively resilient sense-of-self and purpose. This is what he calls becoming existentially born. Being a process, it is never finished. We are perpetually in the process of being born, and simultaneously of dying.

As said before, all theories are based on theories of how to make theories. They can never be assumption-free. In a similar way existentialism and phenomenology are not assumption-free and a model of human development based on their principles must accommodate the principles of phenomenology mentioned above as well as an acknowledgement of the significance of the givens of existence as they are engaged with in their different ways throughout life.

On the simplest level, the notion of 'development' is related to time and hence to chronology and thus to age. In one sense, then, development is about how we move through time, how we get older and what happens as we move from birth through to death. But time can be defined in different ways and each definition will give rise to a different understanding of the term development.

The way existentialists understand time is central to an existential understanding of human development and this difference is what makes an existential understanding of development distinctive.

The existential philosopher who said the most about time was Martin Heidegger. What we usually think of as time, Heidegger would call clock time, and in clock time the minutes go past at the same rate and will always do so. This is a technological linear approach to time, and consists of the past, the present and the future and puts an emphasis on causation in the sense that the past – what has happened – causes the present – what is happening – and that leads to the future which is yet to come. Our involvement with time is passive: it happens to us and is outside of us. We imagine that this is what time is, but it is simply an ontic human invention that only has meaning in particular contexts. It is just convenient and makes everyday life manageable. But this contemporary view of time as clock time was not always so widely held. It can be argued that it is a product of our technological, verbal, linear culture. In contrast, early Renaissance and also Cubist paintings show large spans of time (and space) with the same elements appearing repeatedly within the same image. This is a more experiential, visual, simultaneous view of life. All cultures have their own calendars and ways of measuring time, and Greenwich Mean Time and the International Date Line were only established in the late nineteenth century.

Existentially though, time is integral to the way we structure our meaning world. It is the water we swim in; it is the air that we breathe. It is not something that we passively have or do not have; it is something we are. Temporality is a human quality and it is more accurate, existentially, to say that we are temporal. The ontic and the ontological are entwined in temporality. The way each person understands their own life at each moment represents the ontic dimension of temporality, and the ontological dimension is represented by the fact that temporality is a given of existence for all human beings, past, present and future. Our temporality is therefore both particular and general. We are in a particular time, of a particular age, and also of all time and of all ages. Existentially, the life cycle is not just about how one person lives between birth and death. It is also about that person's life in the context of all other lives, both past, present and future.

Temporality is implicit in our striving for meaning and purpose. We always want to know what comes next. This presents us with a perpetual dilemma that when we project ourselves into the future we find both possibility – of what could happen – and also certainty – of death.

Moreover though, although death is certain, when it happens is not. This leaves us with the problem of having to find a way to live a meaningful life without knowing how long we have got to do it in. Our death gives our lives final meaning and purpose because possibility ceases. There is an end to our temporality but not to time. The world goes on without us.

Life can be experienced as a melody, as a continuous and unfolding story, in which case we become open to possibility and this is what Laing

(1965: 41), who was a very good pianist, meant by 'continuity in time'. But if we come to experience it as a meaningless sequence of separate notes with no particular rhythm, it becomes fragmented and random, and we close ourselves off from possibility.

Projecting ourselves into the future also means that we think about our past – how we came to be who we are right now – our life story and whether such a future might be possible, and when this happens, we become present to ourselves. This is the existential meaning of the present and as such the present emerges instantaneously out of the encounter between the past and the future.

The past is not gone, it is the past-in-the-present, and the future is not to come, it is the future-in-the-present. Although the past, present and future are equally important, if anything, the future is existentially the most important because all our decisions are made in the light of what may or may not happen next. Or as Heidegger says, 'Everything begins with the future' (2001: 159). When we are depressed we say, *What is there to live for?, What's the point?*, meaning that we cannot see a future for ourselves.

By opening to both the present and the future we realise the past can change. Not the material events of the past, which we only have a sketchy knowledge of anyway, but the meaning we currently make of the past. A simple everyday example of this is that when we are happy we find it easier to remember happy times we have had, and similarly when we are sad. Letting go of the idea that we are determined by the past gives us the freedom but also the responsibility to change.

But the present is also never fixed. It is a constantly moving point going in one direction only from the known date of our birth to the unknown date of our death. Our life story is threaded together from the past, the present and the future, and we weave our autobiography out of the way we understand our life at every particular moment. In this sense, then, the past, the present and the future are simultaneous.

An individual life can only be seen as a whole in three ways. One way is by knowing someone all the way from birth through to death, but this is comparatively uncommon and usually only occurs when the other person's life is 'cut short'. Another way is by looking at our own life, but we can only ever do this at the very end of our lives when we know there is nothing else to come. The other way is by piecing it together from the outside, in hindsight, like a jigsaw puzzle, as natural science does. In this way it can indeed be seen as having a number of stages, periods and so on that span several years or decades, and that seem to show some common features.

Existentially though, a whole life consists of an almost infinite number of moments that are characterised by thoughts, feelings, dilemmas, paradoxes and choices, each of which sum up our life up until that moment, and each of which tips us into an unknown future. Every moment has the power, the possibility, of being transformative because every moment demands that we choose how to be from that moment on.

This radically reframes what is meant by development because existentially, development is not about moving passively from one quasi-biological stage to the next, rather than about how we actively meet the paradoxes and dilemmas of existence and how we make choices about the future on the basis of incomplete knowledge about the past and the present, both in the context of how long we expect to be alive for and also in the context of human life in general.

Life certainly has a biological dimension; we are born and then die and always in that order, and we are all subject to maturational processes, but our existential development can be gauged by how much we learn about the givens of existence. It is about how we recover from everyday misfortune, about how we meet our freedom, how we manage our relationships and how we see our place in the unfolding history of humankind.

The developmental model most consistent with an existential-phenomenological view therefore, is a lifelong process model based on the acquisition of the skills of living, knowing not only that life will never be something we can fully master but also that that is what makes it exciting and worth doing.

In our desire to have 'continuity in time and a location in space' (Laing 1965: 41), we actively construct a coherent sense-of-self out of the random events of our lives in order to give ourselves a sense of meaning and purpose. Asking the question about how we work out what stories to tell ourselves, the novelist William Boyd (2010) suggests that we need to impose a narrative template on our experiences and he uses the metaphor that all our experiences are like 'a heedless scatter of millions of iron-filings' and to form an autobiography we need some sort of 'narrative magnet [to] make the filings cluster significantly' so that they make a pattern. In his 2003 novel *Any Human Heart* it was the people the main character loved, but it could have been anything. The story of a life can be told in many different ways, and none of them complete.

In this way we daily encounter our thrownness and realise not only that our life is our own responsibility, but also that it is the product of chance and opportunity and that it has to be remade every moment.

So, when considering human development existentially the question becomes,

> *How do we get from birth, when the dilemmas and paradoxes of existence are not understood, to existential maturity and wisdom – which is by no means guaranteed anyway – when they are understood?*

PART II

3

Søren Kierkegaard (1813–55)

Living with faith

The story of Søren Kierkegaard and hence of modern existentialism begins in the 1750s. It is also a story, as he records comprehensively although not always directly in his writings, that links his life intimately with his philosophy. Although many details are known, his life and philosophy have been the subject of extensive discussion and debate, but Lowrie (1942) is taken as being reliable.

Søren's father Michael was one of nine children born to highly religious serf sheep farmers in the windswept heathland of Jutland. The village, which could not afford a pastor of its own, let a parish house to Michael's family and because surnames were not yet fixed, families were often named after where they lived. This accounts for his name, as Kierkegaard approximates to churchyard.

For economic reasons Michael left home as a child to work outside in all weathers for another farmer nearby and this led to an occasion in which the unhappy, cold and lonely Michael, not surprisingly, cursed God for his lot in life.

It was an action that was to haunt both him and Søren in different ways for the rest of their lives. Not long after this, though, things began to look up when Michael's uncle in Copenhagen took him on as an apprentice in his clothing business. This coincided economically and politically with the dismantling of feudalism and the migration of agricultural workers to the city and the beginnings of industrialisation and the modern era. It was also paralleled by the reduction in Danish military power and the movement of new ideas from Germany, such as Romanticism and the philosophy of Kant and Hegel, and the Danish government saw that a way to ride these changes was to reinforce the link between the church and the state. Michael did so well in business, importing fabric and porcelain from China and coffee and sugar from the tropics, that by the time of his second marriage in 1797 to his long-time maidservant, Ane, who was also from Jutland, he was able to retire in his forties.

A self-educated man, he devoted the rest of his life to the study of theology and philosophy and he died when he was eighty-two. Michael's religiosity, which was always pervaded by guilt and fear of a vengeful God, became even more so. Of the marriage's seven children, the first was born four months after their marriage and only two survived beyond their twenties – Søren, the youngest, and the humourless Peter, eight years older. Søren was born when his father was fifty-six and though Michael's sons had the best education money could buy, Søren was 'favoured' by being taught by his father as well. This took the form of theological and philosophical discussions that stretched the young Søren's imagination and intellectual capacity beyond his years. There were consequently few opportunities for play with other children except with his siblings and he only left the house to go to school. This made Søren a rather odd child, not only because of a spinal deformity, but also because of his old-fashioned clothes. He was teased for this by his schoolmates but he learnt to counter, if not actually provoke, this attention with his sarcasm and wit.

His upbringing was therefore as a special son who was immersed in the world of his sombre and increasingly oppressive father. Reflecting on these times in *Point of View* (1962) he wrote, 'As a child I was strictly and austerely brought up in Christianity; humanly speaking, crazily brought up. A child crazily travestied as a melancholy old man' (quoted in Lowrie 1942: 50). This, however, did not lead him to turn him away from Christianity, but to redefine it. Expanding on this in his *Concluding Unscientific Postscript* (1941: 523), he says, 'To cram Christianity into a child is a thing that cannot be done; for it is a general rule that everyone comprehends only what he has use for, and the child has no decisive use for Christianity.' And on such a Christian education he says in his journal that, 'The most dangerous case is not when the father is a free thinker, and not when he is a hypocrite. No, the danger is when he is a god-fearing man, when the child is inwardly and deeply convinced of it and yet in spite of all this observes that a profound unrest is deeply hidden in his soul.' A consequence of this is that such a child will come to the conclusion 'that after all God is not infinite love' (quoted in Lowrie 1942: 51).

These last points indicate his sensitivity to the issue of what we now call age-appropriate knowledge. He is saying that children are just not equipped to deal with the things that he was exposed to without having their worldview distorted.

At seventeen, and following his father's wishes, Søren went to university to study theology but his real interest was philosophy. By the time he was eighteen, five of his siblings had died, to be followed by his mother when he was twenty-one and his father when he was twenty-five. Peter later became a bishop in the Danish Lutheran Church and they were both openly critical of each other's teachings.

Like many students, Søren appreciated the freedom of university life. He made friends and discovered student politics, theatre and literature, and bought new and fashionable clothes, to the disapproval of both his father and brother. Søren was discovering his freedom. Life was opening up for him.

Towards the end of this time, there was an event that he describes in a story called *The Great Earthquake* in his journals (1976). That it reverberated through the rest of his life is clear enough but exactly what it was is less clear. It may have been that Michael told Søren that he felt he was personally responsible for what he saw as the family misfortune which included the death of both of his wives and five of his children before him, through his sin of cursing God on the hillside some seventy years earlier; or it may have been the shock of discovering his father's sensuality – that his mother had become pregnant before they were married.

Whatever this 'great earthquake' was, he was greatly unsettled and the result was that he put his student ways behind him and he became reconciled not only with his father but also with Christianity, which he had put aside in his student days. Lowrie (1942: 52) suggests that he took his father's death as a sacrifice that he had a duty to honour and this led him to complete his training as a pastor, although he never became ordained. He wanted to be a good Christian but was not at all sure how to do it. The way he chose turned out to be both unique and revolutionary, and addressed the way in which nineteenth-century Danish bourgeois society, and particularly the Lutheran Church, was complicit in undermining true Christianity by reinforcing conformity, and how, through this, people had lost their capacity for personal questioning and commitment. The way conformity is reinforced is no less true today, which is why his thinking is still relevant.

It was not by accident that in his philosophy thesis he examined Socrates' use of irony to facilitate self-questioning, or that he included his own personal experience in its content. As became usual, his examiners were divided, but he passed. His study of Hegel had led him to reject abstract theory building because he wanted to give priority to concrete human reality. He did, however, preserve Hegel's method of the dialectic, but rather than applying it to ideas in general, he saw it as applying to the development of the individual in particular. Each person writes his or her own autobiography dialectically, there is nothing determined, or predictable, except biological maturation.

Like Socrates, he thought philosophers should be judged by the way they lived rather than by what they said. He wanted to be not just a

Socrates for the nineteenth century, but a Socrates who wrote and published: he was in no doubt that he had something to say.

When his father died he inherited half of his wealth and became one of the richest and therefore most eligible young men in Copenhagen and he was to live off his inheritance until his own death in 1855 at forty-two.

At around this time he met a similarly eligible young woman, Regina Olson, who was nine years younger than him. He started to court her in the manner of the time and place by sending her books to read and discussing them with her except that this usually turned into him telling her about them. In 1840, when she was eighteen, he proposed to her and she accepted. Almost immediately he had second thoughts; he finally broke off the engagement a year later and went to Germany for five months to study philosophy. Whatever his reasons, he felt somehow that the life of married respectability as a Lutheran pastor was not what he wanted.

Living off his inheritance he had no need of a job and this suited his solitary nature, and he became ever more solitary, only ever meeting and talking to people while out walking in Copenhagen; he had an easier rapport with children than with adults. He spent his short life publishing an enormous number of books at his own expense and many of these used a method of indirect communication, one of which was the use of pseudonyms which also carried another layer of meaning. These pseudonyms can also be read as having conversations with each other across his books as well as within the books. He gave up using pseudonyms in 1848, preferring to speak with his own voice, giving an account of this in *Point of View* of 1851.

He did not use pseudonyms to disguise himself – Copenhagen was small and before long people knew he was the author, which is what he wanted – but to put forward different points of view that would make the readers ask questions of themselves. This had the effect of making his works more accessible and he gradually gained a small but rather vocal and disorganised following. It was a device that Sartre, Beauvoir and Camus among others were also to use successfully a century later in their development of the philosophical novel. Above all he wanted his books to be readers' books, not writers' books. His spiritual development can be traced through these works and a parallel narrative of his development can also be seen in his mostly undated journals, which he began when he was twenty. Together, his work gives a running commentary on his life, saturated with the tension between randomness and order, chance and opportunity, and trauma and certainty that characterises every person's life story. That he was an unusual if not rather strange person is undisputed, but for Lowrie this enhances rather than detracts from what we can learn from him. He says,

> It was abnormal even to be so deeply engrossed in his own abnormal psychic condition, that he delved deeper than other men into the secrets of personality. In advance of modern pathologists he understood that a study of the abnormal might result in a deeper and clearer knowledge of the normal, that is, of health.
>
> (1942: 131)

At the age of forty-two, after a life of being both ignored and courting publicity, which often turned into ridicule, and with his money gone, he collapsed in the street, having withdrawn the last of his savings from the bank, and died in hospital a few weeks later. While there, he refused to see his brother, but welcomed the visits from his nieces and nephews. He also declined the sacrament because he knew that by taking it he would be accepting the validity of the Lutheran Church. Nevertheless, his funeral was held in the most important church in Copenhagen against the wishes of his followers, many of whom were present, and was characteristically chaotic. His brother Peter conducted the service and had to take care not to inflame the crowd. The dispute about who had a right to speak carried on to the cemetery where Søren was buried, and such was the relationship between them that Peter did nothing to mark the spot and it was only much later that Søren's name was included on the family gravestone.

Like all people, Søren Kierkegaard was far more than the mere combination of his genetic inheritance and his environment. The person he became was the way the givens of existence, the givens of his own particular existence, and his personal choices interacted, and in this way he actively lived his philosophy.

His influence during his lifetime was small and limited to Denmark and in the years following his death, the Danish Lutheran Church gradually became less attached to the state. It was not until the 1860s that his works began to be translated into German but still with little impact. A biography of Kierkegaard was eventually published in Denmark in 1879. Though he wrote at a time of great national and international turmoil, it was not until another period of great turmoil, the end of the First World War, that Karl Jaspers and Martin Heidegger, using German translations, took up and elaborated his ideas on anxiety and temporality. Although they had many differences, not least about the value of religion, by the 1930s Kierkegaard's thinking about freedom, authenticity and bad faith had made an impact on people like Sartre, who gave a talk at the

150th anniversary of Kierkegaard's birth (Sartre 2013). After 1945, world peace seemed as far away as ever and by this time his writings were beginning to be translated into English and his influence had spread to the UK, where he was read by Laing, and to the USA, where he was read by the likes of Rollo May who based his 1950 book *The Meaning of Anxiety* on Kierkegaard's *The Concept of Anxiety* of 1844.

Philosophy

Warnock (1970: 12) describes Kierkegaard as 'the parent of existentialism', because of his desire to free people from what he saw as the 'illusion of objectivity' (ibid.: 8). What Kierkegaard meant was that the human subject needed to be at the centre of any enquiry concerning meaning. He was not interested in creating philosophical systems like Kant or Hegel, rather than in creating a way of making and living philosophy. Philosophy is not a thing – it is not knowledge; it is a life process.

For Kierkegaard, our existence as individuals is intimately connected with our environment and, as such, he anticipates the development of phenomenology at the other end of the nineteenth century, and by shining a light on temporality, freedom and personal responsibility he anticipates the development of existential thought in the twentieth and twenty-first centuries. This is shown when he says (1976: 34), 'The crucial thing is to find a truth which is truth for me, to find the idea for which I am willing to live and die.'

Objectivity and subjectivity

Kierkegaard's central point of departure from the ideology of the day was how they defined truth. He distinguished between subjective truth, which he said was undervalued and is based on what is personally known in a phenomenological sense, and objective truth, which is the basis of natural science and is based on rationalism and consensus. He said that objective truth on its own is dangerous because it encourages people to see themselves as subject to the same rules of determinism as material objects.

Therefore, objectivity is of very limited value when working out how best to live one's life. In the example of mortality, the question, *What can we say about knowing we are going to die?* can either be approached objectively and rationally, or subjectively and personally. In approaching it objectively we use observation and inference, as in: *Living things die + I am a living thing = I will die … sometime.* Approaching it subjectively is far more challenging and involves experiencing how death and temporality runs through every moment of our lives like a thread that draws us closer to death, and in this way we understand what life means by understanding what death means. The two are indivisible.

Subjective, phenomenological, truths are those most directly related to our existence and cannot be taught and this is the paradox – that one creates one's own truth by one's ownership and commitment to it, not by finding it outside oneself, and certainly not by asking someone else. If psychotherapy is a search of truth, then this has huge implications for the role of the psychotherapist. Kierkegaard said this was where Christianity was going wrong, because God is not objective truth; God is ambiguous and must be discovered anew by each person, and being a Christian is an individual subjective passion that cannot be mediated by clergy or by any human artefacts. He said that the most religious people are not be found in churches on Sundays, but going about their lives day by day with passion, humility and personal commitment.

In his dilemma about whether or not to marry Regina Olson, he was faced, as he saw it, with the choice between bourgeois comfortableness and individuality, and he chose individuality. The point here is not so much the nature of his selection, and still less that there was anything objectively or morally better about that particular choice, but that he was confronted with a life-changing choice; not only could no one but Kierkegaard make that choice, but he would have to live forever with his choice. While he did not regret it, he still found it hard to live with.

His overall question then is, *What evidence do we use to make life changing decisions?* His answer is that we cannot just use what feels best at the time, or what most people do. We can only use faith. And that the act of faith is an act of pure freedom through which we choose ourselves. There is no faith without risk. Although desired, certainty is never acquired or possible and there are no guarantees. This freedom evokes anxiety, which he called angst or dread, and is the subject of *The Concept of Anxiety* written pseudonymously as Vigilius Haufniensis (The Watchman of Copenhagen).

For Kierkegaard, anxiety is free-floating; it is unfocused fear and is what reminds us of our freedom to choose. Although Adam was told by God not to eat from the tree of knowledge, he chose to do so and the cost was the anxiety that Kierkegaard (1981: 61) refers to as the 'dizziness of freedom' – when we realise the importance of the present moment. Adam's sin was not that he chose; it was the consequence of his choosing. This points to a difference between anxiety and fear that was taken up later by Heidegger and Sartre, that fear is passive and anxiety is active. We may fear falling off a cliff, but we are anxious in case we jump off the cliff from our own volition.

Our feelings towards freedom and hence anxiety are intensely ambivalent. We want it but we also fear it, and we write our autobiography by the way we negotiate this tension minute by minute, day by day, year by year. Our life task is to recognise this and to meet it, and anxiety 'is an adventure that every human being must go through – to learn to be anxious in order that he may not perish either by never having been in anxiety or by succumbing in anxiety. Whoever has learned to be anxious in the right way has learnt the ultimate' (Kierkegaard 1981: 155).

While we seek the exhilaration that comes from freedom, we know that we create ourselves through choices made at particular times and places, and that these choices will be judged for eternity; they cannot be undone. We alone carry the responsibility for our lives. We cannot not make a decision, and in this Kierkegaard anticipates Sartre.

This is the context in which he made the statement that begins this book:

> It is perfectly true, as philosophers say, that life must be understood backwards. But they forget the other proposition, that it must be lived forwards. And if one thinks over that proposition it becomes more and more evident that life can never really be understood in time because at no particular moment can I find the necessary resting place from which to understand.

We are all of us in the same boat, in more ways than one. We are like rowers on a river facing backwards to move forwards, with occasional glimpses over our shoulder towards what is to come; the unknowable future.

Kierkegaard and human development

For Kierkegaard, human development is not biological; it is a spiritual process of continual becoming. We start from a position in childhood where we are unaware of sin, and our spiritual development only begins after our discovery of sin and therefore freedom. This is about a lack of completeness that is manifested in different ways but never removed, and a realisation that only God will make us complete.

Kierkegaard started to talk about the three stages of spiritual development in *Either/Or*, published in 1843 when he was twenty-nine under the pseudonym Victor Eremita (Victorious Hermit) after his return from Germany where he had retreated after breaking off his engagement. He wrote it not from a position of hindsight, which, as he would have known, would only give it a spurious objectivity, but from being in the turmoil and describing the process from the inside. There are two characters in the book – one simply called A and the other called Judge Wilhelm, who embody the first two stages, the Aesthetic (A) and the Ethical (Wilhelm). These are referred to by Kierkegaard's character Johannes de Silentio (John of the Silence), the author of *Fear and Trembling* (1843), respectively as the personal self and the civic self.

While *Either/Or* is presented as a debate between the two views of life, there is nevertheless a suggestion that the Ethical is an advance on the Aesthetic. Although not included in *Either/Or*, he later added a third stage, the Religious, which is reached after the Ethical. While not being stages in a conventional stage theory sense, there is a directionality in the sense that both the Aesthetic and the Ethical stages have the Religious stage as their final goal. They are also not stages in the sense of rungs on a ladder, because each one dialectically envelops those below: an ethical or religious person can still experience life aesthetically, although this will not be in the earlier way.

The movement from one to another is by no means automatic, nor is it gradual, nor is it biologically or psychologically mediated. It is a spiritual process that is characterised by discontinuity, and transition from one to the next comes about by confrontation with despair related to our relationship with God.

For Kierkegaard, there are three sorts of despair, each one corresponding to one of the three stages. The first, corresponding to the aesthetic, is the despair of not having a self; the second, corresponding to the ethical, is the despair of not being willing to be oneself; and the third, corresponding to the religious, is the despair that comes from willing to be oneself.

Each stage is a mode of being that defines success in its own terms. No one can be persuaded to move – the movement from one stage to another can only come after immersion in the lived paradoxes, dilemmas and contradictions of current everyday life and risking the unknown through what he called a 'leap of faith', which Lowrie (1942: 174) describes as a 'decisive choice that involves the intellect, the feeling and the will'. In *The Concept of Anxiety* Kierkegaard uses the phrase 'glance of the eye', borrowed from Aristotle and to be used later by Nietzsche and Heidegger, to describe the moment when a different future becomes visible, but still has to be grasped. He says, 'In the sphere of historical freedom, transition is a state. However, in order to understand this correctly, one must not forget that the new is brought about through the leap' (1981: 85). The self becomes actualised by the leap of faith that allows a person to embrace freedom and responsibility, and in this way we become closer to God.

The Aesthetic sphere of existence

For Kierkegaard, in the aesthetic sphere we live our lives guided by everyday tasks and concerns, and it is these that come to constitute our identity. He says, 'the man of immediacy does not know himself, he quite literally identifies himself only by the clothes he wears, he identifies having a self by externalities' (Kierkegaard 1980: 53). Being led by immediacy, there is little reflection on living. The aesthetic sphere is appreciated through the body and such a person is like a child bursting with energy and possibilities, and the best way of expressing this is with movement and dance, not words. There is a constant and rather frantic search either for something new to be distracted by or for something familiar to be numbed by. This is also often described wrongly as 'living life to the full'. Pleasure is pursued not for its own sake, but so that boredom, indifference and lack of direction can be kept at bay. It is therefore a cover for despair.

Some people may be largely unaware of their spiritual disconnection, while others may be only occasionally aware, for example when a particular source of stimulation comes to an end. This means that although external stimulation will often be actively sought, life is lived passively and without freedom. When Kierkegaard was writing, the issue was the institutionalisation of Christianity, but in our current era this is added to with determinist scientism, mass communication, the relativism of so-called facts, and a culture that prioritises individualism and consumerism. This makes Kierkegaard's central message about the dangers of losing the authority our own experience and our reflectiveness still relevant, and these issues frequently present themselves in psychotherapy.

In *Either/Or*, Kierkegaard says there are many different ways of living an unreflective aesthetic life. At one end of a continuum there is a wholly unreflective lifestyle driven by sensuality and externality and characterised by cravings for desire and satisfaction through enjoyments that do not require personal challenge, for example alcohol, drugs, sex or shopping. At the other end is an apparently reflective and independent but spiritually apathetic way of life in which activities are cultivated because they do not involve any personal challenge, for their ability to be just interesting enough not to evoke boredom, and not so interesting that they evoke meaningful self-questioning. They are chosen for their numbing qualities, to stop reflection; and wanting to get drunk is no different from priding oneself on one's refined and elegant taste in wine, or collecting expensive works of art. Even, or maybe especially, in a comfortable bourgeois life, whenever such reflective feelings emerge they may be ignored or even forgotten. Activities that involve personal sacrifice and commitment will not be seen as attractive because they do not offer an immediate return, and may be labelled boring. Boredom is a challenge and therefore to be feared. It is almost inevitable that the activity that is chosen to stave off boredom will eventually lose its power to do so. This is because it is being asked to do something it cannot do: to provide spiritual fulfilment. In which case something else will be chosen, not for any intrinsic qualities but simply for its ability to distract. Clients in psychotherapy who start questioning their addiction to one activity often switch to another, imagining they are then free of addiction. In *Either/Or* Kierkegaard calls this Crop Rotation.

Valuing immediacy, the aesthete is inclined to pay little attention to convention, or even to actively reject it, seeing it as unnecessarily constraining freedom in the way that adolescence is often characterised. Using only immediacy as a guide, the aesthete's sense-of-self is no more than a bundle of random events with no story to connect them in time and place and with no solid framework from which to maintain, as Laing (1965: 41) says, 'a sense of being an entity with continuity in time and a location in space'. If the chosen activities do not work as planned the automatic assumption will be that the activity was wrong, not that the choice was wrong. On occasions, though, this excuse will wear thin and when this happens we are tipped into despair, our power will vanish and we will feel victimised by life. At this point life itself becomes meaningless. There is nothing to fall back on.

Sexuality

In *Either/Or* Kierkegaard discusses sexuality as portrayed by the character of Don Giovanni in Mozart's opera who he says gains his satisfaction not so much from the act of seduction, but from engineering the possibility of seduction. Because other people are treated as things, love and sexuality is therefore a rather selfish, narcissistic affair in the sense that the other person is there solely to meet the seducer's needs and make him or her feel whole. The seducer's real aim, therefore, is not to have a relationship of mutuality, but to manipulate, deceive and to take. We lose interest after the seduction and may say, *I did it because I could* or *I did it because I wanted to* as if that justifies it as an act of freedom. If the seduction was allowed to take its natural course, the reality of a relationship of mutuality and trust with another person would emerge and this would not only be extremely challenging in so many ways, but would also mean that reality would impose itself and some (illusory) control would be lost.

The task for the aesthete is to find a way to live with the existential reality of other people's freedom.

Temporality

Temporality is bound up in the aesthetic sphere in the sense that sensations are sought on the basis of their newness, or on their ability to evoke freshness and novelty. It is about birth, but not a birth that leads to something profound and lasting, because there is a need to keep things as they are and for time to appear not to pass.

Ageing is a reminder of temporality and the fear of things fading and of possibilities diminishing. In the aesthetic sphere there will be a desire to repeat the pleasures of the spontaneous first time by replicating it, but for obvious reasons this doesn't work; there is only ever one first time. What is special about the new is not that it hasn't happened before, but that our transformation by it was unexpected. We both desire and fear change in equal measure.

Unrequited, unconsummated affairs are the only ones that last forever. The longing is not for the person, but for the persistence and resilience of hope, of what may be and of what may have been, if .... Affairs that are over are the ones where we know for certain that it wasn't to be. But to understand this we have to own our temporality and embrace the possibility of loss of hope. This is how we can understand the tenacity of 'first love' experiences.

Kierkegaard's attachment to Regina Olson, and the way it persisted throughout his life, was one of these and it gained its power because it was unrequited and because of this he never got to find out whether it would have flourished and been of mutual benefit. As it was, he decided to choose the single life, but was never able to forget the possibility of what his life might have been like if he had made a different choice – the *what if ...?*

It is also difficult not to come to the conclusion that the aesthetic is a description of the freedom Kierkegaard felt when he went to university and when there was an endless stream of new experiences to indulge in that he was starved of at home. When we are young everything is the first time, everything is new and there are lots of first times to be had. As we know, for Kierkegaard, this period of his life ended suddenly.

As we get older we realise not only that are there fewer first times to be had, but also that there will be more and more last times. This suggests that ageing brings not only more occasions for despair, but also more occasions for spiritual development.

The Ethical sphere of existence

Eventually, maintaining the aesthetic way of life gets more difficult. There is a growing realisation that indulging in the spontaneous pleasures of the senses as a way to relieve boredom and stave off despair no longer works.

We are confronted ever more frequently with an inner emptiness which the aesthetic cannot longer fill. We start to wonder how we can bring some more resilient meaning into our lives. This is the ethical way; and by abandoning the reliance on the transient pleasures of the outer world, we turn towards the inner world and start to consider, for perhaps the first time, the effect that our actions have both on ourselves and on others. This prompts us to take responsibility for developing a set of values to live by – for the building of a life project. The ethical is appreciated through the mind and for the first time the person 'has himself as his task' (Kierkegaard 1940: 81). But freedom does not simply arrive; it has to be chosen. As he says, 'Resolution is universally the beginning of freedom' (ibid.: 158).

Initially however, we may feel that moving to the ethical stage will mean that we have to abandon too many of the attractions of the aesthetic life and that the ethical life seems not to have much to offer. The sacrifice may seem too great. It may seem too dull. In such cases, Kierkegaard would say that we are just not despairing enough. Using the example of addiction, the person is still in denial. Things have just not got bad enough; rock-bottom (Kemp 2013) has not been reached. It will be seen as an either/or option, but because of the dialectical nature of change, the ethical way of life is not automatically in opposition to the aesthetic. But this will not be understood because the transition cannot be made with reason, with guarantees. It can only be made with faith.

In the ethical sphere of existence, freedom that was once about maximising possibilities and opportunities now becomes the freedom to choose how to live. The future becomes something to look forward to rather than to fear. There is also a realisation that if no deliberate choice is made, then what follows will be more of the aesthetic mode. The ethical life can therefore offer pleasures that the aesthetic life cannot, and in *Works of Love* (1847) Kierkegaard uses marriage as an example of an ethical life choice whereby it is discovered that commitment to a single alternative is not the enemy of freedom and that this commitment can lead to a greater and more profound experience of the sensual. The body is not lost after all. It will be remembered, of course, that this was not the choice that Kierkegaard himself made. For the ethical person, love is expressed through a freely chosen commitment and devotion and this for Kierkegaard is the interpersonal meaning of love.

Such a transition to the ethical may also happen in early adulthood, and is most usually connected to marriage, but also when a person becomes a parent and realises that whereas before they only had to think about themselves, they now have responsibility for another life. This always produces anxiety because of the realisation that, regardless of how many books they may read, or how much advice they may get, they still do not know how to do it; they are on their own in a brand-new world.

For the first time they realise that their own pleasure has to take a back seat to doing what's right for their children. While they may try to use reason, ultimately they have to rely on faith. A parent may do what they think is best, but they will not find out for a decade or more what difference it made.

In this way, our actions in the ethical sphere therefore begin to have a consistency and coherence that they lacked in the aesthetic sphere.

The human desire for a solid foundation to life means that we will often embrace the teachings of a pre-existing body of moral law, and although there are some major differences between the aesthetic and the ethical, there is one important similarity. While the aesthetic is followed unreflectively and the ethical is chosen, the similarity is that they are both accepted whole as sources of meaning. In this way the ethical can be mistaken for the religious, but this is not the true religious life because it is based on belief and reason, not faith. Some may hope to become religious merely by following the teachings, while others will use the teachings as justifications for acts of tyranny. In both cases there is be a belief that the teachings are objectively true and morally good, and following them word for word will absolve us of responsibility for their effects. Instead, we sacrifice our subjectivity for objectivity.

The Religious sphere of existence

Sooner or later the answers gained in the ethical sphere become less and less convincing. The social conventions and moral codes that were once thought to be absolute are now found to be relative, and the benefits of money and social inclusion are found not to be as spiritually nourishing as was hoped for. Successful socialisation does not lead to a contented life.

The final transition to the religious sphere strikes at the heart of Kierkegaard's distinction between objective and subjective truth. Objective truths are discovered by reason and are believed. They are facts. Subjective truths are different; they are personally meaningful and chosen. Kierkegaard's God is a personal God that cannot be believed in like we believe in a chair, because this makes God earthly and not transcendental. Since God is essentially unknowable this means that we can only approach God through faith, not reason.

The move from the ethical is prompted by the realisation that there is still a despair that cannot be removed except by embracing it with faith. The person is therefore confronted with the paradox that the only truths that really matter are the truths that cannot be known. Despair in the religious sphere is associated with the guilt of failing to undertake this final freedom of faith.

Kierkegaard illustrates this in *Fear and Trembling* (1843) with the story of Abraham who was told by God to sacrifice his son, Isaac. This action clearly goes against all conventional moral codes, but Abraham nevertheless puts his faith in God who, as we know, intervenes at the last moment to stop it. Therefore Isaac is saved not because of chance or choice, but because of Abraham's faith in God – through divine intervention. Although faith is needed to make the transition between the aesthetic and the ethical, faith in God is needed to make the transition between the ethical and the religious.

The absurdity of faith is that we always act without knowing what is going to happen. On many occasions we try to get round the difficulty of faith by making the future predictable. It never works. For Kierkegaard, freedom in the religious sphere is characterised by the 'knight of faith' who embraces the absurdity of faith, committing himself to finite life while maintaining an awareness of the infinite (Kierkegaard 1983).

Addiction

Kierkegaard says in *Fear and Trembling* that if we were just finite and subject to causation and divine intervention, at the bottom of everything would be a vast pointless emptiness. Life would indeed be something to despair over. It would be truly absurd. But this, he says, is not our situation. Instead, humankind is a synthesis of necessity and possibility, finitude and infinity, eternity and temporality, and it is our responsibility to make ourselves within these parameters that evoke anxiety and despair.

Psychotherapists who work with addictions know that the differences between them, whether from alcohol, drugs, sex, food, shopping, hoarding and so on, are just artefacts of the qualities of the addictive object, and existentially what they have in common is that the drug is an external object that is then given the responsibility to do something it can never do: bring about permanent relief from despair. At a deeper level the drug is hiding the need for a connection with God and recovery can only begin with the realisation that the only option is to face despair.

This is what is known as rock-bottom (Kemp 2013) and that the addict's ability to avoid it and to maintain the delusion that recovery is possible without it is enormous. Rock-bottom is the despair that engulfs the person when they realise that what they have been doing – chasing sensation and avoiding themselves – has been futile and counterproductive. It is when they realise that there are only two developmental options open to them: death, which means a fast or slow suicide; or life – recovery. It is when they make a decision about whether to live or to die. No one can persuade a person of this, or teach anyone about this despair; it has to be experienced in its full force before the person can find something 'for which I am willing to live and die' (1976: 34). In this sense, addiction is a choice (Schaler 1999).

The importance of facing the tension between necessity and possibility has been paraphrased by the ethicist Reinhold Niebuhr (1892–1971), who asked us to have 'the serenity to accept the things we cannot change, the courage to change the things we can, and the wisdom to know the difference', and this has been taken up by Alcoholics Anonymous and its variants. These organisations also know, as Kierkegaard did, that confrontation with this despair is not just necessary for recovery, but necessary for the development of inner resources to sustain us through other despairing times. As the second step of the twelve-step approach says, recovery can only start when addicts come to 'believe that a Power greater than ourselves could restore us to sanity'. Also, as Kierkegaard knows, this restoration is never complete; it has to be repeated moment by moment, one day at a time.

The paradox of the self in relationships

As said, objective truths involve facts and certainty, whereas subjective truths involve faith and doubt. Just as the act of faith is not fixed, not once and for all, the self is not fixed either; it has to be remade every moment. For Kierkegaard this is the nature of the self, and we become spiritual by embracing the anxiety of despair. When we open ourselves to transformation by the unexpected, by God, with faith, every moment becomes a new moment.

The self is not discovered by a leap of faith – as one jumps from one stone to the next, the self is the leap itself; the self comes into being by the constantly repeated action of faith in the face of doubt.

In the aesthetic sphere love is about possession; in the ethical sphere it is about duty; and in the religious sphere it is about sharing and giving. For Kierkegaard, any act of love between people is a leap of faith because it has to be given freely with no expectation of a return. Therefore a commitment to be with a partner *till death us do part* can only be a choice based on faith not reason. That this is both a real and a symbolic moment in life is shown by the social and cultural rituals that surround it: engagement, marriage, and joy and excitement. In a similar way there are equivalent rituals when faith is found to have been misplaced: disappointment, divorce and acrimony. Love is not a thing. The act of giving with no condition of return is the act of love and has no life beyond the present moment; it has to be constantly renewed. When it is not, or when conditions start to be imposed, we become stale, complacent and resentful and may seek the instability of affairs based in the aesthetic, imagining that we are being free.

Just as the pleasures of the aesthetic are not lost in the ethical, just transformed, the pleasures of the aesthetic and the ethical are not lost in the religious. Love is expressed in many different ways, and it is always risky. But by the same token we know there is no real alternative.

4

Friedrich Nietzsche (1844–1900)

Living with power

Friedrich Nietzsche's question is essentially the same as Kierkegaard's, which is how to be an individual; how we can preserve our autonomy in the face of the normalising effects of society and religion. But he came to a very different conclusion.

He was born near Leipzig in what was then Prussia eleven years before Kierkegaard's death and like Kierkegaard grew up in a pious household. Nietzsche's father was a Lutheran pastor, as were both his grandfathers, and Friedrich, who was named after the then king of Prussia, was the eldest of three children and like Kierkegaard his early life was comfortable and settled. But he knew loss early in life; in his case it was his father who died after a short illness when he was five to be followed soon after by his younger brother. This resulted in his mother moving with Friedrich and his younger sister Elisabeth to live with her mother and two sisters in nearby Naumburg. He always spoke with great warmth about his father, describing him in his autobiography *Ecce Homo* (EH) written when he was forty-four as 'delicate, kindly and wise' (2007: 1) and that it was 'a great privilege to have such a father' (ibid.). In contrast to this he described the treatment he received from his mother and sister for his whole life as filling him 'with unspeakable horror' (ibid.: 10).

In his teens he went to a prestigious boarding school in a Cistercian monastery building close by and received a classical education learning Greek, Latin, Hebrew and French. At this time he was still a practising Lutheran but also interested in the classical world of Greece and Rome. Nietzsche's mother and sister clearly had Friedrich lined up to follow in his father's footsteps as a Lutheran pastor and at twenty he went to study theology and the new discipline of philology at the University of Bonn. While at school he had shown some desire for autonomy and individuality by studying the early nineteenth-century unfashionable and troubled Romantic poet Friedrich Hölderlin and on one occasion he returned from an outing drunk thereby losing his privileges (Hollingdale 1999: 21). His study of philology at Bonn entailed interpreting classical texts, including the Bible, which he read in the original languages, not as truth but as myth and this contributed to him losing his faith, to the dismay of his mother and sister, and he spent the rest of his life investigating the implications of this loss of faith. Another important landmark in his life at Bonn was his discovery of *The World as Will and Idea* by Schopenhauer. Although he was to disagree with Schopenhauer's conclusion about the nature of happiness, this work awakened his interest in philosophy and in particular in Schopenhauer's idea of the significance to humanity of non-rational forces.

After military service in the Prussian army he became Professor of Philology at Basel University in 1869 at the age of twenty-four and during this time, he met the composer Richard Wagner who was the same age his father would have been had he lived. He was much taken with Wagner; they both saw art as making life worthwhile and music as the greatest art form. Although respected at Basel, his highly original first book *The Birth of Tragedy* (BT) in 1872 did little to cement his academic reputation, and in 1876 at thirty-two he left Basel, initially temporarily, because of persistent and increasing ill health. He was not to return and spent the next thirteen years travelling round Europe in an effort to find a climate that would improve his health. He said in his later autobiography (EH) that his health had declined when he was thirty-six, the age his father died. During this time he wrote prolifically although with little or no impact beyond a small circle of friends. Prussia had by this time been absorbed into a greater Germany but because he did not agree with Bismarck's project, he declined German citizenship, preferring to be stateless and he alternated between spending the winters on the Mediterranean in Italy or France and eventually spending many summers in the Swiss Alps in the village of Sils Maria near the border with Italy. His symptoms included headaches, nausea, difficulty concentrating and trouble with his eyesight which he self-medicated with opium and chloral hydrate that he often obtained by writing prescriptions and signing them 'Dr. Nietzsche'. His poor health was due at least in part to a slow-growing tumour on the brain behind his right eye that eventually led to his death in 1900 (Huenemann 2013). This accounts at least in part for his aphoristic writing style after he left Basel, which was similar to the pre-Socratic philosophers he greatly admired, because he was only able to write for short lengths of time.

His religious upbringing and subsequent loss of faith had led him to be preoccupied with the possibility of transcendence without religion, and he sought its origin elsewhere. His relationship with Wagner led him to the possibilities of the ecstatic communal experience of opera, especially considering that the plots of Wagner's operas were based on German romantic nationalist myths of tragedy and were, he felt, a perfect integration of the ancient Greek Apollonian and the Dionysian spirit. Performances of Wagner's work were the nineteenth-century equivalent of twentieth-century stadium rock music or large sporting occasions. This route was short-lived as he soon saw the communal experience as being just another sort of conformity. His book *Human, All-Too-Human* (HAH) (1878) marked an end to this idea and to his relationship with Wagner because he was openly critical of Wagner's anti-Semitism. He was becoming more and more preoccupied with the relationship between individuality and transcendence. In 1882, at thirty-seven, he met Lou Salomé in Rome and became infatuated and proposed marriage to her but she was too much of a free spirit to be married to anyone; she rejected him and took up temporarily with his friend Paul Rée instead, moved to Berlin and eventually became an associate of Freud's. Irvin Yalom's (1992) subjunctive novel *When Nietzsche Wept* starts at this point, when Lou Salomé realises that Nietzsche is in a bad way and arranges for him to meet with Joseph Breuer who is also very confused – by what Freud later called transference – and for each to give the other therapy, unbeknown to the other. She subsequently wrote insightfully about her time with Nietzsche and his philosophy (Salomé 2001). The model of psychotherapy presented in Yalom's book is one where Nietzsche is extremely challenging and not at all sympathetic to Breuer's self-pity. It is also a model that relies for its effectiveness on being challenging to both client and therapist.

In 1889 he had a physical and psychological breakdown in Turin and after a brief spell in hospital went to live with his mother in the house he had lived in as a child. His writing career was over. Meanwhile his sister Elisabeth and her husband had been trying to establish an Aryan, anti-Semitic colony in Paraguay and after his mother's death in 1897, his sister who had returned from Paraguay in 1893 after her husband's suicide, took responsibility for Nietzsche's welfare and proceeded to promote a distorted version of her brother's philosophy. In 1900, at fifty-six, he died of pneumonia following a stroke and is buried in the family grave beside the church in the village where he was born.

Reading Nietzsche

Reading Nietzsche presents some unique challenges. His elliptical, repetitive, poetic style is more akin to philosophising than to formal philosophy and his imagery and tendency towards hyperbole introduces an ambiguity and an intensity that can be both excitingly clear and frustratingly opaque. He was not likely to say *'I don't know'* about anything. It is rather like trying to make out a landscape illuminated by flashes of lightning. Things become momentarily vivid only to be plunged into darkness, only to be lit up again from another direction. Although clear, one wonders if one saw accurately. This metaphor is not accidental as it is employed by Nietzsche himself in *Thus Spoke Zarathustra* (TSZ) (2006a). Is it philosophy, is it psychology, is it cultural criticism, is it political polemic, or is it religious teaching? It is all of these and all the time. But it is also autobiography and not just because he often wrote in the first person.

Nietzsche's interest in autobiography, and biography in general, was long-standing; he wanted to know how people lived their lives and anyone reading Nietzsche's more formal, for him, autobiography (EH) – it was not written in aphorisms – expecting a sequential and factual account of his life will be disappointed. He says in *Beyond Good and Evil* (BGE) (2006b: 6) that 'every great philosophy [is] the personal confession of its author and a kind of involuntary and unconscious memoir'. What he means is that whether the writer intends it or not, there is an intrinsic and necessary connection between the moral purpose of the philosopher and their writings. In this he anticipates the phenomenological concept of reflexivity. This theme is explored at greater length by Nehamas (1985: 13) who agrees, saying that 'Nietzsche's thinking is inseparable from his writing and that coming to terms with his style is essential to understanding him at all.'

Freadman (2001: 61) suggests that a major factor in the writing of all autobiography is the will to power and that Nietzsche exerts this will, as Kierkegaard did, by rejecting the stable ego of the unitary authorial voice, in favour of a number of constructed and highly rhetorical narrative selves in both first and third person, singular and plural, as well as active and passive voices, and each making a bid for its own centrality in the world.

This brings in another important idea that Nietzsche called perspectivism. In this idea he again anticipates phenomenology and stakes another claim to be one of the first phenomenologists. What he means is that we adopt perspectives on reality whether we are aware of it or not; we can only ever see things from where we are. Our reflexivity is the only way to save our perspective from being a solipsistic delusion. Therefore the conclusions we draw about our existence are always defined by current circumstances, of which we actually know very little. This is what Sartre and Beauvoir were later to call our 'situation'. Nietzsche talks about this in *The Will to Power* (WP) (1968), when he says that there are no facts, only interpretations, and that even this is an interpretation. He goes on to say,

> In so far as the word 'knowledge' has any meaning, the world is knowable; but it is interpretable otherwise, it has no meaning behind it, but countless meanings.—'Perspectivism.' It is our needs that interpret the world; our drives and their For and Against. Every drive is a kind of lust to rule; each one has its perspective that it would like to compel all the other drives to accept as a norm.
>
> (WP: 481)

Schacht (1994) suggests therefore that truth, as defined by perspectivism, has to accommodate all the currently knowable viewpoints that illuminate an idea in apparently contradictory ways, but on closer examination reveal only contextual differences. Truth is neither solely objective nor subjective but phenomenological, and is continuously created by integrating different perspectives together (Nehamas 1985: 3). One can never have enough perspectives and, like a novelist, Nietzsche continually generates more perspectives to make his work progressively richer, or as narrative theorists call it, thicker. Like Kierkegaard he had no wish to construct a unifying philosophical system, so those who look for it will be disappointed, and those who try to make one misunderstand his project.

Nietzsche was as prone to distortions of perspectivism and inadequate reflexivity as anyone else and this is nowhere more so than in his analysis of gender differences. Sceptical about the possibility of equality in sexual relationships, he talks on many occasions with his usual certainty about the ways that sexual love can manifest such that 'the lover wants unconditional and sole possession of the longed-for person' (e.g., The Gay Science (GS) (2001): 14) but also more speculatively and rarely that:

> Here and there on earth there is probably a kind of continuation of love in which this greedy desire of two people for each other gives way to a new desire and greed, a shared higher thirst for an ideal above them. But who knows such love? Who has experienced it? Its true name is friendship.
>
> (ibid.)

It is, however, unlikely from the biographical evidence available that Nietzsche had much actual experience of such friendships with women or even any sort of relationships with them except of course with his mother and sister, which, as said, were rather different.

Nietzsche's antipathy towards women, and especially his view that women are incapable of friendship in a section called 'On the friend' in TSZ, have to be read in the context of four factors that collectively constrained his reflexivity. They are firstly, that during the writing of TSZ he was still smarting from his rejection by Lou Salomé; secondly, his relationship with, or rather the way he had constructed his relationship with, his mother and sister seems to have been entirely negative; thirdly, that the undervaluing of women was a significant trend in nineteenth-century Christian-influenced thought; and lastly, that he idealised the pre-democratic Greek social organisation in which women were thought to be inferior to men.

Because there is a wide variety of perspectives within Nietzsche any summary of his thought will be an interpretation not only because it will depend on what perspectives are chosen to make the summary from but also because they will be added together in new ways. This is true of this book too. Its truth is no more or less accurate than any other summary, but is represented instead by the intention of the writer, me, not to deliberately mislead, and also by the degree to which it resonates with the reader's experience. That is to say, what you, the reader, do with it.

Above all therefore, his books are readers' books. They demand attention and it is this that has led him to be misunderstood sometimes through ignorance, and sometimes wilfully, for example in the way his sister edited his unpublished notes in WP to suit the emerging Nazi ideology of the early twentieth century. In this context it is slightly alarming to learn that Heidegger felt that WP was the most complete summary of Nietzsche's thought (Heidegger 1979) and it is the reading of WP that has led to a connection being made between his ideas and those of Ayn Rand.

Philosophy

The mid to late nineteenth century was a time of great change based on industrialisation, science and rationality. The established order was being challenged from all directions. Marx had published the *Communist Manifesto* in 1848, Darwin had published *On the Origin of Species* in 1859 and Dostoyevsky had published *Crime and Punishment* in 1866. In *Twilight of the Idols* (TOI) (1990), Nietzsche called Dostoyevsky 'the only psychologist, incidentally, from whom I had something to learn; he ranks among the most beautiful strokes of fortune in my life' (TOI: 45). What Nietzsche saw around him, though, was just the speeding up of a historical process that was given an extra push by the Enlightenment, whereby the Dionysian forces of emotion, imagination and creativity of earlier eras were being gradually weakened and were in danger of being completely submerged by the nineteenth-century Apollonian forces of reason and order. But one of the consequences of this rise of rationalism was even more catastrophic for humanity, and that was the decline of religion.

He wanted to revive the ancient Greek purpose of philosophy as a practical discipline intimately bound up with the promotion of *eudaimonia*, of human happiness and flourishing. He was not only the first philosopher to write about the human condition in the light of modernism but he also anticipated post-modernism with his views on the nature of truth and the self (Thompson 2004) while also giving a vigorous critique of it that resisted both the dead-end of easy secular humanism and also the simplistic glorification of human self-assertiveness. He did this by focusing on the transformative power of the tragedy of human existence (Deurzen 2010).

For Nietzsche, 'life is an endless struggle, where moments of ease and happiness are the exception rather than the rule' (Deurzen 2015: 181).

'God is dead'

When Nietzsche coined the phrase 'God is dead' in *The Gay Science* (GS: s125) he meant that science had destroyed the Christian value structure of European society leaving a Christian-style ethical system devoid of spirituality. He continues, 'We have killed him – you and I. All of us are his murderers ... God is dead.'

With God as no longer a source of absolute moral authority, objectivity and science had deprived humanity of three fundamental qualities; there were no ultimate values to believe in and be guided by, there was no solution to the fear of death, and there was also no ultimate moral code to live by. This has led him to be described rather crudely and inaccurately as a nihilist. For Nietzsche though, it was the death of God that followed from the advances in science that was nihilistic.

He says in *The Will to Power* (WP: 13) that nihilism is 'a pathological transitional stage' and by this he means that it is pathological to assert that there is no meaning at all to life, and that if nihilism is not transitional it is only because the person is not strong enough to overcome it. Nihilism is therefore something that we must experience and pass through. It is not the end, but a beginning; it is an opportunity to revaluate inherited moral codes and create new personal ones. Nihilism is a necessary shattering process that enables transformation, a process that is both life-depressing and also life-enhancing (Jenkinson and Adams 2007).

But even without the influence of modernity Nietzsche was highly critical of Christianity. He saw Christianity as a malign and fundamentally unhealthy influence whose focus on the next life rather than the present life robbed the here and now of its sublime meaning and possibility.

Christianity and slave morality

He first explored his criticisms of Christianity in *On the Genealogy of Morals* (GM) (1969) where he said that Christian morality is a slave morality because it focuses on the worst off in society. By denigrating human power and mystifying weakness into strength it results in a culture of blame in which people are praised for the amount of suffering they can endure. This mystifies victimhood into a human achievement and litigation and public shaming comes to be seen as a legitimate way of establishing blame, exacting revenge and becoming famous, but not through any personal striving. While it is supposed to make life safer it actually leads to a culture of mediocrity and a relationship with strength and power that is both ambivalent and confused. Being guilty about our own power and fearful of being held responsible for someone else's misfortune, we become risk-averse and retreat into conformity. This is the contentment of what he called the herd, for whom mediocrity is satisfactory. If society is to survive, he said it needed the great individuals that slave morality was holding down.

He was not against compassion, but it needs to be derived from the knowledge that all people share the same struggles with living, not from a delusion of superiority and specialness on the part of the carer. The latter is not empathy; it is pity. For compassion to be valuable we have to start by being compassionate towards ourselves. He says, 'Help yourself, then everyone will help you. Principle of brotherly love' (TOI: Maxims and Arrows 9). And with an eye on the future profession of psychotherapy he says, 'Physician, help yourself: thus also you help your sick' (TSZ: 102). If we do not, our compassion will make the sick more powerless.

Slave morality is also responsible for what he called *ressentiment.* Nietzsche adopted the French word for resentment as there was no equivalent in German. This is both a psychological and a cultural phenomenon whereby those who identify as weak in society develop a persistent and fixed pattern of resentful and impotent, passive aggressive, hatred towards the strong, who in turn despise the weak. A dangerous competitiveness then follows where we compare the power and status we have with what we feel we are entitled to, and thus deprived of. It leads to a denial of complicity and a righteous indignation that prevents the weak from becoming strong in their own right because they see the strong as the cause of their weakness (Scheler 1915). Nietzsche said it was largely a phenomenon of modernity because in pre-industrial societies power and status were seen as hereditary and this had the effect of mitigating envy. Industrial, post-Christian democracies have 'replaced the yearning of salvation in the afterlife with the clamour for affluence and security in this world, breeding extravagant needs and expectations' (Burston 2003: 5).

Nietzsche was tapping into and disputing the dominant ideology of the time that we need to suffer on earth in order to have a better life in heaven. It was a message in which our natural Dionysian human drives were considered to be an affront to God and were made into something to be ashamed of and to be denied. This, he said, showed an institutionalised hatred of our natural humanity.

The body

This led him to place an importance on the body as the origin of and the centre of knowledge. He was not just talking biologically; he meant the unity of body and soul, thereby rejecting the Cartesian separation of body and soul, or body and mind. He says in TSZ in the section 'Of the Despisers of the Body', that 'I am body entirely, and nothing beside; and soul is only a word for something in the body. The body is great intelligence, a multiplicity with one sense, a war and a peace, a herd and a herdsman.' In case this sounds reductive it is not because he goes further than this to consider the nature of the self, and says in the same section, 'Behind your thoughts and feelings, my brother, stands a powerful commander, an unknown wise man – he is called self. He lives in your body, he is your body.'

He was saying that the combination of science and Christianity has conspired to separate us from our body, from our sense of wisdom. The mature view is to recognise that soul and body are one, and that what is called the soul is an aspect of our physicality. Moreover, that we can choose to listen to or to ignore the wisdom of the body. It will be remembered that Nietzsche had little physical strength. What happens if the body is ignored he talks about in a section called 'The Pale Criminal', again in TSZ. He says, 'What is this human being? A pile of illnesses that reach out into the world through his spirit: there they seek their prey Whoever grows ill now is befallen by the evil that is evil now; he wants to hurt with that which makes him hurt.' We ignore our body at our peril because by ignoring it we give ourselves illnesses, feel victimised by our own body and then blame others for not curing them. On the other hand, by listening to our body we connect with our human spirit and find our power. Our emotions are how we feel in our body and we create problems for ourselves by labelling some emotions negative, because this suggests that they are unnecessary or damaging, at a huge cost to our humanity.

Instead of devoting energy to overcoming them we need to learn to use them. To do this we need to know them.

The human spirit

Whereas Kierkegaard's model of human development resulted from putting faith in God, Nietzsche's solution was about discovering the power of the human spirit by continually confronting and overcoming life's obstacles and that far from needing God to find ourselves, in fact God takes us away from ourselves.

Life is indeed a struggle, but it is more accurate to say that life is struggle and that paradoxically, it is this struggle that makes life so fulfilling. It is how we discover our spirit. He says, 'There is much that is difficult for the spirit, [...] but the difficult and the most difficult are what its strength demands' (TSZ: s1). In typical fashion he also says, 'Out of life's school of war: What does not destroy me, makes me stronger' (TOI: Maxims and Arrows 8). Rediscovering the resilience of the human spirit is linked to his phrase, 'Become who you are' (GS: s270) and by this he means that we cannot be more than we are. There is nothing extra or more that we need to aspire to, simply who we really are, since most of the time we are selling ourselves short. And when he says, 'who you are', he does not mean it in any fixed sense, but in the sense of possibility: what we can become through struggle. Anticipating Heidegger, he said that every individual is a piece of fate; every individual has something given to them and it is up to them to make something of it by choosing what challenges to take on. Some people know what they have to do but choose to do nothing; they seek safety. These are people for whom stasis is comforting, and change – beginnings and endings – is terrifying.

Nietzsche and human development

In struggling, the spirit undergoes three metamorphoses and although he talks about this developmental process explicitly only in one brief chapter in TSZ the implications reverberate throughout his work. In GS he talks about the genesis of TSZ. In 1881, on his travels round Europe he found himself in Sils Maria. At last he had found a place where he was able to think and write in peace. Like all his work, Zarathustra has strong autobiographical elements and in the character of Zarathustra he is describing a process of personal transformation he had when he was forty that also has universal resonance (Yates 2011: 66).

He begins Zarathustra like this,

> When Zarathustra was thirty years old, he left his home [...] and went into the mountains. Here he had the enjoyment of his spirit and his solitude and he

> did not weary of it for ten years. But at last his heart turned – and one morning he rose with the dawn, stepped before the sun, and spoke to it. Thus began Zarathustra's going down.
>
> (TSZ: 1)

He wanted and felt able to tell the world about his realisations, but as with his own writings, no one wanted to hear what Zarathustra had to say.

The human spirit he calls the reverent spirit, meaning that the spirit reveres the tasks it is to undertake and it is this reverence that draws the spirit on its journey of transformation which is never directed towards prescribed ends, rather than to take on heavier loads. It is this spirit, this strength, that makes us truly human and when we deny our spirit, we deny our humanity.

He talks about it in WP (s. 1067) and sees it as pure energy. It is

> a monster of energy, without beginning, without end; a firm, iron magnitude of force that does not grow bigger or smaller, that does not expend itself but only transforms itself, [...] this world is the will to power, and nothing besides! And you yourselves are also this will to power, and nothing besides.

Always keen to get away from materialism he also describes it using the simile of an ocean wave constantly moving back and forth, forever seeking crevices to explore. He says, 'That is how the waves live – that is how we live' (GS: 310). For Nietzsche, the self is not a thing; it is a process that has no endpoint any more than the movements of the waves have a fixed form or an endpoint. Every act is transformational and changes the self, changes our story, because our self is nothing other than our striving.

The three metamorphoses

Nietzsche describes a metaphorical process of three spiritual transformations from the immature spirit into the camel, then from the camel to the lion, and then from the lion to the child, which characterises the flourishing life (TSZ: s1). Like Kierkegaard's, his model is directional, but not one-way, automatic or gradual.

Consistent with his multiple viewpoints these stages can be seen as applying on a psychological level as much as on a societal or political level and each will have to be treated in a different way by the psychotherapist because each has different characteristics and different needs.

The first stage: the camel

The defining quality of the camel is to fulfil the tasks it is given. It can be thought of as corresponding chronologically to childhood although there is no guarantee that it will ever transform to the next stage, the lion. Some people may choose comfort and stability and spiritually remain in childhood forever. The camel stage is a time for obedience, of receiving instruction and of internalising society's requirements in order to live a socially responsible life. It is when we learn self-discipline. It is in the camel's nature to say 'Yes' to obligation and burden without reflecting on its relevance, purpose or personal meaning. The camel is so immersed in its task that it has no understanding of context or alternatives. It accepts everything as normal.

The child's life story is to a large extent written by others. As such, the child's duties and responsibilities follow society's values as refracted through the family. Some of these may be healthy influences, but others may reflect the pathologies of that particular society. While the camel at least at the beginning takes pleasure out of taking on heavier and heavier loads, as time goes on it becomes increasingly more isolated both from others and from its reverent spirit. But as a child gets chronologically older and gets to experience other ways of being it starts to reflect, to question how far its will to power is being exercised. A child may well feel that he or she is not being treated correctly but will not have the power to do anything about this and consequently feel that his or her perceptions are wrong and/or wrongly take responsibility for the mistreatment. This can persist through life in the way people can take on the characteristics of their abusers. The point at which the camel's spiritual task transforms is when it finds its work most meaningless and it no longer serves its original purpose.

While taking on loads is the camel's nature, it is not its true spirit. This distinction between nature and spirit is important. For a camel, taking on loads is easy, it is what it does, it is far more difficult for the camel to unload itself, but this is what it needs to do.

The camel's spiritual task is to take on the heavier burden of not taking on more loads. We know that in everyday life we only change when we become so dissatisfied with what we are doing that we cannot continue – when we realise that facing nihilism and risking an unknown future seems more preferable than staying put.

The second stage: the lion

The transformation of the camel spirit to the lion spirit represents how the reverent spirit asserts its fundamental independence by showing it can overcome the burdens it has taken on. In contrast to the camel's 'Yes', the lion's nature is to say 'No' in an equal and opposite way. Although angry and necessarily so, the lion does not act out of its own rage, but because the camel has unquestioningly accepted too much. It is a reactive anger and the heavier the load that the camel has taken on, the greater will be the lion's anger.

Nietzsche calls all the outside influences the *'thou shalts'*. Using mythical imagery he says, '"Thou shalt" is the name of the great dragon. But the spirit of the lion says, "I will." "Thou shalt" stands in its way, gleaming golden, a scaly animal, and upon every scale "thou shalt!" gleams like gold' (TSZ: 1). Each scale represents one of the *'thou shalts'* that the camel spirit has grown up with believing as fact. Some are particular to the child's family situation and some are cultural and historical going back many centuries, like Christianity. But whereas the camel, as a child, submitted to the *'thou shalts'*, the challenge for the lion spirit, the youth, is to find the courage to throw them off, and the dragon has to be slayed, scale by scale.

There is a clue here to the nature of what we call adolescent rebellion, and the risk of adolescence is that in throwing off inherited values nihilism will be confronted and will leave the young person with nothing, with no values. But this is a risk that has to be taken in the name of autonomy, and the freedom thus created will not give rise to new values themselves, rather than the space for new values to emerge. This is true self-discovery.

And so, when all the *'thou shalts'* are overcome and the dragon is thoroughly slain, the rage evaporates and the lion can gain the courage to reject its easy destructiveness and move on to the next challenge.

The third stage: the child

In the child spirit there is at last the possibility of something completely new and original emerging, rather than something reactive. Nietzsche says, 'The child is innocence and forgetting, a new beginning, a game, a wheel rolling out of itself, a first movement, a sacred yes-saying' (TSZ: 1). What he means is that having faced nihilism with courage and survived, the spirit is now free both of its dependence on the past and of its rage against the past and is not in need of future redemption. In this way we become able for the first time to develop a personal moral code to live by.

This is how he understands self-sufficiency. It is the ability to be independent of the herd and free of the reactive obligation to say *yes* or *no*. The motive for truly heroic behaviour is not to gain the praise of others, nor is it to feel victorious over others, but so that the spirit can delight in its own strength. Only the child spirit is able to say this unconditional and sacred *'Yes'* to life and thus gain the right to make his or her own life story.

For Nietzsche the greatest load to bear is this responsibility and he called this attaining the state of the *Übermensch* or 'overman'.

According to Nietzsche, the turning point of evolution is not between animal and man, but between man who is still an animal, and man who is truly human. He says, 'Mankind is a rope fastened between animal and overman – a rope over an abyss. [...] What is great about human beings is that they are a bridge and not a purpose' (TSZ: 4). We are nothing but possibility. But Nietzsche is not a Darwinian; the *Übermensch* state will not happen by itself but by the individual's effort to substitute choice for causation and to rise above his own tendency towards mediocrity. As such it is available to all but guaranteed to none.

It is not the pinnacle of struggle after which no struggle is necessary; it is the struggle itself, and as soon as we become complacent our spirit diminishes in strength, much as our physical strength diminishes when we cease exercising, and we slip back into being spiritual couch potatoes.

The Nietzschean psychotherapist will therefore hold onto the ideal of the importance of struggle, and will be unlikely to accept the avoidance of struggle embodied in such statements as *'I can't'* challenging the client to translate them into *'I won't'*.

She will also be guided by the principle that although periods of calmness and tranquility are valuable so we may regroup, when extended they are often a cover for self-deception. Happiness, such as it is, comes not from these moments, but from the satisfaction we gain from defining a difficult task for ourselves and mastering it, and then defining and mastering another more difficult task (Deurzen 2008). Happiness is also connected to creativity, and creativity does not come from out of nowhere – this is a romantic view – but is preceded by a lot of hard and frequently rather dull work and also much trial and error, think a musician practising scales or an artist filling sketchbook after sketchbook (Crawford 2010a: 51). Although the finished work will probably provide some moments of satisfaction, by the time it is finished the artist will be on to the next challenge. Or if there is no next challenge, the last work will just get repeated and subsequent works become ever more dull and mediocre. It is not just artists and musicians that have to master their technique before their personal skill can develop and they are able to produce something original. We all do.

The 'last man'

Nietzsche contrasts the *Übermensch* with what he calls the 'last man'. He was not a fan of post-Enlightenment egalitarian democracy because he saw it as fostering a disabling desire for comfort and in this he is echoed by Fukuyama (1992). He said a post-Christian technocracy would be like a non-secular religion that celebrates the mundane.

Nietzsche would recognise the consequent symptoms of *ressentiment* in our contemporary consumerist world, where options masquerade as choices, where sexuality is commodified, where art becomes a product to be bought and sold, where the ambiguity of reality is reduced to trivializing soundbites, where political debate is more concerned with manufacturing an oppositional either/or dichotomy, and where legitimate questioning is reframed as fear-mongering or 'fake news'. In the same way, redemption, transcendence, is never achieved by winning the lottery, and the fame that is gained by being on reality TV is empty. The contemporary rhetoric of freedom and taking back control undoubtedly has great appeal, except that the freedom on offer is a freedom from 'them' that 'we' are alleged to be under attack from. He anticipates Beauvoir's (2015) idea of the 'adventurer', who is a charismatic leader who promises to 'return' power to the electorate, but actually intends to use it for his own purposes. The slave morality is being invoked again and we are being asked to trust those who brought it about in the first place, to remove it.

Übermensch is an embodied and embodying process that can only be undertaken by people who are authors of their own change process. As Western European culture has evolved to become more technological and cognitive, we have become dependent on what might be and distanced from our own experience.

He wanted us to keep asking the deeply moral question of how we should live and what the point of our lives is. He says, 'one must still have chaos in oneself to be able to give birth to a dancing star' (TSZ 1: 5), meaning that a life without struggle will lead to true nihilism. And goes on to say, '"What is love? What is creation? What is longing? What is a star?" thus asks the last man, and blinks.' The 'last man' is incapable of appreciating the value of mystery and wonder. Aspiring only to continuity and comfort the last man renders the emergence of the *Übermensch* impossible.

Time, temporality and eternal recurrence

As said, the three transformations are not unidirectional, automatic or linear; they are better thought of as cyclical. Nietzsche's conception of time and temporality is encapsulated in the thought experiment of eternal recurrence that he developed at Sils Maria and it is associated with the proposition that our fear of death is derived from of our fear of an unlived life. He says in GS, published a year before TSZ,

> What, if some day or night a demon were to steal after you into your loneliest loneliness and say to you: 'This life as you now live it and have lived it, you will have to live once more and innumerable times more; and there will be nothing new in it, but every pain and every joy and every thought and sigh and everything unutterably small or great in your life will have to return to you, all in the same succession and sequence [...]. The eternal hourglass of existence is turned upside down again and again, and you with it, speck of dust!' Would you not throw yourself down and gnash your teeth and curse the demon who spoke thus?... Or how well disposed would you have to become to yourself and to life to crave nothing more fervently than this ultimate eternal confirmation and seal?
>
> (GS s.341)

He expands on it in part III of TSZ and it is presented as a struggle Zarathustra has with a malign dwarf he calls the spirit of gravity. The image is that of a mountaineer with a dwarf (*gravity*) on his back and the further he climbs, the more the dwarf draws him back to the abyss and the further there is to fall. This makes Zarathustra recognise the need for courage:

> Courage also slays dizziness at the abyss; and where do human beings not stand at the abyss? [...] Courage is the best slayer; courage slays even pity. But pity is the deepest abyss, and as deeply as human beings look into life, so deeply too they look into suffering. But courage is the best slayer, courage that attacks; it slays even death, for it says: 'Was that life? Well then! One More Time!'
>
> (TSZ: 3.1)

This is important for psychotherapy because courage in the face of the unknown is necessary for change because courage destroys giddiness at abysses and annihilates self-pity. Insight is the consequence not the prerequisite of change. By facing adversity with courage we discover we are free and why the spirit of gravity cannot anchor us in the world of fate, necessity and causation. Nietzsche presents the idea of eternal recurrence as a choice between two paths approached through a gateway: one path stretches endlessly behind, the past; and the other endlessly ahead, the future; and the name of the gateway is 'moment' (TSZ: 3.2). The word he uses means literally 'glance of the eye' and is a term borrowed probably knowingly from Aristotle and then Martin Luther, and certainly unknowingly from Kierkegaard. It was a term Heidegger was also to use.

The dwarf argues that since history is determined the notion of choice is irrelevant. Nietzsche makes it clear though that such a conception of time implies a crushing fatalism (Kaufmann 1950: 178) that reduces life to causation and ignores choice and agency: the ability to choose a different path.

Instead, because the past, present and future are experienced as interconnected and simultaneous, every moment in time can be such a moment but we rarely make it so because of our desire for comfort and anaesthetising predictability. In this way we actively but unwittingly repeat our past mistakes giving ourselves excuses like *I couldn't help it* or *its genetic* or *it's my parents' fault.* All of these are variations on circular recurrence or serial determinism in which we cast ourselves as slaves, as victims of circumstance, of other people, or even of life itself. Each and every moment can be the gateway to a different past and a different future, but instead we spend our time passively waiting for the right moment to arrive with guarantees for the future, not realising that no moment will ever be more real than the present moment and that there will never be any guarantees.

Nietzsche's theory of lived time enables the possibility of outgrowing behaviour patterns that lead to unsatisfactory ways of living.

To return to the question Nietzsche left us with earlier: if we are able to look at ourselves and answer honestly that we have not ducked any of the challenges life has thrown up and that we have lived in such a way that we would be happy for all the events, actions and decisions of our lives to be repeated in exactly the same way for eternity, then we are truly living authentically and *Übermensch* has been achieved, but only up until that moment. Life is about a never-ending succession of such present moments that can be enjoyed and relished for what they are and is not about striving for a future promised land either on earth or in heaven. He uses the phrase *amor fati- 'to love ones fate',* which is derived from Epictetus, to describe the attitude in which we see everything that happens in our life, including suffering and loss as beneficial for our learning.

But if our answer is *no,* a fixed autobiography based on causation begins to be constructed out of the way we only brush the surface of existence. Only by experiencing the intensity of the present moment do we become aware of our choices and gain the power to change the course of our lives. If we are always focused on what we have done or what we are going to do, what we regret or what we expect, there is no current world to experience, and hence no coherent sense of self. It is by having the courage to go through the gateway that we open ourselves to being.

On many occasions we can rise to the challenge with courage, but trauma results when we are forced out of our habitual comfort into the unpredictable present by an instance of randomness and chance such that the foundations we grew to rely on are suddenly found to have collapsed. Trauma is when meaning evaporates and we fall into the abyss.

Ever optimistic, Nietzsche sees this as an opportunity. It is when we realise perhaps for the first time that we have a choice. It is the gateway of the moment to an authentic life of presentness and a deeper understanding of existence (Jenkinson and Adams 2007).

It is only in the dismantling of old ways of being that we create new meanings. This questioning and revaluation of values, whether through courage or chance, is not some arcane intellectual exercise; it is the stuff of therapy. It is the way we develop and only by accepting and loving our fate are we are able to come to terms with our history and escape the inertia of the past.

This is relevant not just to living, but also to dying, as he says in 'On free death' in TSZ,

> Many die too late, and some die too early. The doctrine still sounds strange: 'Die at the right time!' thus Zarathustra teaches it. To be sure, how could the person who never lives at the right time ever die at the right time? But he had not yet matured. A youth loves immaturely, and immaturely too he hates mankind and earth. Still tethered and heavy to him are his mind and the wings of his spirit. But in a man there is more child than in a youth, and less melancholy; he knows more about death and life. Free for death and free in death.

If we are able to live at the right time, in the moment, then we are also able to die at the right time. Not too early or too late.

5

Martin Heidegger (1889–1976)

Living in time

Born in Messkirch in rural southern Germany near the Swiss border in the year of Nietzsche's breakdown and raised as a strict Roman Catholic in a predominantly Protestant area, Martin Heidegger was the eldest of three children. In contrast to his mother who was outgoing and good-humoured, his father was very quiet and reserved and was a woodworker. As the sexton of the local church he also had the responsibility for maintaining its fabric and for bell-ringing. After a period in a Jesuit seminary near Konstanz, he studied theology at the University of Freiburg some 70 miles from Messkirch but soon changed to philosophy and studied with Husserl. A small wiry man with piercing, bewitching, eyes – he filled out in later years – and a good skier, he met his wife when she was studying politics at Freiberg University and they married when he was twenty-eight and she was twenty-four. She was a Protestant and after the marriage they both broke with their respective churches, which greatly disappointed both sets of parents. Nevertheless he was buried, at his request, in the Catholic graveyard at Messkirch. Heidegger never lost his attachment either to the possibility of transcendence or to the practical rural life. Heidegger and Merleau-Ponty are the only major existential philosophers to have had children and he had two, both boys but his second son, Hermann, was not biologically his, being the result of an affair his wife had with a local doctor. Although intellectually able, his wife had little involvement in his philosophical work, but Hermann was more interested in his father's work and became Martin's literary executor.

Heidegger was influenced in his early career by both Husserl and Brentano and his best-known work, *Being and Time* (1927), was written during the German depression but prior to the rise in German nationalism and Heidegger's Nazi affiliation. It was not published in English until 1962. The relationship with Husserl was both personal and philosophical. He was about the same age as Husserl's son who died in the First World War and *Being and Time* was originally dedicated to Husserl. He also took over Husserl's post when he retired from the University of Freiberg in 1928. In 1933 he became rector of the university, which strained his relationship with Husserl, who was Jewish. It was a job that required him to enforce new Nazi laws that included removing Jews from university posts, which he did. However, he resigned from the post a year later and spent the rest of his life out of formal academic life unable to teach until 1951 when his rehabilitation began. Safranski (1998) suggests that his association with the National Socialists was both philosophically and politically naïve in that he thought his ontology could be transposed directly onto the ontic national context. Safranski (ibid.: 232) also suggests that his wife was more keen on his Nazi affiliation and that Heidegger himself was bewitched by Nazism, feeling that it would release Germany from the tyranny of the Nietzschean 'last man', and that he resigned and retired from public life when he realised this could not be done. As a result of the post-war denazification hearings, which prevented him from teaching until 1951, he had a breakdown in 1946 and was treated by a colleague of Ludwig Binswanger (ibid.: 351).

In 1922 his wife had come into an inheritance and she supervised the designing and building of an isolated four-room 'hut' at Todtnauberg, 16 miles from Freiberg in the Black Forest mountains. This south-facing 'hut' had no utilities until the 1960s; water came from a nearby spring and all heating and cooking was done on wood-fired stoves and Heidegger had wood-cutting rights in the forest. It had few books or furnishings, and although he always kept his house in Freiberg, after his resignation he spent more time life in it, receiving few visitors. The 'hut' is still owned by the Heidegger family and has come to have equal architectural, biographical and philosophical significance (Sharr 2006).

His younger brother, Fritz, who he was very close to and who worked in the bank in Messkirch all his life and who was in some ways his opposite, more like his mother – he had a good sense of humour – always helped him by typing out his lectures and manuscripts. Fritz also understood his brother's work very well but had no aspirations to be a philosopher himself. His breakdown also signalled a movement in his thinking towards a more spiritual transcendental dimension to existence, of belonging (Young 2002). Where Sartre and Beauvoir turned to travel, politics, the novel and the theatre for their revelation of ontology, Heidegger turned to the rural life and poetry.

The Swiss psychoanalyst Medard Boss was introduced to Heidegger's work in the 1930s by Ludwig Binswanger who was applying Heidegger's ideas to psychiatry (Binswanger 1975). Boss was becoming gradually more disillusioned with the epistemological basis of psychoanalysis and it was in the early 1940s, during Heidegger's academic exile and when Boss was serving in the Swiss army, that Boss, fourteen years younger than Heidegger, began to read *Being and Time* and to consider its relevance to psychotherapy. After the end of the war, in 1946, he wrote to Heidegger (Boss 1988) about these implications, and although Heidegger used to receive many letters, he apparently answered very few. On this occasion, however, Heidegger responded to Boss's letter with enthusiasm. This led to Boss visiting Heidegger where a kinship developed and it was followed eventually, after the teaching ban was lifted, by Heidegger travelling regularly to Switzerland to give lectures to medical students in Boss's house in Zollikon, just outside Zurich. These lectures became known as the *Zollikon Seminars* (Heidegger 2001) and lasted for ten years until 1969 each being attended by between fifty and seventy of Boss's colleagues and students. In his later years as he became more infirm, he spent less time at Todtnauberg and more time back in the Freiberg house and he died at eighty-six in his sleep at home.

Philosophy

Heidegger felt that the nature of existence had been overlooked since the ancient Greeks and he wanted to return to this question. His often quoted, 'Why are there beings at all, and why not rather nothing' (Heidegger 1998: 289), which was also raised by Leibniz in the eighteenth century, illustrates his fundamental question.

He begins *Being and Time* (1962) in this way,

> For manifestly you have long been aware of what you mean when you use the expression 'being'. We, however, who used to think we understood it, have now become perplexed.

By this he did not mean, *what is the nature of your being or my being?*, but, what is Being, with a capital B.

The word he used for Being was Dasein and it referred to the fundamental and universal conditions of human existence: the ontological dimension of human existence. In contrast, the everyday concrete, changing and practical aspects of our everyday life he called the ontic dimension and every ontic experience has an ontological correlate.

The inclusion of 'there' (*da*) in the meaning of Dasein reinforces the notion that Being is never outside looking at the world, but always in and of the world. His phrase being-in-the-world sums this up in the sense that it describes not just our permanent connection with all that is, was, and will be, but also that Being opens us to the givens of existence. Macquarrie (1972: 69) says that man 'stands out as the only one that not only is, but takes over its being in awareness of who or what it is and of who or what it may become'. Humankind alone is able to imagine the implications of life as well as death. Dasein takes on the responsibility for its own existence. Dasein is not just about existing; it is about knowing that I exist. We all have this potentiality and in this sense, the world matters to us. Our fundamental stance towards the world, Heidegger says, is one of Care (*Sorge*), the English translation of which has ontic implications that are not intended.

An analogy is that Being is the ground while the human being is the plant that grows out of the ground in which it is rooted. A plant is not the same as the ground, but will not grow unless it is in the ground. And in the way that the ground supports life, Being supports being (Karban 2017). Hence, Being is the ground of being.

This way of thinking about existence has far-reaching implications.

Temporality and anxiety

As said earlier, time is not something we passively have or don't have; it is something we are; it is personal. We are in time and time is in us; we are temporal. Just as it never stops, we never stop; we are not static; we are continuous; we are continuity. More than this though, our awareness of our temporality reminds us that we are only temporary – that we are not here for long and that there was an infinitely long time before we were born and there will be an infinitely long time after we die.

Experiencing time as continuous opens us to Being, but if, for any reason, we experience life as fragmented and/or discontinuous, we are unable to be open to Being. Experiencing life temporally evokes what Heidegger calls Anxiety that is best spelled with a capital 'A' because its origins are ontological and this distinguishes it from our own everyday, ontic anxiety, for example stress, depression, agitation and so forth. Anxiety, ontological anxiety, can only be tolerated at best for a short time and we can evade it by deferring to what he calls the 'they' or *das man* which involves abdicating responsibility and following what we imagine to be the majority opinion. This is the *they-self* and is recognisable in everyday life when we find ourselves justifying an action by saying things like, *This is what one does* or, *Everybody thinks this* or by asking *what do people usually do now … What's normal?*

In therapeutic practice we work on understanding the relationship between everyday ontic responses like stress, depression and agitation and our fundamental existential anxiety. It can be said that one-third of suffering is ontological and the other two-thirds is because we cannot accept the one-third.

Authenticity and inauthenticity

Heidegger uses the word thrownness to describe the existential fact that we are born into this world with no say about where or when or even if we come to life; our life starts from a position of randomness and chance. We gain much of our daily meaning from our constant striving to make something personal and meaningful out of the short but uncertain period between our birth and our death.

Authenticity is the English translation of a neologism (*Eigentlichkeit*) coined by Heidegger, and the clue to its existential meaning is in the first four letters 'auth', as in authorship, ownership. Authenticity therefore does not refer to what is real or genuine, nor can it be standardised or normalised; these terms are only valid in a natural scientific sense. It is about the responsibility we have for ourselves and also for others in our world, for they are functionally inseparable. In authenticity we open to Being and also to being, which is about the responsibility we have to make our own life story.

But authenticity is not sustainable for any length of time because it evokes ontological anxiety, which we avoid and inevitably slip back to inauthenticity, which is our more usual mode of being. As Cox (2009a: 88) says, authenticity is not like being an Olympic champion when you remain a champion for at least four years whether or not you run another race. Authenticity hardly lasts beyond the present moment. In inauthenticity we close off from Being and being. It is an attempt to reduce anxiety and hence to stop time. But by doing this we also deny possibility, and we always know this. This is existential guilt. A characteristic of inauthentic living is that we see ourselves as being caused and that life is a technical problem to be solved. But this too eventually becomes intolerable and we respond with what Heidegger calls the 'call of conscience' by owning up to our responsibility.

Anxiety at the responsibility of making something of our lives is always present and by constantly looking to others for a lead we fall out of touch with our autonomy and possibility. He calls this our fallenness and we often confuse thrownness with fallenness in an attempt to avoid responsibility. We find it easier to invoke causation as an explanation for our actions than to admit that we chose to limit ourselves. As such, it occurs prereflectively. It is easier to say *They stopped me doing it* than *I chose not to do it.* When we own our fallenness we open ourselves to choice.

It is more accurate to talk about the single idea of authenticity/inauthenticity. However, simply by using a textual language, as Heidegger did, where words are placed in a particular order to create a given meaning, a linearity in the relationship between authenticity and inauthenticity is reinforced that is not intended. In contrast, representing ideas pictorially, graphically, as they were prior to the growth of the written word, enables the ideas to be grasped as a whole and simultaneously, and the reader/viewer can then move around the image in any order they choose. This attempt to transcend linearity is behind Deurzen and Adams (2016: 107) simplified Cycle of Authenticity. As such therefore, both authenticity and inauthenticity has the other as its possibility. They are, as he says, equiprimordial, meaning that each is as basic to our being as the other. His reluctance to express a view about their relative value to successful living can be seen as a product of his overall project, as a philosopher primarily concerned with the ontological. Existential psychotherapists have other priorities and Cohn (2002: 124) notes that, 'However great Heidegger's reluctance may have been to tell us what to do, there can hardly be any doubt that he considered "choosing existence" to be a choice of surpassing value.'

Authenticity can therefore be an aim of psychotherapy as long as we remember firstly, that it is a general statement of intent and direction rather than an expectation of a particular end result; secondly, that it is not a norm; and thirdly, that we can never rid ourselves of inauthenticity, and any claims to have done so are inauthentic.

Heidegger and human development

On the face of it, with respect to human development, the work of Martin Heidegger does not look very promising. The details of his life are not as well documented as the other philosophers and there are almost no references in his work to any particular times of life, to human development or even to human beings as such. Safranski's (1998) biography focuses on his philosophy. Heidegger is much more interested in temporality than age. He had little personal or philosophical interest in individual history or biography and in this way he was a classical philosopher in that he concentrated on the abstract, on ontology – Being – to the exclusion of the personal, the ontic – being. For example, although he refers to how our emotionally laden relationships connect us to the world and are therefore existential clues to our being-in-the-world, this is the closest he gets to lived experience. As Kearney (2010: 150) notes, 'Dasein does not eat, sleep or have sex.' Being able to talk about the ontic as well as the ontological is necessary when thinking about human development.

In his philosophy he was a phenomenologist, and his philosophy is nothing if not a reflection on the nature of existence. But although his project was about reflexivity, he did not see any reason to include himself in his philosophy; there was no space in his work for his own personal reflexivity. This is in contrast to Kierkegaard, Nietzsche, Sartre and Beauvoir for whom it was an integral part of their work and for Merleau-Ponty for whom the links were more subtle. This may go some way, post-1945, to account for his reluctance to talk about his former Nazi affiliation.

Because he did not make the connections this does not mean that no links between his life and his philosophy can be made (Stolorow 2011), and he gave us enough building blocks to use in order to propose some implications for human development. Some of these are directly applicable to particular ages and some to life as a whole. For Heidegger development is linked to temporality rather just than to time. Time, as technologised in the clock, is impersonal, whereas temporality, the effect of time on my life, is personal.

The meaning and development of death awareness

For Heidegger, being thrown into temporality brings to light the inevitability of a personal moving into the future towards a death that is expected but is never known. A key question for human development, then, is how our understanding of death and non-being, and by implication life and being, changes as we go through life.

Philosophers from Socrates onwards have placed death at the centre of their thinking (Gray 1967). The seventeenth-century writer La Rochefoucauld (1959: Maxim 26) noted not just how hard death was to think about but also how paradoxical our relationship with it is when he said, 'Neither the sun nor death can be looked at steadily'. This has been variously translated and finds its way into the title of Yalom's (2008) *Staring at the Sun*. The title of Yalom's (2015) *Creatures of a Day*, which has the same subject, is from Marcus Aurelius, again variously translated.

In more recent times starting with the Enlightenment and on into the modernist era there was an emphasis on scientific objectivity and progress through reason, and accordingly the personal and subjective meaning of death became sidelined in favour of the biological and objective meaning of death which manifested in the attempt to control and dominate nature. Death is regarded as an illness to be treated and overcome. One example of this is in Cryonics whereby people elect to be deep-frozen until such time that technology can restore them to full health and extend their life. It is a twenty-first-century version of the Faust story and is a desire to defy time. It took the emergence of existential thinking in the nineteenth and twentieth centuries to bring death back onto the philosophical agenda (Cooper and Adams 2005). Heidegger, drawing on the work of Kierkegaard and Jaspers (1932), gives the most detailed study of existential meaning of death and an understanding of Heidegger's meaning hinges on two points: firstly, that death is not to come, it is already here. Heidegger says that since we are aware of our death as a potentiality, it is not the 'end' as such; it is a part of life and he calls this our *Being-towards-death*. He contrasts it with our *Being-at-an-end* (1962: 293) which is our demise; our physical end (1962: 295). And secondly, that death is personal. Heidegger says, '[D]eath reveals itself as that possibility which is one's ownmost, which is non-relational' (1962: 294). What this means is that I will always die my own death. No one can do it for me, or be able to tell me what it will be like. It is an utterly and uniquely unsharable life experience. It is an absent presence in our lives. Jaspers (1932) described it as a 'limit situation' we cannot escape or evade that forces us to make decisions. But we also have the freedom to choose our stance towards it. For Firestone (2015), death is the ultimate resistance.

All these points evoke anxiety, which we try to evade and deny in various ways (Becker 1973; Cooper and Adams 2005). Although these may bring some temporary relief they need constant maintenance; we always know what we are evading and denying.

However, we should guard against going down the simplistic route of pathologising all death denial, because depending on our reliance on them, these strategies can take us towards either authenticity or inauthenticity. An example of this is in Yalom's (2008: 83) idea of rippling. He says that,

> Rippling refers to the fact that each of us creates – often without our conscious intent or knowledge – concentric circles of influence that may affect others for years, even for generations. That is, the effect we have on other people is in turn passed on to others, much as the ripples in a pond go on and on until they're no longer visible but continuing at a nano level.

The important phrase in this for us here is 'without our conscious intent or knowledge'. Accommodating the idea that more than likely we will have an effect after we have gone which was neither planned, hoped for, nor expected and because of this is beyond our control and subject to randomness and chance is humbling and also authentic. In a similar way, what went before our birth exerts its influence in ways we are barely aware of. Trying to control our legacy from beyond the grave is inauthentic. Maybe karma is no more than the unexpected and unpredicted consequences of our actions.

There is a paradox and a dilemma at the centre of death. The paradox is that although physical death will kill me, the denial of death will destroy the time I have left, while the idea of death will save me in the sense that it will prompt me to live my life more resourcefully and more fully (Byock 2002; Deurzen and Adams 2016). Fear of death is not so much about the fear that life will end, it is about a fear of an unlived life, that not enough has been done in life. The dilemma is that mortality is a constant fact of our lives and we are reminded of it every time something comes to an end.

The question that our awareness of death asks is, *How can I live my life fully while knowing I may die at any moment?*

Physical death is not the same as existential death. We know what physical death is, but existential death is when we close ourselves to the world of paradox, dilemma and uncertainty. It is when we stop living. And it can happen at any time.

However, Heidegger only considers what is to come; he does not consider the equal mystery of where we came from even though his initial question, 'Why are there beings at all, and why not rather nothing?' (Heidegger 2014: 1), suggests it. The overriding mystery of existence is that the inanimate can transform to the animate and back to the animate at all.

Vladimir Nabokov (1999) begins his autobiography like this: 'The cradle rocks above an abyss, and common sense tells us that our existence is but a brief crack of light between two eternities of darkness. Although the two are identical twins, man, as a rule views the prenatal abyss with more calm than the one he is heading for.' It seems that it is equally difficult although less anxiety-provoking to contemplate non-being before birth, than after death. The difference of course is that birth brings being into existence whereas death removes being from existence.

Although Heidegger does not mention natality, the Jewish political philosopher Hannah Arendt, with whom Heidegger had a very secret affair when she was his student in the three years prior to the publication of *Being and Time*, until she broke it off, has talked extensively about the existential significance of natality, of beginnings (Arendt 1998) as has O'Byrne (2010) who prefers the term finitude to mortality.

Arendt, who understood the political life in a way that Heidegger did not, says that if freedom means anything at all it means that we have the capacity to begin, to start something new and that all human beings have this simply by virtue of having been born. Action as the realisation of freedom is therefore rooted in natality, in the fact that each birth, each new moment, represents a new beginning and the introduction of novelty into the world. She says, 'the new beginning inherent in birth can make itself felt in the world only because the newcomer possesses the capacity of beginning something new, that is of acting' (1959: 9).

Natality reminds us that everything starts, everything at least has the potential of being different from what was, whether we want it to be or not. It is a reminder of the new, the unspoiled, the free, of pure potential. Of pure wonder and awe at the becomingness of things. Our wonder at the fragility and smallness of, for example, a baby's fingernails is not simply because they are small. It is because the baby represents potential, that a completely and utterly new consciousness has arisen out of nothing, and of what may become if it. There is a fantasy, a dream, a delusion within natality that some sort of completeness of potential may or will occur. Compare this with what it is like to hold the hand of someone very old, whose hands show all the signs and scars of living. In natality there is a mixture of hope, optimism and anticipation of beginning and potential that is also tinged with sadness and melancholy because we know that before long it will fade.

Mortality reminds us that we have only a short time to decide what we want to do, find out how to do it and then to do it. It reminds us that everything is transient, everything finishes. It is a reminder of the winding down and eventual expiring of potential. It is more often tinged with sadness and melancholy, people don't like to be reminded of it, but can also be tinged with hope, optimism and anticipation that what has been done has made a difference. There is a reminder of this in the phrase from the Burial Service in the Book of Common Prayer and echoed in other religions, 'dust to dust, ashes to ashes'. The body may die but the soul, however it is defined, lives on.

In a full realisation of mortality is the realisation that not only did completeness never happen, but that it was never going to happen either. And that this is not just unfortunate or a personal failing (although it may be on some level) but it is necessary that the next generation try for completeness and fail.

To concentrate on mortality is to concentrate on the transformation of the animate, the human, into the inanimate, the material. The other side of the equation, which precedes it, is the transformation of the inanimate, the material, into the animate, the human.

Existentially life is informed by the tension between natality and mortality. Between beginnings and endings. With the eventual realisation that they are not separate or different, that neither beginnings nor endings, neither birth nor death, can happen without the other and rather than being in opposition to each other they are dialectically connected.

This is represented in Roman mythology by Janus, the god of beginnings, transitions and endings, who has two faces, one looking to the future and the other to the past. Being two sides of the same coin they are a constant reminder of our temporality.

An everyday example of this is gardening, which is often thought of as being an old person's activity but it is also as old as civilization, indeed it probably defines civilization. Not only does gardening involve heavy physical work, digging and so on, but it also embodies a close relationship with and understanding of the life of the seasons as well as the seasons of life.

Before time was taken over by the distancing effects of technology and became identified with the ticking of the clock, it was measured by the seasons and the phases of the moon, by natural events. Gardening involves understanding this, that even though an individual life will stop, life goes on, and it is only an old person's activity because this is when the cycle of life starts to be fully understood. Gardeners also know that not only are they are working with transience, but also that their work will not look at its best until many years after he or she has died. In this sense, we garden today, for tomorrow. Successful gardening also involves understanding that in the battle between the human and the natural world, the latter will always win; it resists human intervention, and is unforgiving and unrepentant. As such, as a gardener, I need to understand that a plant's survival is not just dependent on my care and skill but also on randomness and chance: weather, disease, animals and so on. These paradoxes and dilemmas make gardening an existential activity.

Existentially, a creative life is informed by the way we meet the tension between natality and mortality, beginnings and endings, the way we understand temporality. A life can be dominated by either mortality or natality. A life dominated by natality will be one that focuses on beginnings and potential. It will be dominated by thoughts of birth, of plans, hope, optimism and of openness. Life is a glass half empty and filling. A life dominated by mortality will be preoccupied by thoughts of death, ending, finality, closing down and loss, and of pessimism, and unfinishedness. Life is a glass half empty and emptying.

Young(er) people tend to be preoccupied by newness and potential and tend not to be bothered by things ending. There's plenty of time for everything. Transience is fine. Old(er) people tend to be concerned with maintaining things as they are or even of trying to return things to the way they were. This helps to stop the awareness of time passing and hence awareness of mortality. Every new thing means that an old thing, something familiar to me, will disappear. And the more things like this that disappear, the more I disappear.

But there is another huge contrast between mortality and natality. Heidegger says that death is personal, everyone dies their own death, we do it on our own. Natality is the opposite. We can only be brought into physical being by the activities of others and we are also brought into existential being through our relationships with others and the world. We are our relationships. This is the meaning of being-in-the-world.

Natality, as such, has been little studied and the differences in our awareness of death as we go through life were not addressed in any way by Heidegger but this absence has been filled by other writers and the way it has been studied is instructive. Yalom reviewed the literature concerning children's awareness of death until that date and he notes that there is a 'marked discrepancy between the importance of death to the child and the attention accorded death' in the child development literature (1980: 75).

There have been many studies and reviews in the intervening years (e.g., Kane 1979; Speece and Brent 1992; Grollman 1992; Kenyon 2001; Andrikopoulou 2004; Slaughter and Griffiths 2007; Edwards and Titman 2010). Most are not on the personal meaning of death, but on demise, on the impersonal and biological facts of death.

While there is an acceptance that children may well understand the biological meaning of death, another aspect is adults' reluctance to talk to children about the meaning of death (e.g., Dimattia and Regazzo 1995) and although factors like religious doctrine come into it, Yalom (1980) suggests this reluctance is either because they think that children will not know anything about it, or will be upset about it, or will not be able to understand something as abstract as death. And this is mirrored by a reluctance to talk about birth. That they are curious about it is shown by their enthusiasm for Halloween. When birth and death are talked about it is usually biologically rather than existentially and if the child's natural existential curiosity is met with unease or mystification, the child will quickly learn not to raise the subject again. In fact, children probably have a greater understanding, an embodied understanding, of the meaning of death than adults. They are after all closer to non-being than adults because they have only just been born into being out of non-being and they are also dependent for their being on adults.

A preoccupation with the utter mystery of birth and coming into being is shown by this comment made to me by my granddaughter, then aged four years and one month, which came apparently out of nowhere:

When I was a tiny tiny baby in my mummy's tummy, me and daddy lived in a house near the woods.

If I had said, as she already knew, that she moved from that house just after she was born it would have been factually true but I would have missed her point, which was that of the mystery of what came before and of how something can come out of nothing. As it happened she did not need a reply; she was more interested in her trampoline. As Yalom (1980) notes, it did not come out of nowhere; children of that age think of these things all the time.

This was followed two months later when she initiated this conversation with her grandmother.

Granddaughter: *My daddy came out of your tummy.*

Grandmother: *Yes.*

Granddaughter: *Just like a chicken comes of an egg ... but not every egg becomes a baby chicken does it.*

Grandmother: *That's right.*

Again, she not asking about biology, she is trying to understand the existential mystery of birth, but this time she has added into her consideration the equal mysteries of randomness, chance and death: non-being and non-becoming.

Her preoccupations with these themes continued, as shown in this conversation with me, again initiated by her, when she was four years and eight months:

Granddaughter: *Papa?*

Me: *Yes darling.*

Granddaughter: *You're very old aren't you?*

Me: *Well, I wouldn't say very old, but yes I'm old.*

Granddaughter: *That means you are going to die soon doesn't it?*

Me: *I hope not very soon.*

Granddaughter: *I don't want to die.*

Me: *No I don't want to either.*

She clearly knows about the biological meaning of death, but more than this she knows that it applies to herself as well. She knows, as Heidegger says, that death is personal.

Given that smaller children know about and are curious about death, how can we understand that older children appear not to be curious? Yalom

(1980: 91) suggests that as the child gets older curiosity appears to diminish only because death denial defences have become more established.

Later on in what we call adolescence these defences start to break down and the young person becomes far more preoccupied with existential issues including death (Fitzgerald 2005). This increasing awareness of death is evidenced by the tension between risk-taking and fearless notions of immortality on the one hand, and a developing sense of rationality and excitement about the unfolding of life's possibilities on the other hand. Adolescents are also increasingly exposed to death in a way that it becomes more personal (Noppe and Noppe 2004).

Later on into adulthood death anxiety takes on a different form when, among other things, people become or consider becoming parents. Death becomes personal in a different way because we start to think of the approaching death of our own parents at the same time as taking on the responsibility for a fragile new life. Parenthood is a lifelong project. When our parents die we becomes the next in line to death. It is another realisation that death is personal, that there is probably less time left than we have had.

What has become known as 'mid-life' is largely about an increasing personal meaning of death (Steffen 2007). Although called mid-life it is rarely halfway between birth and expected death because it is to do with death awareness, not chronology. Jaques (1956), noted a difference both in the nature and in the process of the work of creative people, and the time that this happened he called mid-life. He noted a change from the more spontaneous 'descriptive and lyrical content' of early adulthood to the more sculpted 'tragic and philosophical content' of later adulthood (ibid.: 504). This book is a sculpted work and the most important thing to know when sculpting is when to stop. Mid-life, for Jaques, is when we realise that we have stopped growing up and that we have started to grow old and this forces us to reassess our life story. Our life changes from being spontaneous to being sculpted. He illustrates this by drawing on *The Divine Comedy* by Dante. Written when Dante was thirty-seven it begins, 'In the middle of the journey of our life I came to myself within a dark wood where the straight way was lost.' This is a model of therapy because he is met by Virgil, the therapist, and although he cannot show Dante the way, he can, because of his personal knowledge of the vicissitudes of human existence, do something better, and that is to help him find his own way.

Jaques says the emotional task of mid-life is the transformation of beliefs about the goodness, or badness, of man into beliefs about the goodness and badness of man. From the either-or to the both-and.

In his view, attempts to deny death by asserting youth and youthfulness are more likely to be present in people who feel underachieving by the time they realise that they have less time left than they have had.

An alternative approach is to see ageing and death not in terms of loss – this is to look backwards – but to see life as a whole, and also to see one's own life as a continual striving for but never reaching perfection, that 'life and the world go on, and we can live on in our children, our loved objects, our works, if not in immortality' (Jaques 1956: 513).

With increasing age, death becomes more and more personal. Landmarks like peers dying, reducing physical capacity, failing health and retirement all remind us not only that time is passing, but that it will soon run out. This touches us all, no one is immune; the young just have it to come. We gradually come more face to face with death and our greatest challenge is to face non-being in a world that will carry on after we've gone. That this is not necessarily a cause for despair is shown by Yalom (2008, 2015) who notes that probably at no other time in life is there as potent a force towards self-awareness operating as in old age. Paul Wong (2000: 28) agrees, saying that 'life is a task-master while death is a master teacher', but the latter is in no way automatic and the challenge of successful ageing in the face of death is to face the reality of death and he says there are three consequences. One he calls escape acceptance and it is when ageing and death are so intolerable that suicide and profound depression seem the best option. Another is neutral acceptance and is when we accept death on a cognitive level only. He is clear about the best option and he calls it approach acceptance and it is when we can acknowledge the completion of our mission in life and look forward to a rewarding afterlife. Therefore, he gives an overtly Christian meaning to our response to death whereas Yalom's notion of rippling is more secular.

Wong's point about death showing us how to live is also shown by the experience of the musician and actor Wilko Johnson (2013) who after being diagnosed with terminal cancer said,

> The things that used to bring me down, or worry me, or annoy me, they don't matter anymore – and that's when you sit thinking, Wow, why didn't I work this out before? Why didn't I work out before that it's just the moment you're in that matters? Worrying about the future or regretting the past is just a foolish waste of time. Of course we can't all be threatened with imminent death, but it probably takes that to knock a bit of sense into our heads.

In his case, after spending a year planning a farewell tour and 'calmly accepting the idea I was going to die', the cancer turned out to be operable and that death was nothing like so imminent after all. He said, 'If there's a moral to this story it's that you never know what's going to happen.' We have to remember though that not all people will respond like this.

Boss (1994: 121) says that the 'most dignified human relationship to death consists in keeping the knowledge of personal mortality constantly in awareness, neither fleeing from it nor hiding it' and it is hard to maintain but when we do this we realise that we have responsibility for every moment of our lives. This is authenticity.

The relationship between happiness and psychological well-being over the life cycle was also investigated by Blanchflower and Oswald (2007) using international data. They found not only that happiness was lowest in middle age but also that it increased with age, suggesting the prevalence of Wong's second and third options. This finding was corroborated by a UK study (ONS 2016) which found that people aged sixty-five to seventy-nine tended to report the highest average levels of personal well-being and that those aged ninety and over reported higher life satisfaction and happiness compared with people in their middle years.

Three dimensions of temporality

All three dimensions of temporality – the past, the present and the future – can be approached authentically or inauthentically and whichever is chosen is relevant to our development.

The future

For Heidegger, the primary time dimension is the future. We are future directed and the principal issue we have to deal with is the uncertainty that we never know what is going to happen next.

Inauthentically we approach the future by 'awaiting' (1962: 397), by passive expectation, by a feeling that, *My life will get better without me doing anything about it.* In this way we disown responsibility for our lives. By waiting for the future to come to us, we unwittingly repeat previous patterns and thus reinforce the illusion of causation, often blaming others or events for our difficulties and disappointments.

In contrast, he says that authentically we approach the future with 'anticipation' (1962: 306). This is characterised by the introduction of every episode of *Star Trek*: 'To explore strange new worlds, to seek out new life and new civilizations, To boldly go where no man (*sic*) has gone before.' When we actively put ourselves into new ways of being we transcend determinism and are then able to consider the future as full of opportunities for acts of self-defining freedom. In this way we actively make the future different from the past. It is not hard to recall moments in our lives when we have done this and to remember both how exciting and also how affirming it was. It is how we develop existentially.

The past

With respect to the past, the principal issue we have to deal with is our thrownness and inauthentically we approach the past by 'forgetting' it (1962: 388). He does not mean that we cannot remember what happened, although this may also happen; it means that we forget its significance, its meaning for who we are now. We stop asking ourselves questions about it because we have already decided on its meaning and if events are remembered at all they will be remembered as interesting stories that have little significance except to fix history. There is a belief that either *I am not my past* or *I am caused by my past*. We feel fated. The flow of being becomes fragmented and discontinuous and this evasion of temporality will lead us into believing we are doing something different although we are just copying it.

In contrast, the authentic way of approaching the past is with 'repetition' (1962: 437). But he does not mean repeat as in copy; he means it in a more profound experiential sense because it is only by repetition that we can reacquire the past as a tradition and it is only by being part of a tradition that we can become free. What was once inauthentic fate becomes authentic destiny. It is a paradox that we can only transcend the past by owning it. In repetition we come face to face with our past and understand that it is not gone at all; it is present and informing our every act. In repetition there is the possibility of breaking the ties of inauthentic determinism. It is how we develop existentially.

The present

In the present, the principal issue we have to deal with is our fallenness and the need to be aware of the complexity and transience of being. Heidegger says that the inauthentic way of approaching the present is by 'making present' (1962: 388). The use of the word making is in the sense of pretending. The way we talk to each other is with 'idle talk', and by making present we hold someone else or something else responsible for our current circumstances by being either a victim, a persecutor or a rescuer. It is about passively evading and denying responsibility.

In contrast, the authentic way of approaching the present is with a 'moment-of-vision' (1962: 437). The literal meaning of Heidegger's word is *glance of the eye* and is a term borrowed from Martin Luther, Kierkegaard and Nietzsche and can be traced back to the Greek word *kairos*, meaning the right or opportune moment. This is when there is a profound sense of the simultaneity of the past, present and future and that we are on the edge of a new way of being should we be courageous enough to choose it. These moments are always unexpected. We may say something like, *I've been making this same mistake my whole life ... and I don't have to do it anymore*. We become able to actively choose the future rather than let it passively happen. We change the course of our life story. It is important to clarify the existential meaning of choice here. The everyday meaning of choice is when we select between options, whereas the existential meaning of choice is when we take personal responsibility for a course of action. The existential question is not which option shall I pick – *Shall I take this job or that job?*, or *Shall I marry this person or that person?* – but can I be committed to whichever one I choose? An existential choice can be made without there being options, because existentially there is only one question. As Shakespeare's Hamlet says, 'To be or not to be, that is the question' (*Hamlet* 3: 1), whether to embrace life and the consequences of our actions, or whether to try evade and deny them. The former will lead to authenticity, a greater and more passionate engagement with life; and the latter will lead to inauthenticity, passivity and blaming, and a sense of pretence, fragmentation and discontinuity. It may also lead to us opting out entirely.

Therefore, passively not choosing has just as strong a consequence as any active choice we may make. We can never blame anyone else for the consequences of our actions and this also applies to the positives: if we can own them, they cannot be dismissed as chance and we can take some credit for them.

A 'moment-of-vision' comes about not by inauthentic 'idle talk', but by the sort of mutual attention that leads to a more profound sense of the present that allows us the space to make an existential choice and hence take responsibility for what happens next. This is true dialogue.

Following Cohn (2002: 124), the existential psychotherapist takes special note of the way the client relates either authentically or inauthentically to the past, the present and the future, and challenges the degree to which these actions are actively chosen.

Authenticity and our relationship with the material world

As said, the world matters to us in the sense that our identity is tied up with it and when we forget this connection, we forget the meaning of our own being and also the meaning of Being; we fall into inauthenticity.

Heidegger says there are two ways of encountering objects. One way is to consider them as nearby, as 'present-at-hand' and the other as useable, as 'ready-to-hand' (1962: 98). Of these, he considers 'ready-to-hand' to be primordial, original, not necessarily because it comes easiest, or is easiest, often it is not, but because it is most important for our well-being.

Borrowing probably from his experience of watching his father at work, Heidegger uses the example of a hammer. Towards the end of his life he might have used the example of football; he was much taken with the play of Franz Beckenbauer (Safranski 1998). Seeing a hammer on a table sees it as 'present-at-hand'. This is the stance of a natural scientist, someone who sees the world objectively. The hammer is there simply as an object. I may recognise it as a hammer, but it only becomes 'ready-to-hand' when I use it. A hammer that is not being used is not a hammer; it is just a hammer-shaped object. When I pick it up I may find out that it is too heavy for the use I have for it, or the handle is too big for my hand. I instantly know more about it through my relationship with it. When I use it I can then say that this hammer is not just a hammer, but is my hammer. It has become a part of me. It is owned.

We all know stories about someone who has had the same hammer for thirty years and has replaced the handle three times, the head twice. There are two parts to this, one is the continuity through time of the hammer and the other, just as important, is that the person has changed the handle or head himself. He (for it is usually a he in the case of a hammer) has used his knowledge of the behaviour of materials and of his own requirements to make the hammer his own by his skill at manipulating the external world to his own ends. A hammer is only useful if we have the skill to use it. Otherwise it is dangerous. We also all know stories about how someone who owns a box full of tools, usually power tools, but does not know how to use them. Probably the most useful carpentry skill is to know how to sharpen a chisel.

Developmentally, as infants we first see things not as merely nearby, but as usable and in-the-world with us and consequently we get a fuller understanding of our temporality in the sense of what we can do with them in the future. In evolutionary terms our understanding of time arose through our ability to see the potential in the objects around us, to make, use and repair tools.

When the world is 'present-at-hand' we observe it and find it interesting and we act on it with techniques but when the world is 'ready to hand' we engage with it and it becomes important; we understand it and it has meaning for us. We discover skills.

This distinction between skills and techniques is also important with respect to psychotherapy (Dreyfus and Wrathall 2014; Adams 2016). In its simplest form a technique is a way of operationalising a theoretical principle. The danger is that by mechanising the theoretical principle into an action and then generalising it into a technique we stop being human beings and become technicians. Techniques are about seeing the world as nearby, as 'present-at-hand', and lead to inauthenticity. Skills on the other hand are owned ways of being; they are about seeing the world as useable 'ready-to-hand' and lead to authenticity. Our skills are the way we enact our beliefs.

Moreover, skills become owned not only by perseverance but also by experience of failure. This repositions human development away from the rather ambiguous, abstract and curiously passive 'change' to the more active 'learn', and learning is a process. With skills we have to be careful because when we become complacent, what was once an owned skill can revert to being a disowned technique. When this happens we are often shocked and disorientated to discover how much we do not know. Like physical fitness, skills need constant practice to maintain.

It is inevitable that at different ages, times and places, different skills will need to be acquired; what we need changes as we go through life, but living with meaning and purpose at all points between birth and death is a process of skills acquisition rather than technique acquisition.

Everything we learn involves understanding ourselves and our place in the world differently. From the moment of birth, or maybe before, a newborn baby is actively, not passively, learning – learning what different sounds, tastes, touches and so on mean. Total engagement with every moment, every experience, transforms the baby's way of understanding its being-in-the-world.

Children can do this easily; they are more comfortable with their dynamic sense-of-self. Actually, anyone who has noticed how small children learn will have noticed that their natural curiosity leads them to persevere with problems until they have solved them. And then they move on to another. The only interesting problems are the difficult problems.

Adults believe they have understood their place in-the-world, children know they have not; they are too busy being-in-the-world. As we get older we imagine we know things and perhaps we do, but often we decide we know enough and actively stop ourselves learning. When we stop learning, we stop living and start dying, existentially.

Adults slip into the natural way of seeing easier than children. We actively stop putting ourselves into situations, relationships, ways of being that will challenge what we think we know.

Just like the relationship between authenticity and inauthenticity, which it tracks, skills acquisition is more fulfilling but riskier than using techniques because it relies for its success on openness and rigorous reflexivity.

All learning, whether it involves doing a jigsaw puzzle, using a hammer, being a client in therapy or coming to terms with the givens of existence, involves a process whereby unowned techniques become owned skills through confronting and overcoming feelings of incompetence that if persevered with will evolve into competence (Adams 2013a).

In his later work, no doubt influenced by his hut, Heidegger moved his focus from an analysis of temporality, being, to an analysis of presence, dwelling (1971), showing, like Nietzsche, his indebtedness to Hölderlin. And in his writings on technology (1977), he is not concerned so much about the specific uses technology can be put to, but the way it detaches us from our being. He says that by viewing the world only technologically, as raw material for our exploitative technical operations, we not only deplete the world's resources but also reinforce our inauthenticity.

Crawford (2010a) takes these ideas of 'ready-to-hand' and 'present-at-hand' further and gives them a socio-political dimension. He notes that the disappearance of manual skills from the education system is the beginning of a slippery slope to a wider ignorance not just of how things work, but also of our relationship with the things we make use of and incorporate into our lives. By understanding how things (objects, relationships, etc.) work and developing skills through overcoming failure we develop humility, agency and respect. He talks about how important it is to our sense of ourselves as creative beings to be able to say, *I made this* or *I did that*. This explains the success of IKEA furniture for adults and Lego for children – except that Lego is better because many different things can be made with the same pieces. When we lose the sense of ourselves as creative beings our lives get smaller, and we feel depressed and anxious. 'Ready-to-hand' connectedness tempers our 'present-at-hand' individualism and our narcissistic expectation of perfection and specialness.

Since the 'ready-to-hand' is primordial, if it does not find a healthy ontic manifestation it will find a pathological manifestation in which the crucial features will be evaded, denied and mystified, for example in the way that sex can be a thing to be done or got, rather than an aspect of a relationship and that choice and freedom are seen as products to be bought and sold. The kind of freedom that is sold is not freedom at all; it is the opposite, and we are complicit in our falling into inauthenticity. The trust we (mis)place in technology is the same trust we disown in ourselves. The crucial point is that the person's agency has not been tested or engaged; it has been subverted.

Removed from the process of manufacture into the anaesthetising process of consumption we nevertheless have a basic need to own, in the sense of making one's own, the objects in our world. As, for example, making our own clothes becomes less common, our involvement in those things that make us 'us' – for example our clothes – degenerates into the next best thing – shopping for clothes. As anyone who has worked with a client with a shopping issue knows, this is not a solution to the problem. The new item only satisfies temporarily because the gap it fills is nothing to do with clothes. The new item of clothing is given a transformational life-changing value it cannot possibly live up to. The problem instead is one of feeling powerless to generate owned meaning and purpose. In fact, all addictions are about relying on an external object for producing mood change, rather than on personal agency and the acquisition of the skills of living.

Although Crawford talks specifically about the value of manual work, hands are a metaphor for personal agency and although as psychotherapists we do not work with our hands as such, what we do is equivalent in that we quickly discover how inadequate technical advice is. We work on our own account. We are thrown back on our abilities with the existential choice being whether to accept the responsibility or not. If we do, we carry on, but if we do not perhaps we should get a job that relies more on technique.

Thrownness and the development of Dasein

Our life task is to acknowledge our thrownness, and in doing so we open to Being and become beings-in-the-world, but with the exception of a few short references (Heidegger 2001), he does not say or show much interest in how this opening occurs. Indeed, in most of his writings, 'Dasein remains essentially ageless' (Harrison 2014: 5) and in this sense Heidegger's Dasein is by default an adult Dasein.

But, being a psychotherapist, Boss (1994: 243) knew that this account was incomplete and suggested that while the infant 'is not yet an independent Dasein capable of carrying out its own being' it nevertheless contains its own potentiality of being, of becoming existentially born.

Using a rural metaphor, Heidegger (1962) described Dasein as a light or a clearing (*Lichtung*) and this suggests the kind of clearing we find in a forest when the trees thin out and let the light in. And in this sense Dasein develops by discovering the way its presence 'lightens' the world it is a part of. Moreover, because Dasein is brought into being not by its past but by its future possibilities, there can be no fixed plan for human development, or as Dreyfus (1991: 188) says, there can be no 'genetic account of the development of Dasein'. Rather than being a developmental milestone, Dasein is a never to be completed understanding of how we continually illuminate and create our meaning world. This means that stages like adolescence or early adulthood are culturally mediated ontic artefacts of this process of illumination.

Building on some short references in the Zollikon Seminars (Heidegger 2001), both Dreyfus (1991) and Reuther (2014) suggest that at the beginning of life, the infant's fledgling Dasein is fully and necessarily absorbed for its survival and its future in the caregiver's Dasein, and generally speaking, as Laing says (1965: 41), it is a process that is 'taken for granted' and the world is taken to be largely benign. In this way, starting from birth and because of our dependence on others for life, the 'human organism starts Daseining gradually', and starts taking 'a stand on itself by pressing into human possibilities' (Dreyfus 1991: 187). Daseining, to use Dreyfus's term, is about discovering and experiencing the opportunities offered by attunement to the world and is therefore always mediated through our relationships with others.

In infancy and childhood our lack of experiential knowledge of existence reinforces our dependency on caregivers for systems of meaning and significance and the nature of this immersion in the world of others gives a personal context to our fallenness.

Our individual patterns of falling therefore begin to be formed at birth and an implication of this is that we cannot understand how a person came to be how they are without looking at the way they constructed the whole of their life from that moment onwards.

Another implication is that throughout life we will defer to authority, real or imagined, when confronted with uncertainty and by doing so we fall out of touch with our autonomy and our authenticity.

Because falling is prereflective, embodied, rather than cognitive, it will feel given rather than chosen. We rarely even have words for such experiences and on occasions they may be so harmful to our autonomy that they lead us into self-destructive actions like addictions. Keeping with the metaphor of *Lichtung*, we all learn early in childhood that there are certain emotions that are dangerous to refer to or even to experience because they may jeopardise the relationship we have with our caregiver(s), and hence our link with Being. Everyone has a unique emotional palette, and because of the child's need to preserve the relationship with the caregiver, the child frequently takes on the responsibility for maintaining the relationship and the problematic emotion becomes darkened in a futile attempt to remove it as a source of anxiety. In this way, we selectively shed light on or move light away from elements of our meaning world and learn to define ourselves and write our autobiography.

Generally, consistent and reliable care gives structure to a chaotic and unpredictable world and if this happens, resilience can grow, difficult situations can be resolved and anxiety, loss, separation, freedom and autonomy can be managed if not actually sought and valued. The child is dependent on the caregiver for a relationship to Being and as a protection from existential anxiety.

But if the primary caregiver is inconsistent or rejecting there is a struggle for a felt-sense of security and safety and a connection, a dependence, will be maintained because the alternative of no relationship is much worse. The child will be permanently anxious about the caregiver's unpredictability and this will limit the child's ability to open to the world and explore its possibilities. Wrapped up in the unreliable caregiver's unreliable Dasein, the child is constantly confronted with non-Being.

Children frequently ask questions about life – if adults are prepared to listen, but less frequently ask questions about how to live, that is, until adolescence. Adolescence is often described as a time when reflection begins in earnest and questions start to be asked and answers sought about the nature of the 'they' world that the person is a part of. It is when, as adolescents, we asked existential questions like *So what?* and *What right have you got to tell me what to do?* Maybe this is why adolescents upset adults so much – because just when the adults thought the child was becoming organised and biddable, they discover that he or she was not. Whether characterised by anxiety or excitement, the questions and particularly the responses, herald the emergence of existential guilt which is when we start to understand that our life is our own responsibility rather than the responsibility of an other, as it was earlier in childhood (Chessick 1996).

Our life task then becomes one of learning to live with freedom, choice and responsibility, and discovering what it means to have an authentic life as a permanently developing Dasein.

The paradox is that an immature Dasein needs a resilient and reliable Dasein to fall into in order that it may open to its own existential possibilities. The corollary is that if the caregiver is not resilient or reliable, the ability of an emerging Dasein to take on the challenges of being in the world will be constrained. Heidegger calls the way we relate to each other 'solicitude' and he distinguished between two different sorts, but they are better seen as two ends of a continuum. The first translates somewhat awkwardly into the English term 'leaping-ahead solicitude', often shortened to leaping-ahead and the second into 'leaping-in solicitude', or leaping-in.

Leaping-ahead is a more human way of relating in which we acknowledge and respect the autonomy of the other at the same time as respecting our own, and it gives rise to the sort of authentic relationship that enables a mutual awareness of temporality that opens out being. It is a relationship of love, that is based on faith.

In contrast, leaping-in is a more inauthentic and technical way of relating which essentially involves directing, advising or controlling the other person, usually with overt or covert suggestion, in a way that does not respect their autonomy and that reduces awareness of temporality and closes down being.

Heidegger (1962: 158) describes the consequence like this:

> In such solicitude the Other can become one who is dominated and dependent, even if this domination is a tacit one and remains hidden from him. This kind of solicitude, which leaps in and takes away 'care', is to a large extent determinative for Being.

6

Jean-Paul Sartre (1905–1980)

Living with nothingness

Jean-Paul Sartre's autobiography, *Words* (1964), starts in 1850, but could have begun even earlier. It begins, 'Around 1850, in Alsace, a schoolteacher with more children than he could afford was willing to become a grocer. This unfrocked clerk wanted compensation. Since he was giving up the schooling of minds, one of his sons would school souls.' One son, Charles, Sartre's grandfather, had other ideas so it was left to the other son, Louis, to fulfil this wish twice over. His son was Albert Schweitzer.

This book, which does not pretend to be a historical record, even if such a thing was possible, was written and rewritten over a period of a decade or so, unusual in itself for Sartre, and was eventually published in 1964. Although very short by Sartre's standards, it is a rich and many-layered work (Whitmire 2006). On one level it is about his first twelve years, but it also spans over a hundred years and has multiple viewpoints. It is an existential analysis. Divided into two sections, *Reading* and *Writing*, it asks the questions, *What is autobiography?* and *What can be said about a life?*

Sartre was an only child and when he was two his father died from tuberculosis and he went with his mother to live with her parents in Paris. Of his father he says, 'The death of Jean-Baptiste was the big event of my life: it sent my mother back to her chains and gave me freedom' (1967: 18). The brief period of relative independence she had from her powerful parents while she was married came to an end. When he was three he developed an eye infection that lost him most of the vision of his right eye and he was to lose the sight of his other eye as well in his last years. Although he said he did not miss his father – he had no father to miss – his grandfather Charles stepped in and introduced him to books and to literature and it is because of him that Sartre became fluent in German, but not English. Barnes (1974: 2) describes his grandfather as an 'indulgent tyrant, who assigned to his grandson the role of pampered prodigy' and in *Words* Sartre describes how he saw himself from a very young age as a writer, as a creator of stories. Meanwhile, his mother became like an older sister to him. Of his mother he says,

> Anne-Marie, the younger daughter, spent her childhood on a chair. She was taught to be bored, to sit up straight, to sew. She was gifted: the family thought it distinguished to leave her gifts undeveloped; she was radiant: they hid the fact from her. [...] Fifty years later, when turning the pages of a family album, Anne-Marie realized that she had been beautiful.
>
> (ibid.: 14)

When he was twelve his mother remarried and they moved to La Rochelle on the Atlantic coast. He was very unhappy there and was never close to his stepfather, and in 1917 returned to Paris to go a boarding secondary school and was eventually to graduate from the prestigious École normale supérieure in 1929, where he had met Simone de Beauvoir and Maurice Merleau-Ponty and gained a reputation for philosophical brilliance as much as for his sense of humour. The relationship between Sartre and Beauvoir was to become one of the most talked about relationships of the period. They were a striking couple, him just over 1.53m (5 Feet) and with thick lenses in his glasses to correct his poor eyesight, and her, tall and imperious.

Like Heidegger, Sartre was influenced by Husserl, and relating the moment in 1933 when Sartre was first introduced to phenomenology by his friend Raymond Aron, Beauvoir says, 'Here was just the thing he had been longing to achieve for years – to describe objects just as he saw and touched them, and extract philosophy from the process' (1966: 162). This moment led him to study phenomenology, as Aron had, at the French Institute in Berlin. What drew him to phenomenology was that he could find a correlation between consciousness and the objects of consciousness. It held the promise of realism and a move away from the abstract philosophy he had studied until then. Like Kierkegaard, he shared Socrates' view that philosophy should be actively and passionately lived, not merely thought about. Sartre's overall philosophical project was to make a description of human existence based on the phenomenological study of consciousness: how we make sense of, and live in, the world.

Like Kierkegaard, he wrote in many different genres, philosophy, politics, autobiography, fiction, drama and film scripts but unlike Kierkegaard he also earned his living from writing and was never anonymous. His decision to live his life in public was a lifelong philosophical choice; both Sartre and Beauvoir opposed any kind of censorship and France had strong censorship laws; it is why there is little tradition of biography in France. On being interviewed when he was seventy-two he said, 'I think transparency should always be substituted for secrecy. [...] It is impossible to accept the fact that we yield our bodies as we do and yet keep our thoughts hidden, since for me there is no basic difference between the body and the consciousness' (Sartre 1977: 11). Rowley suggests that for him 'the notion of privacy was a relic of bourgeois hypocrisy' (2007: xi). If he were alive now, he would surely be writing a blog and on social media.

He eventually found a publisher for his first novel *Nausea* in 1938; it was published in English in 1949 and is often taken as the model of a philosophical novel (Cox 2009b). In the Second World War he was posted to a weather station and was later taken as a prisoner of war for nearly a year, before being released as unfit for service. Interestingly, Heidegger was also posted to a weather station when he was in the German army, but in the First World War. It was while a prisoner of war that he became influenced by Heidegger's *Being and Time* and began to write *Being and Nothingness* as well as *The Roads to Freedom*. Heidegger inevitably came to know of Sartre's work and the two were curious about each other, but the only meeting between them, in German, took place in Heidegger's house in Freiberg in 1953. Seeking to regain his place in philosophy Heidegger had more to gain, but the meeting did not go well and neither was keen to repeat the experience (Safranski 1998; Bakewell 2016: 205). They were very different sorts of people, Heidegger was a poet who valued seclusion and who didn't understand politics, whereas Sartre saw his writing as the legitimate expression of his political commitment. This was in fact the essence of the difference Hannah Arendt had with Heidegger. It was that although Heidegger's philosophy was nominally about being-in-the-world, his analytic model paid little attention to the world, and Heidegger's misguided association with Nazism was just an example of this (Tubali 2018). Heidegger's turn towards dwelling and presence in the 1950s only emphasised this. Because of their analogous ways of seeing the moral purpose of philosophy this places Arendt closer to Sartre, Beauvoir and Merleau-Ponty.

Many of *Nausea*'s themes are echoed in *Being and Nothingness* that appeared in 1943 and was published in English in 1956. He felt he was able to express his ideas more clearly in his novels, plays and his autobiography because they were about the everyday paradoxes and dilemmas that people lived (Cox 2009b).

Previously indifferent to politics, the years of imprisonment and occupation politicised him and many of his plays have strong political texts and subtexts and this underlines a major difference he had with Heidegger in that he was much more interested in the psychological, in the concrete conditions of a person's life (Cannon 1991: 6). Faced with a choice between his fiction and his philosophical writing he felt his literature was more worthwhile because it 'catalogues the present world, whereas philosophy does not possess an absolute value in itself' (Beauvoir 1985: 153).

After the end of the war he extended his belief that philosophy was about action in the world with others – about being *'engagé'* – by founding the left-wing political and literary journal *Les Temps modernes* in 1945 with Beauvoir and Maurice Merleau-Ponty, named after the 1936 Charlie Chaplin film. *Les Temps modernes* is still in publication. For Sartre, our being-in-the-world means that we are always *engagé*. Our existential task and our choice is therefore to find a way to put this into action that stays true to our situation and to the givens of existence.

In 1964 he was awarded the Nobel Prize for Literature, which he refused because he did not acknowledge the validity of official honours. Never a member of a political party, his position was always one of a libertarian socialist, rather more akin to a cooperative form of anarchism. He became more and more preoccupied with the political dimensions of philosophy, trying to reconcile the freedom of existentialism with the determinism of Marxism (1968, 1979, 2004) and when he fell out with people it was almost always over disagreements over political ideology, and most usually with men – a point Beauvoir (1985) picks up on.

He became the public face of existentialism, which was incidentally a word coined mockingly by Gabriel Marcel and that he only reluctantly accepted, because of a talk (Sartre 1973a) he gave in 1945 just weeks after the liberation of Paris in which he positioned existentialism as a practical discipline that addressed the contextual nature of human issues. His talk caught the mood of the time perfectly, and this mood continued to reverberate across the subsequent decades. He made philosophy a matter for everyday discussion and he is still the most widely known existential philosopher.

Sartre's influence on French politics while he was alive was always strong: he was judged by the OAS, the extreme nationalist group opposed to Algerian independence, to be enough of a danger to their cause that they bombed his flat in 1961 and again in 1962. He was out on both occasions. And later on both Sartre and Beauvoir played an important part in the uprising of May 1968, coming as it did just three years short of the centenary of the Paris Commune. In later years the status of existentialism as a fashionable philosophy was passed to structuralism and post-modernism and Sartre temporarily lost some of his importance. He was not greatly worried by this and readily adapted to changing times and was on friendly terms with younger philosophers like Michel Foucault. Although Foucault was not in Paris in 1968 – he was teaching in Tunis at the time – Foucault's work became more overtly political after 1968. Overall though, since his death, Sartre has had a more lasting impact on philosophy and culture than on French politics.

French laws of inheritance mean that all property, including intellectual property, goes to the dead person's family, and as he was an only child, he never married or had children, one way of getting round this was by legally adopting his former student and friend Arlette Elkaïm in 1965 when he was sixty. He continued to write prolifically but his work had been gradually getting less sharp for some years and by the time he was seventy he had almost completely lost the sight in his one good eye but he was still passionate about work and had many plans for new projects. He was interviewed at seventy-two (1977) on a wide range of topics including his failing eyesight by Michel Contat and the interview concludes,

Contat: *What still has real interest for you?*

Sartre: *Music, as I told you. Philosophy and politics. […] I have not been disappointed by anything. I have seen people, good and bad – moreover, the bad are never bad except in relation to certain goals – I have written, I have lived, there is nothing to be sorry about.*

Contat: *In short, so far life has been good to you?*

Sartre: *On the whole, yes. I don't see what I could reproach it with. It has given me what I wanted and at the same time it has made me recognize that it isn't much. But what can you do?*

(The interview ends in a fit of laughing brought on by the disillusioned tone of that last statement.)

Sartre: *The laughter must be kept. You should put: 'Accompanied by laughter.'*

He had always had high blood pressure, and no doubt not helped by his consistently unhealthy lifestyle and diet; in his last few months his health regularly failed and he never recovered, and eventually after a day or so in a coma he died in hospital with Arlette who had taken over sitting with him from Beauvoir and her friend Sylvie le Bon only three hours before.

On his death at seventy-five, Arlette Elkaïm took responsibility for his literary inheritance and copyright and to many peoples dismay, including Simone de Beauvoir's, she imposed extreme restrictions on the use of his works, especially unpublished works although she did cooperate with his biographer Annie Cohen-Solal. He did not wish to be buried in the family plot in the Père Lachaise Cemetery and his funeral and interment in the Montparnasse Cemetery in Paris, very near to where he and Beauvoir had always lived, was on a cold drizzly April day and was attended by 50,000 people. The interment was an occasion of 'spontaneous disorder' (Cohen-Solal 1987: 523) – at one point a man fell into the grave – because there was, at his request, no police presence, but this meant that there was also no crowd control. In a way this was fortunate because there was no formal ceremony, again on his wishes, emphasising the existential truth that death is the limit of all experience.

Philosophy

While Sartre shared Heidegger's starting point of our thrownness, he did not share Heidegger's conclusion that temporality, being-towards-death, was the central organising principle of existence. His phenomenological analysis revealed that we come into being, into existence, as nothing; and our responsibility as beings is to make something, our essence, out of what we are given. At birth we meet facticity, the world will not do exactly as we wish, but we also meet a world of possibility in the sense that we have the freedom to choose how to respond towards it. Since we are nothing, we could be anything.

This freedom is an obligation and this is what he meant when he said, 'To be free is to be condemned to be free' (2003: 152). This is the radical freedom of early Sartre. We are thrown into freedom and choice, and we have responsibility for our lives whether we like it or not. The only choice we do not have is not to choose.

The way he put it in his talk in 1945 was,

> What do we mean by saying that existence precedes essence? We mean that man first of all exists, encounters himself, surges up in the world – and defines himself afterwards. If man as the existentialist sees him is not definable, it is because to begin with he is nothing. He will not be anything until later, and then he will be what he makes of himself.
>
> (1973a: 28)

Making something of ourselves continues till death. When he said, 'at the moment of death the chips are down, there remains not a card to play' (2003: 138) he meant that a life is only complete on death. For Sartre, an eighteen-year-old life is as complete as an eighty-year-old life. The phrase 'the chips are down' is also the title of a screenplay (*Les jeux sont faits*) that he wrote (1951) for a film of the same name and is a French gambling expression meaning that after the bets have been placed, no changes can be made. All bets are possible, but only until death. The plot of the film reinforces the principle not only that we have to take responsibility for the consequences of our choices but that they can never be reversed.

As he showed in his play *In Camera*, of 1944 (aka *No Exit*) freedom is only for the living; death puts a final stop to our freedom and to our projects, it is when we have to surrender our lives to the judgement of others. We have to trust what Yalom (2008) calls rippling. It is often forgotten or not understood that this play, which is the origin of the much quoted 'hell is – other people' (Sartre 1990: 223) is set in the afterlife where people are without freedom. Hell is the condition of being without freedom. He did not say or ever mean that other people are hell. Risky and fascinating maybe, but not hell.

A life cannot be judged until death, and probably not then either, and certainly not by the person who has just died. Sartre's works were rarely finished because he felt conclusions were an artificial literary device that give the impression that he has said all he could say on a topic (Sartre 1977). And he always had something else to say. All a work, a life, can aspire to, is to be a true record up till the present moment.

A primary distinction for Sartre is between the world of things and the world of beings and this gives rise to three simultaneous modes of being. One is to do with our relationship with the material world. Objects here have no consciousness, they cannot be anything other than what they are; their natures are fixed. A chair is always a chair; it can never decide not to be a chair. He called this mode of being, being-in-itself (*être-en-soi*).

People are different; we are not fixed like chairs, we have responsibility for what we become. He said, 'Life is nothing until it is lived; but it is yours to make sense of, and the value of it is nothing else but the sense that you choose' (1973a: 54). The strength of this statement is enhanced in the original French as the word '*sens*' means something more like 'way' or 'direction' rather than the more abstract 'sense', as in the translation. For him, consciousness is always embodied consciousness; there is no such thing as a body without consciousness, nor a consciousness without a body. He called this mode of being, being-for-itself (*être-pour-soi*) and it is analogous to Heidegger's 'Dasein'. Our responsibility for choosing our lives evokes anxiety; we know that when we choose one possibility we reject another. We try to evade this by pretending we have a fixed essence and while this reduces the anxiety of freedom, it puts us into a position of bad faith and since it is an action, we always know we have done it. Self-deception is therefore never possible since we cannot deceive ourselves of something we already know; we are complicit. Lying to others is damaging to our relationships but lying to ourselves is worse because it damages the relationship we have with ourselves and with reality. Authenticity, or good faith, is when we acknowledge and embody our nothingness in all its uncertainty without turning it into a nothing thing, but it is unattainable. It is what we mean by God: omnipotent, omnipresent and omniscient.

The third mode of being is about our relationships with other people. He calls this being-for-others (*être-pour-autrui*). While we all have the responsibility and freedom to make choices about our lives and this gives us a sense of personal agency we also know that other people have it too. In fact it is other people's freedom that make them both exciting and threatening, and the tension between the need for certainty and the desire for freedom is played out between people in the dynamics of their relationships.

He explored this vision of human relationships in which people's freedoms are in perpetual conflict philosophically in *Being and Nothingness*. His trilogy *The Roads to Freedom* (2002), published at around the same time, describes in fictional form how the various characters relate to their freedom.

Sartre and human development

His interest in psychology and biography led him to ask pertinent questions about human development. Always familiar with Freud's work, one of his co-editors on *Les Temps modernes* was the psychoanalyst J.-B. Pontalis, and his existential psychoanalysis in *Being and Nothingness* is a response to psychoanalytic ideas and he also wrote a screenplay (1985), which eventually was not used, for the John Huston film of Freud's life. His fundamental disagreement with psychoanalysis was not with the observed phenomena, but their explanation (Sartre 1979: 37).

But what he meant by psychological was not traditional because he did not consider individuals as such, but individuals in a situation, in a context. He coined the term 'singular universal' to mean that each person is both a contributor to his or her era at the same time as being an expression of his or her era. We are all singular; utterly unique, as well as being universal; of our time. As such an individual can be taken as an example among many, but never as the example of many.

He also felt that the versions of human development that had dominated both literature and psychology were based on a false notion of a character developing gradually, inevitably and by causation as a result of the joint influences of heredity – nature, and environment – nurture. Sartre argues that they took no account of freedom and responsibility. Causation is an artefact of the research method. Events only appear caused when viewed in hindsight because of the illusion that one particular event seemed to inevitably lead to or cause, the next particular event. By basing the future on looking back, alternatives are excluded in the way that they are not when looking forward. In *Nausea* he has the biographer Roquentin give up his project because he does not want to impose a narrative of coherence and purposiveness on a life that is actually characterised more by randomness and ambiguity. If we look at human development without taking into account randomness, freedom and choice we are likely to buy into retrospective and prospective determinism (Cannon 1999: 29).

He therefore abandons the idea that human development is linear, causative and related to age. One of the implications of existence before essence is that the human being is a meaning-making agent from birth. He views age more as a distraction and suggests instead that 'a life develops in spirals; it passes again and again by the same points but at different levels of integration and complexity' (1968: 106). This is not only philosophically consistent but it also corresponds to experience. Moreover he looks for the distinctive shapes and key moments on which a life turns; those moments in which a person makes a free choice that changes not just the meaning of the past but also the course of future and thus transcends determinism. He wanted to show how people chose themselves by choosing between opposing passions in times of crisis (Barnes 1974: 72). At these moments we catch a person in the very act of turning fixed essence into free existence. His own *Words,* which rarely mentions chronology, illustrates this.

But he does not discount childhood at all and he places great importance on decisions made in childhood and his biographies on Baudelaire (1967), Flaubert (1981) and Genet (1983), all focus on the subjects' early years and their consequences. His concern with chronology is only with respect to the life of the person he is writing about.

There are consequently a number of areas directly relevant to human development.

The sense-of-self and the original project

Sartre's questions about the sense-of-self are, *What is it?* and *How does it come about?* Following Husserl, he said that consciousness is like a light that illuminates the world; it has no content of its own, and our never-ending stream of random and context-dependent experiences are first of all captured by our prereflective consciousness. This has no sense of temporality or spatiality, of context, and is not weighed down by responsibility or the need to be consistent. Such things that are captured by prereflective consciousness are 'individual but nonpersonal' (Barnes 1993: 42). What she means by this that while they are to do with a particular individual, they have not yet been made personal and owned by reflection. Childhood is often characterised and idealised by adults in this way, as free, and as something that has been lost and that needs in some way to be regained. Our prereflective consciousness can be captured at the times when we say, *I can't help it ... it's the way I am.* There is enough of a memory to know that I did do it, but not enough to make it personal and owned.

These experiences are then gradually made sense of, made personal, by our reflective consciousness which objectifies and fixes the world and our relationship with it. In contrast, our reflective consciousness can be captured at the times when we say, *I know that I did it and I take responsibility for it.* Both prereflective and reflective consciousness are present throughout life.

It is in this sense that what we think of as our 'self' is a matter of interpretation and choice that changes throughout life and is the result of the way we meet the fundamental givens of our personal existence moment by moment, rather than being a product of nature or nurture. As Barnes says, 'we should not be asking what kind of self I am, but what kind of self my consciousness has created' (1993: 43). To emphasise the fluidity of the sense-of-self this quote should perhaps be continued with ... up until this moment.

From birth we encounter a world of facticity and the family that we are born into has its own particular quality of facticity. Also, our vulnerability and dependency as children mean that we are necessarily immersed in and absorb this world and we largely accept it without question. Sometimes we never question it.

But finding out that the world will not behave as we wish forces us to reflect, and out of this we get a sense of temporality and spatiality and start to make our autobiography. We are natural storymakers and storytellers; we look for patterns and make up stories about how and how we came to be this way. We use photos, memories and conversations with others, including therapists, to locate ourselves in time and place and to form a sense of coherence between our personal past, present and future, to create as Laing says 'a sense of being an entity with continuity in time and a location in space' (1965: 41). It helps to give us meaning and purpose but it also introduces a bogus fixity. This is the fundamental dilemma of bad faith because as Barnes says, 'At the same time as the self is seen as fixed, the interconnected of beings is lost and denied' (1993: 43).

Because of our need to maintain a stable narrative, to be able to say *This is who I am*, we start very early to impose, choose, patterns of coherence on our experiences and it is these that constitute what Sartre calls, depending on the translation, our original or fundamental orientation to the world, our original choice. Although less often used, I have come to prefer the term original because it has implications of 'first', whereas fundamental has implications of 'basic' in a quasi-genetic sense which is not the case at all, although it may feel like that. Original is more experience-near.

Countless similar choices gradually coalesce into our original project of how to be in the world and all our subsequent life projects are based on this original project. What we come to call our personality is no more than a summary of choices, actions and decisions that are consistent with our original project, which although made at a particular time and place for a particular purpose is then expected to last for all time.

It is a mistake to think of the original choice and project as being intellectual or cognitive or even as something that we can easily put into words. Although we have the possibility of translating it into such terms later on as our language skills grow, since the original experiences were emotional and existential they will be sensed or felt; they will be embodied. If reflected on at all, the conclusions will seem obvious – as if we always knew them because they occurred prereflectively. They will come to have a factual, thing-like, quality about them. Which is to say that we will not be aware that we made them. In this way the original choice is seen as given, whereas it is actually constructed.

Throughout life we have an ambivalent attitude to our original project. On the one hand we believe that *this is me and this is the way I am*. But on the other hand there is a nagging sense that there is nothing fixed about it at all, that *maybe my life could be/have been entirely different*. We cannot help wondering, *What if…?* This is often the underlying question clients have when they enter psychotherapy and the ability to ask it is a source of hope. Without this sense of our temporality, life would be literally hope-less, because there would be no future to have hopes for.

Although the original project can be reversed or remade, as we get older we tend to find it increasingly difficult to do. This does not mean it is any more true; it has just had longer to get fixed or as Sartre (1991) says, mineralised, as if set in stone. In part this is because there is more life to look back on and a life looked back on will seem determined, but it is also because we tend to look for opportunities that match the demands of our original project and then pick them imagining they are the only ones available. Because of our need for coherence, the determinism implicit in storymaking also involves us editing out or forgetting events that conflict with the original project. We prefer to see them as exceptions to the rule. In this sense the world reflects back to us our earlier decisions and the original choice becomes like a self-fulfilling prophecy as we become more and more alienated from our responsibility for it.

Nevertheless because the original project is a choice and not a given, it can be changed and Sartre calls the moment of significant change on which life turns, the 'psychological instant' (Cannon 1999: 51). Sartre calls these moments 'presence to being' (2003: 121), and are products of what Cannon (1991: 148) calls pure reflection. Sometimes they are forced on us by circumstance, and sometimes we encounter them by contemplation or through interpretation in therapy, but these are the moments when are able to stay with the question, *What if…?*, and they can never be planned or scripted. As Sartre says, consciousness is 'perpetually threatened by the instant' (2003: 488). We are always aware of the possibility that the fixity of the original project will be shown to be an illusion.

The psychological instant is a moment of 'double nothingness' (2003: 488), because we become pure possibility. Freed up from both the fixed future and the fixed past we become aware of the responsibility we have for our life and these moments are as significant for human development as they are for therapeutic practice and are as desired as much as they are feared. Desired because of the hope that follows when we assert possibility over fixedness, and feared because we are exchanging something known for something unknown. They may well reverberate for some considerable time.

These are the moments when we gain perspective and we see our current life against the horizon of our whole life. We see the current problematic aspect of our life not as being a one-off, or as or bad luck, or as someone else's fault, but as being as example of the past in the present, of a pattern that had threaded its way through our lives giving the illusion of being determined, when it was actually chosen.

Therapeutically, the psychological instant is when a symptom that has been hidden or embodied is suddenly seen in the context of the original project: as a choice and not a fact. Indeed, Sartre says that the goal of existential psychoanalysis 'must be to discover a choice and not a state' (2003: 573).

By daring to have a different future, we also come to have a different past. This is what Sartre means when he says 'My past comes to meet me out of the future' (Cannon 1991: 153). Freedom replaces causation. It is for this reason that the past can take on different meanings at different times of life or at various stages in the course of psychotherapy. This echoes Sartre's earlier comment about life developing in spirals.

Resistance therefore can be reframed as the fear of the freedom of an unknown future, and not simply a fear of a particular feeling. A person facing divorce may well be scared of being lonely, but in addition there is a fear that they will have to construct a different identity by rewriting their future as well as their past. The psychological instant reminds us in the most direct way that the self we seek to create can never be fixed.

It is necessary that we trust our imagination and spontaneity if we are to have a stance towards the future such that we can develop our life projects, and when we choose to give up on having projects we commit existential suicide.

There is such an instant in the film *High Fidelity* (Frears 2000) when the character Rob Gordon is reflecting on his inability to commit to his girlfriend Laura. He says, 'I can see now I never really committed to Laura. [...] and that prevented me from doing a lot of things, like thinking about my future and I guess it made more sense to commit to nothing, keep my options open ... and that's suicide ... by tiny, tiny increments.' Existentially, choosing means being able to own and commit ourselves to whatever decisions we have taken and when we are able to generate and carry out self-defined projects we become existentially born. But when we have no projects or a project comes to an end, either planned or accidently, we start existentially dying. By refusing to commit to either being with or not being with Laura, Rob was dying existentially.

The philosopher at the end of Woody Allen's (1989) film *Crimes and Misdemeanors* says,

We are all faced throughout our lives with agonizing decisions and choices. Some of these are on a grand scale, some are on a lesser scale, but we define ourselves by the choices we make. We are in fact the sum total of these choices.

The influence of early experience

Sartre's interest in human development was in how we create our lives through our own choices and actions. And as such, everything is significant and can only be understood in context. He was keen to develop an existential analysis that could understand this process and this project unifies all his work from *Being and Nothingness* in 1943 to his biography of Flaubert, *The Family Idiot* in 1981.

Central to his thinking is how the child's situation affects their awareness of freedom and agency and how this leads to the formation and choice of their original project. For Sartre, parental and family influences are as significant as in psychoanalysis but he treats them differently.

He uses the term 'prehistory' (Barnes 1993: 54) to refer to the person's parents, grandparents, siblings and other significant people. Birth order is important since, for example, a first-born will have a different experience in the same family from a second-born and so on. He calls the early years of childhood, our 'protohistory' and this refers both to the emotional relationship the infant has with his mother and also to the way the infant sees his position in the family, how the child makes his life personal.

The vulnerability and dependency of the child means that the child is more in touch with the fluidity of nothingness and possibility. This means that the child has little sense of a fixed self, whereas the adults at least appear far more certain about who they are, and act as such.

Sartre calls the child's need for approval by parents and significant others 'valorisation' and he is unequivocal about this. He says,

> This is not a matter of conjecture: a child must have a mandate to live, the parents are the authorities who issue the mandate. A grant of love enjoins him to cross the barrier of the moment – the next moment is awaited, he is already adored there, everything is prepared for his joyful reception; the future appears to him as a vague and gilded cloud. [...] If later on with a little luck he can say: 'My life has a purpose, I have found purpose in my life,' it is because the parent's love, [...] has revealed his existence to him as a movement toward an end; he is the conscious arrow that is awakened in midflight and discovers, simultaneously, the distant archer, the target, and the intoxication of flight ... If this happens] living will be the passion – in the religious sense – that will transform self-centeredness into a gift; experience will be felt as the free exercise of generosity.
>
> (1981: 133–134)

Sartre's point about having a mandate to live is important. We know that some people appear almost effortlessly to be able to take on the opportunities that life gives them and to live actively, whereas others are racked with doubt, are not able to take them on and in consequence, live passively. The love of the parents, which Gibson (2017) sees as an expression of authentic love, therefore guarantees that the child will grow up with a genuine feeling that he is of value and has an unquestioned right to be alive and an active agent, with all that that implies. Without this mandate, Cannon (1991: 102) says that the child 'will be left afloat in a meaningless universe where physical laws perhaps point to a sense of a future but where one's own existence appears senseless or wrong'. Time, for such children, 'becomes a slack succession of present moments that slip back into past' (Sartre 1981: 134). In this way, unvalorised children find it hard to experience themselves as agents because the past holds no nourishment and the future holds no promise.

Cannon (1991: 34) raises the question about whether the valorised child's sense of purpose is an expression of bad faith because it rests not only on the mandate of the parents but also on the fact that the parents are promising something that cannot be delivered: certainty. She also notes the paradox that this mandate to live is, in fact, a necessary deception that makes the later encounter with the truth of existence tolerable. The paradox is that a lie makes it possible to acknowledge the truth. But significantly, this truth 'must be revealed slowly [at the] end of a long delusion' (Sartre 1981: 136).

For the parents to reveal the truth of a random contingent existence too early through neglect or hostility will lead to an unintegrated past and the loss of a future. If they reveal these truths too late through a misplaced desire to protect the child, no doubt derived from their own problems with truth, it will lead to the overprotected child not being able to be spontaneous for fear of making mistakes. And a child who is given too much responsibility too soon will also learn to distrust his spontaneity, concluding that the future is to be feared.

Therefore to reveal existential truths either too early or too late through inaccurate valorisation is to subject the child to the impression not simply of being unjustified but also of being unjustifiable, that is, unable to find a purpose in life. Such children will be unable to form an authentic project of being towards the unknown future and may instead make a project out of trying to get the love they felt they had a right to but did not get. Extreme examples of these are characteristic of borderline conditions (Cannon 1991).

Our agency, our overwhelming need to carry out a 'significant autonomous act' (Cooper 1967: 58), is primary and we will do anything to keep hold of it. It is what makes us human. The extent to which the child is valued by significant others is crucial in determining whether he or she will grow up to be an active agent or a passive agent; to be irresponsible or to be responsible. But we should not go away with the idea that it is a simple either/or dichotomy. There are many graduations in quantity as well as in quality. We are both embodied, relational, psychological and also ethical beings and can be relatively active and responsible in one of these dimensions while being relatively passive and irresponsible in another. Having said that though, in striving for meaning and purpose, for joined-up living, the more ethically active and responsible we are in one dimension, the more active and responsible we will be in the other dimensions.

There are many ways that the child's fragile and emergent autonomy can be constrained, many ways that well-meaning parents can accidently misjudge and mistime their actions and many ways in which the contingency of the world will intervene. In the case of Flaubert as a singular universal, Sartre suggests that Flaubert's mother, immersed as she was in the unreflected legacy of her own prehistory and protohistory, was both overprotective and unloving and he grew up feeling in the shadow of his cleverer, older brother, among others. As an 'underloved' (Cannon 1991: 177) child, he had a consistent experience of himself as a thing, dependent on and with a responsibility for the parents' welfare, and consequently there was no sense of reciprocity. The result was that he developed a passivity that underpinned his original project. Simone de Beauvoir (2009) shows us that this passivity takes on a different quality for men compared with women.

In Flaubert's case it led to a sense of impotence, resentment and self-doubt that he did not know what to do with. He did not know how to translate his agency into future action. His need to commit a significant autonomous act remained; and it led him in adolescence to reject the expectation that he would follow his cleverer brother – this was never going to work – but to follow the strategy of a passive agent. He therefore chose to demonstrate his inferiority, to decide to fail. Hence the title of Sartre's book. He needed to think of himself as active – we all do, it is ontological – but the way he chose to be active was by choosing to be reactively passive. It was a project of bad faith ... but at least it was his, and not someone else's.

This is how we can understand the impotence and anger associated with depression and also the more overt self-destructiveness of addiction: as the autonomous act of a passive agent that incidentally has a personal cost. It is slow suicide. The gain is a sort of autonomy and a fraudulent independence. The loss is seen as being worth the imagined gain. Addicts only change when they decide to do it themselves. No one can do it for them and if they do the addict will prove them wrong if it's the last thing they do – which tragically it sometimes is. No one can win against another person's self-destructiveness, against someone's freedom.

The Look

The parents' mandate to live is mediated through what Sartre calls 'the Look', and Cannon (1991: 102) subdivides the Look into three different forms:

> the look; how we look at others visually and how we perceive the way they look at us, the touch; how we touch others and how we perceive the way they touch us, and the word; how we talk to others and how we perceive how we are spoken to.

These are of significance throughout life but are of particular significance in the early years because of their part in the formation of the original choice and project.

The visual look

There are a number of references to the visual look in Sartre's writing, perhaps the best known is the example of the man who when looking through a keyhole suddenly realises he is being watched (2003: 283). Whereas before, he was simply looking at the scene on the other side of the door, he suddenly becomes aware that he is being seen by someone else. Sartre was a great fan of the cinema and the image of the keyhole was a frequently used plot device in early cinema. The metaphor is of the moment when we are objectified by another person. Although Sartre says there are three possible responses, shame, pride or fear, this much-quoted example is misleading because the Look, as such, is not always objectifying because it allows us to appreciate, for example, why it is that feeding or holding an infant in a position that allows eye contact facilitates psychological growth and why games like hide and seek are so important and highly charged. It also goes some way to explaining why a conversation between two people in which one person is wearing mirrored sunglasses can have an awkward dynamic.

Eye contact is significant at all ages to communicate attention and it is harder to lie with the eyes than it is with words because the meaning is embodied.

The touch

Sartre says that touch and the language of touch are especially important from earliest infancy and he talks about this in *The Family Idiot* (1981: 47).

He says that maternal love is a relation, an action and not a feeling, and it is expressed in the way a mother nurses an infant and in this action she cannot help but embody her own prehistory and protohistory. In the early months of life, our care, our respect for the infant's fundamental freedom and emergent autonomy is expressed through touch. Although only dimly differentiated in earliest infancy, the mother's touch is thus intimately connected with the infant's awareness of his own body and is how the infant discovers himself as a part of a relationship.

If it is done in a consistently insensitive way the child will see himself as an object for someone else whose freedom and autonomy are overridden. If the child is, for example, cared for on the adult's timetable the child will fail to make the association between need and satisfaction and may never learn the pleasure of being satisfied. This is seen in eating disorders with people who have lost or learnt to deny – for we are all born with it – the ability to know whether they are hungry or not. Food comes to mean something more than simply food. It becomes a corrupted and confused form of love. But if done in a consistently sensitive way the child will grow to see himself as someone whose freedom and autonomy is respected.

Without a consistently sensitive early experience of touch, the child will find it hard to develop a sense of owned physicality and Cannon (1999: 105) suggests that many disorders that relate to one's own body as active, passive, disgusting, pleasurable and so on derive from this period.

This early knowing of person-to-person physicality will form a template which will develop eventually into the way the person comes to know and trust another person in the physical sense and manifest in patterns of adult sexual behaviour.

The word

Sartre was introduced to the literal world of words by his grandfather and as would be expected from a person who made his living from writing, he places great importance on the meaning of the written and spoken word. It is important to remember though that he is also talking about the meaning of the unwritten and the unspoken word. Although his autobiographical *Words* (1967) is in two sections, *Reading* and *Writing*, he means them to go together. Reading is an act of imagination and when we read, we also write, we interpret, we make up stories about what we have read and how we might be in the stories.

In any family, the words, spoken and unspoken, form the backdrop to the child's prehistory and protohistory. It is one of the concrete aspects of our thrownness. From birth or even before, the adults in whose world we are immersed are using words to describe and direct how the world is to be experienced. In a less benign form it can prescribe our life plan. As Franz says in Sartre's play *The Condemned of Altona*, 'Nine months before my birth they had chosen my name, my career, my character and my fate' (1973b: 84).

He illustrates this too in his biography of Genet (1983) where a turning point in Genet's life was when he was discovered stealing and was named a thief, and from that moment he decided to become one. The naming changed the theft from something that he had done to something he was: a thief. In his case his free existence changed into fixed essence.

Although naming is inevitable, and clearly praise is preferred to criticism, the sense of violation of freedom and autonomy only comes if the naming is inaccurate and or does not match experience. For example, *What a good little girl you are*, depending on context can become less of a praising description and more of an instruction that can stifle spontaneity and freedom. In Sartre's case he tells us in *Words* that his experience of the applause of adults had transformed him into a 'fake child' whose playacting 'robbed me of the world and of human beings' (1967: 84). Both Laing and Esterson (1964) and Laing (1970) refer extensively to the effect of the spoken and unspoken word.

The truth is that even in the most benign forms, the words of others have the power to distort experience. This too is inevitable if we are open to the world; it is a part of discovering the resistance of the world. On many occasions though, consistently inaccurate naming serves to restrict and mystify our emotional range and close us off from others. Recognition, or accurate verbal reflection, therefore becomes a critical factor in the formation of our sense-of-self.

In *The Family Idiot*, quoted in Barnes (1999: 52), Sartre gives an analysis of the implications of practical jokes. Noting that it is through the world that I come to know myself, he says,

> Most of the time I exist with the assumption that things are indeed roughly what they seem. Despite my knowledge that my senses have on occasion deceived me I cannot live without assuming that there is a broad area of daily life in which they can be trusted. Yet I retain a slight awareness of the ultimate unknowability in the things of which I am conscious. While the anguished awareness of this uncertainty is not present in every act, it exists as part of our global insertion into the world.

The practical joke is a deliberate attempt to evoke a rupture in the normal world of the person who is fooled. The joker is playing God and deliberately making the world seem other than it is in order to disorientate the victim. What we call a practical joke is only a relatively benign version of the mystifying effects of inaccurate naming. When a child is told, *You did not see what you saw*, or *you did not feel what you felt*, there is a fracture in the emerging sense of self and a doubt placed in the reliability of their perception and at the moment of the practical joke the victim appears

> as a stranger to myself, my customs are disqualified, my past abolished, I am naked in a new present which is lost in an unknown future.
>
> (Barnes 1999: 52)

To be the victim of one practical joke especially if the context is benign and the consequences are minimal is unlikely to have serious long-lasting effects. They may even be enlightening; they are a way of reminding ourselves that things may not be the way they seem. This is why people are both attracted and repelled by magicians and conjurors – as long as the issue is of little consequence like playing cards and as long as it is done on someone else.

This is also one of the attractions of fiction and of film, which are of course willingly entered into, and it is always an important moment when the book or film ends and we return to our everyday life. In a similar way at the end of a play there is always a moment when the cast appear together out of role. A horror film is only truly horrible if it never ends and starts involving the viewer in the plot.

But a prolonged series of mystifications and inaccurate namings perpetrated on the same victim especially if it is a child can have serious consequences and might well induce, Sartre says,

> an artificial psychosis by forcing him to live his normal adaptation to the real as a permanent disadaptation.
>
> (Sartre 1981: 1314)

This echoes Bateson's (1972) idea of the 'double bind' that he used to describe the complexity of human communication and that was taken up by Laing and Esterson (1964) and Laing (1965). While it is unlikely that Sartre knew about Bateson's work, we know that Laing knew the work of both Sartre and Bateson. We also know it as gaslighting in the interpersonal arena and 'fake news' and 'alternative facts' in the national and international arena.

Sartre suggests throughout his work that the value of reading as well as writing, and this goes for other literary media such as film, is to broaden our experience of the world. As we read we start to identify with the characters who have different lives from us; we cannot move into the fictional word without modifying our own world. Reading helps us to empathise and phenomenologically we get to see the world from a different point of view, with a different horizon. We grasp both the characters' free consciousness and our own free consciousness and we ask ourselves, *Suppose that was me, ... What would that be like? ... Would I do that, or not?* Research too has corroborated Sartre's intuition that reading fiction broadens the mind. Kidd and Castano (2013) and Appleyard (1991) talk about the different ways we use fiction throughout the life cycle.

Relationships with others

With respect to our relationships with others the perpetual question is, *How can I be with other people?* Sartre's thinking about this develops the implications of the Look. Although our autonomy, our freedom, is fundamental, it is also true that we all get our meaning and identity from our simultaneous connectedness to all other beings and to the world. It is in fact this connection that protects us from complete isolation, but it is our need to be different that preserves our individuality. This is the perpetual dilemma and one of the questions everyone has to answer as they go through life is, *How can I be me and also be connected to others?*

The problem of mutuality and love is founded on the parallel facts that we are both different from each other and the same as each other. In conflict, the other person's freedom is feared because of its difference, but in cooperation it is loved because of its difference and it is this movement from conflict to cooperation that constitutes human development in the interpersonal arena and Sartre (2003) and Cannon (1991) describe three objectifying either/or strategies and two cooperative both/and strategies we use to manage the unpredictability of relationships.

The first of the objectifying strategies is when we retain our freedom at the expense of the other's freedom. We make the other into an object, and this is an aggressive act committed on the other's freedom in order to preserve our own. Sartre calls it sadism. The second is when we sacrifice our freedom for the sake of the other's. We make ourselves into an object, and is an aggressive act committed on our own freedom. This is self-destructiveness. Sartre calls it masochism. A frequently quoted example is of the woman on a first date who does not respond when her hand is held. She disembodies herself to deny her situation (Sartre 2003: 78). The third is withdrawal or indiffe-rence. This arises out of the failure of the other two. By trying to avoid conflict we attempt to isolate ourselves from relationships entirely (Cannon 1999: 86).

Fortunately, or unfortunately, these strategies only ever work temporarily because our overall task is always that we need to find a way to live with the existential reality of other people's freedom.

Laing: Engulfment, Implosion and Petrification

Laing (1965) was greatly influenced by Sartre and he takes Sartre's idea of the Look further and relates it to the anxiety felt in relationships. For Laing, existential birth begins at physical birth and is mediated by the capacity of early relationships to promote trust rather than mistrust. In contrast, existential death is mediated by an objectifying Look such that we experience ourselves as separate, as reified and 'partially divorced from the body' (ibid.: 42), that is, as not being fully embodied. We are in the world, but we are not in-the-world.

He acknowledges with Sartre that the quality of our relationships is constitutive of how secure we feel and that if the threshold of what he calls ontological security has been reached then relationships with others will be risky perhaps, but there will be a belief, a faith, that the risk will be worth it and that mutuality is both possible and worthwhile.

But if we have not reached this threshold for whatever reason, our task will be self-preservation and we will deem a relationship to be successful if we have not lost something, and actually gaining something may be either not conceivable or actually threatening. It is not just that we feel temporarily uncomfortable; rather that intimacy is dreaded in case our fragile sense of autonomy and sense-of-self is lost. Such people may not feel sufficiently differentiated from the rest of the world, so that their identity, their sense-of-self, is in question and they may feel as not being fully embodied. Bearing in mind that we are permanently in-the-world and not separate from the world, a person whose relational world cannot be trusted, cannot by definition have a secure sense-of-self.

Laing suggests that this anxiety can be experienced in three different forms – engulfment, implosion and petrification – and is connected by individual either/or dilemmas and an overarching but ultimately self-defeating paradox, that 'to forgo one's autonomy becomes the means of secretly safeguarding it; [...] to feign death becomes a means of preserving one's aliveness' (Laing 1965: 51).

Although he related this explicitly to development of psychosis, he also notes (ibid.: 46) that none of us are immune, even those of us above the threshold can go below it in adverse circumstances; it is part of the human condition; it is ontological.

Engulfment

In the anxiety of engulfment (ibid.: 43), the consequence of relationships is that they can 'engulf, swamp and smother' (ibid.: 45) and to avoid it we isolate ourselves from others. The choice is either to withdraw from others or to be engulfed by others. This includes all relationships, especially those in which the other person is loving. Indeed love is seen as a more duplicitous form of hatred because it is felt to come with conditions. These are the ties that bind.

As Laing notes (ibid.: 45), the therapist must manage the relationship minute by minute such that there is an optimum amount of intimacy between therapist and client and the client not feel engulfed or abandoned by the therapist's care.

Implosion

In the anxiety of implosion (ibid.: 45), we feel empty. This is not an emptiness within, rather that we are the emptiness. The choice is between the no-thing-ness of emptiness and the nothingness of annihilation, and relationships are felt as collapsing being rather than filling being. This experience of emptiness is likely to be reversed into claims of completeness, or to feelings of envy. Attempts to fill the emptiness may be made with overeating; filling the emptiness, or undereating; denying the emptiness, or other addictive behaviour the purpose of which, regardless of the addictive object, is to address the sense of emptiness. They are never successful.

Petrification

In the anxiety of petrification (ibid.: 46) we experience ourselves as an object, that our subjectivity has been drained away by the other person's freedom, by their Look. We may retain a vestige of autonomy by reifying ourselves before the other does it. The choice is between petrifying ourselves or being petrified by others.

Mutuality and love

While in his early writings Sartre talked mainly about the consequences of objectification, in his later writings (1991, 1992), no doubt prompted by personal experience he also suggests that by valuing freedom (2003: 434) a way can be found out of the sadomasochistic circle.

These are described by Cannon (1991) as the two cooperative options. The first is when two people look at the world together; this is the sense of 'we' that people can get when involved in a common project (1991: 98) and is the basis for comradeship and trust whether in intimate relationships or not.

The second is the experience of positive reciprocity that Barnes calls the 'Look-as-exchange' (Barnes 1974: 64). She regards such a Look as 'a mutual affirmation of respect for the other as subject'. The 'Look-as-exchange' involves the acknowledgement not just of the other as other, but also that understanding the other's world can enhance both self and other. The prototype of the 'Look-as-exchange' is the contented mutual gazing of the mother–infant pair and is marked not by hostility or fear but by mutual receptiveness. As such, development is mutual.

Psychotherapy is an example of two people learning to know and to trust each other.

By conducting relationships cooperatively we remain open to the other person and acknowledge the rights of ourselves and of the other, together. However, this approach rests on finding the ability to tolerate greater degrees of unpredictability and anxiety as we allow and encourage the other to make their own choices and decisions in the full knowledge that those decisions might be painful for us. This more cooperative approach is when intimacy with another is felt to be freeing and not constraining, and although more challenging, it is also more fulfilling since it acknowledges both partners' autonomy.

This both-and solution can be summarised as: 'I have the responsibility to do what I want in a world of others, but so does everybody else and it works best if we take each other into account' (Deurzen and Adams 2016: 75).

Human development therefore is about learning to live with our own freedom at the same time as living with the freedom of others. It is a perennial question and being a question it is never solved once and for all. And it takes on a different form depending on the particular relationship we are in and also the time of life we are in.

7

Maurice Merleau-Ponty (1908–1961)

Living with embodiment

The importance of the relationship between Sartre and Merleau-Ponty cannot be overestimated; they were intellectual equals who influenced each other both philosophically and politically. Like Simone de Beauvoir, he was younger than Sartre by three years and was a teenage friend of Beauvoir's before either of them met Sartre later when they studied at the École normale supérieure, where he also taught from 1935 to 1939. He is referred to in Beauvoir's autobiographies by his own name and also by the pseudonym Jean Pradelle. There has been no biography written and much of what we know of his life has been documented by and is therefore through the eyes of Sartre and Beauvoir.

He was born in 1908 near Bordeaux, and after the death of his father when he was five, he, his brother and sister and his mother moved to Paris. He served as a lieutenant in an infantry division in the early years of the Second World War before being wounded days before the armistice between France and Germany, whereupon he returned to teaching in Paris. Shortly after, he married and had a daughter. Unlike Sartre he spent his life in academia and became Professor of Child Psychology and Pedagogy at the Sorbonne in 1949, and then Chair of Philosophy at the elite College de France in 1952, until his sudden death from a heart attack nine years later, at fifty-three. Of all the philosophers in this book he was the only one to work in academia for all his professional life. He was outlived by his wife Marianne by nearly fifty years – she died at ninety-six – and was buried in the Père Lachaise Cemetery in Paris. His death was marked by a special edition of *Les Temps modernes* including a long and warm appreciation by Sartre (2013).

Although they shared many friends, his closest collaborations with Sartre were political rather than philosophical, and these began with their involvement with the resistance in Paris during the occupation although Sartre was too well known even then to be actively involved. He arranged for the funding to put on Sartre's play *The Flies* in 1943

(Sartre 1973a) and he then published a review of it emphasising its theme of freedom – itself a risky thing to do in Nazi occupied Paris. (Stewart 1998: xx). After the end of the war they founded *Les Temps modernes* on which they were co-editors and Merleau-Ponty was the political editor. Although Sartre said later (2013) that he regarded Merleau-Ponty as his major political influence, their stances about the relationship of philosophy to politics were rather different. Whereas for Sartre commitment was about commitment to a cause, Merleau-Ponty argued for the philosopher's commitment to truth: he was sceptical of easy dichotomies (Goehr 2004: 318). These differences came to a head around what *Les Temps modernes'* policy should be towards Stalinism and led to Merleau-Ponty's resignation in 1953, to their moving apart, and to his book *Adventures of the Dialectic* (1973) on the relationship of philosophy to politics. They had different ways of defining *engagé*. Whereas Sartre saw objectification by others as ontological, Merleau-Ponty saw it as cultural. He said the 'I-other problem [is] a Western problem' (1968: 221) and he saw difference as an opportunity for people to 'fathom each other by delving more deeply into the shared world they inhabit' (Mazis 2016: 169). In spite of how much he shared with Sartre, they were rather different sorts of people; they had different temperaments. Where Sartre saw anxiety and struggle, Merleau-Ponty saw excitement and mystery. Where Sartre was intense even when joking, Merleau-Ponty was relaxed. While they both had bourgeois childhoods, Sartre saw little of value in his, but Merleau-Ponty's was enjoyable and he valued his. While Sartre valued words and language, Merleau-Ponty valued the senses. While they both liked music, Sartre was a good pianist and singer, Merleau-Ponty liked to dance and he was a good dancer (Bakewell 2016: 237); he knew how to move through space and make it his own. He wanted to live the music. He also had a family life he valued and the relationship between his life in philosophy and his life in politics was more subtle than that of Sartre's (Whiteside 2014).

Philosophy

Ultimately Merleau-Ponty was a phenomenologist who valued the primacy of reflection. He says,

> Reflection does not withdraw from the world [...]; it steps back to watch the forms of transcendence fly up like sparks from a fire; it slackens the intentional threads which attach us to the world and thus brings them to our notice; it alone is consciousness of the world because it reveals that world as strange and paradoxical.
>
> (2002: xv)

Philosophically, Merleau-Ponty was influenced by Husserl before Sartre, attending Husserl's 1929 Sorbonne lectures, and in 1939 he studied at the Husserl archives and was instrumental in setting up a centre for Husserl studies in Paris in the years of occupation, itself a risky operation. While staying close to Husserl's overall project he also developed it and consequently the existential strands in his work have a particularly strong phenomenological base and Warnock (1970: 72) assesses him to be more philosophical in tone than Sartre. Whereas Sartre, although immensely well read, often did not reference other writers, Merleau-Ponty did and he drew from a wide variety of sources like child development, psychological research, anthropology, neurology and psychoanalysis, and tackled a wide variety of subjects. In turn, his ideas have influenced a wider variety of fields, for instance, art criticism and practice, and also architecture. With respect to his thinking on child development, Welsh says that, 'his use of psychology is not meant to affirm its validity or worth over and above philosophy but to indicate that if philosophy is serious in taking up the real concrete historical situation of humankind it must begin with the living, situated, subject' (2013: xvii). In this way philosophy and psychology have a natural meeting place in phenomenology.

Above all, he did not wish or expect to solve any questions, simply to be phenomenological and try to put into words what is ordinarily not put into words, or as he said about Montaigne, to gain 'not self-satisfied understanding but a consciousness astonished at itself at the core of human existence' (Merleau-Ponty 1960: 203; Bakewell 2016: 237).

His first book, *The Structure of Behaviour*, which anticipated his whole project, was a critique of natural science as a way of looking at human phenomena; of the artificial dualisms of mind and body, subject and object, inner and outer. In this, he notes that while all animals manifest behaviour, it is only human beings that can choose their responses by an act of will. The meaning world is therefore not wholly physiological nor is it wholly psychological, nor in any way determined, by individual physiology or psychology.

Perception and embodiment

What excited him were not issues like anguish or authenticity, rather than apparently simpler but actually more complex issues like how we get the sense of being a body in space. While the different senses, sight, touch and so on may seem distinct, their simultaneity and the translation of one to another makes them an organised totality, they are 'not simply logically symmetrical, but form a real system' (Merleau-Ponty 1964: 120).

Perception is not simply visual; it is how we make sense of the world and it is always both from the body and in terms of the body. An early example of this is that when a small child draws a picture of a house it invariably takes the form of the human face; a building is as much of an enclosure of space as a body. Some buildings we call home and when people do not feel at home in their body, they feel immense unease. In this way our sense of being embodied underpins our entire existence. It is the basis of our awareness of ourselves in space, from simple things like using a knife and fork, to negotiating rush hour travel, to playing games like football or tennis, to making love rather than just having sex. It is the way we 'see' the fragility of a pane of glass, or 'feel' the springiness of a branch of a tree that a bird has just left, or imagine what a bed of nails would be like to lie on (Welsh 2013: 56). It is how we 'feel' warm when we see a picture of people on a sun-drenched beach or cold when we imagine swimming in an icy sea, rather than just remembering the warmth or coldness, cognitively. In the example of driving a car it refers to the sense that I know the boundaries of the car as I know the boundaries of myself. It is something we take for granted as adults and we only notice it when things go wrong. Although we know it as a sense, we learn it through trial and error and it is how we learn to take responsibility for our actions. Embodied knowledge can break down under the influence of, for example, alcohol or drugs, which reduce our reflectiveness, and this is also when we are inclined to deny responsibility for our actions, to blame others for them.

He went on to develop these ideas in *The Phenomenology of Perception*, which can be seen as a philosophical response to Sartre's *Being and Nothingness* of two years earlier. In turn, after *Being and Nothingness*, Sartre focused more and more on the influence of contextual issues and this can be seen as an acknowledgement of the influence of both Merleau-Ponty and Beauvoir.

While Sartre conceptualised consciousness as a light we shine on the world, and Heidegger said it was a like a clearing in the forest, Merleau-Ponty (1968) suggested two images for the relationship between consciousness and the world. One is that our consciousness makes folds in the world in a similar way that we make folds in a piece of fabric when we move it (Merleau-Ponty 1968: 196; Bakewell 2016: 235). Every time we perceive the world we make a fold in the fabric of the world. And it straightens out again when we move our attention away. Because of habituation we get used to seeing the same folds and imagine that they are always there. Merleau-Ponty calls this sedimentation; it is when we act as if truth is fixed and knowable. It is not, and since meaning is only ever constructed in the light of possibility, truth is therefore perpetually ambiguous.

The other image takes us even further away from dualism and is that of a 'chiasm', similar to the way one hand simultaneously holds and is held by another hand. Consciousness and the world are folded each into the other.

This abandons the idea of the discrete psyche known only to the owner in favour of a consciousness apprehending and finding meaning in actions in the world. He says, 'My consciousness is turned primarily toward the world [...], it is above all a relation to the world' (Merleau-Ponty 1964: 116). We are all intersubjectively connected bodies in space, permanently enclosing and being enclosed by the world; 'a body is not an object, it is a grouping of lived-through meanings' (2002: 177).

We all slide from the womb to the birth canal to an equally close and total immersion in the world and it is this immersion that he calls our 'total situation', in the same way that Sartre and Beauvoir mean, and neither body nor world can be seen as the cause or the effect of the other and our embodied spatiality constitutes the natural boundary to our freedom. Truth is not out there to be found; it is my embodied perception of the world that creates a truth that is dynamic and ambiguous.

While the body is a spatial object it also has a relationship to time, because without the continuity of the body in time we would not be able to make sense of the (changing folds in the fabric of the) world. Indeed, the ontological primacy of spatiality leads us to spatialise time into past, time behind; present, time here; and future, time in front. For Merleau-Ponty neither space nor time are things, they are qualities that we inhabit. Just as Heidegger says that we do not have time, we are temporal, Merleau-Ponty says that we do not have space, we are spatial.

Merleau-Ponty and human development

Few philosophers since Rousseau considered childhood worthy of interest at all, but for Merleau-Ponty it was a serious philosophical issue. He felt it was the job of philosophy not just to find out about what is, but also how it came to be so. In the light of this it is curious that there is only a passing reference to of his contribution in some standard reviews of his work (e.g., Carman 2004, 2006).

Merleau-Ponty (1964: 108) says that from the time of birth, the infant is moulded by his environment, and in this way parental authority is exercised. Lymer (2011) suggests that the environmental influences begin before birth but regardless of the timing, the infant is still dependent on his context for his physical and existential survival. Therefore a child can never be independent of his context. Such a pure state does not, cannot, ever exist. The child is always actively making sense of his sensations and in this way he structures his surroundings.

Therefore, the development of perception cannot be understood without reference to the human capacity to attribute meanings to the world and to imagine possibility. If development is not causal in adulthood, it cannot be causal in childhood.

Merleau-Ponty's ideas about child development are concentrated in 'The Child's Relations with Others' (1964) that is part of a lecture course he gave at the Sorbonne although there are frequent references to childhood and development in other works. There is a different chapter of the same name in *Childhood and Pedagogy* (2010), which although it has more background material has no substantial differences. He argues in these chapters that child development must be understood as a cumulative dynamic process rather than as a sequential achievement of stages. He also says that the view that a person's subjectivity, however acquired, determines the way he sees external reality is too simplistic and linear. There is a connection but it is not causal, it is correlative; it is subtle and fluid. Instead, because we are in constant interaction with our world, we gradually move at birth from a fragmentary, undifferentiated and unintegrated sense-of-self to a more integrated but actively constructed sense-of-self, but which is never complete.

While he maintains that the course of development is flexible, this does not mean that no patterns exist. His theory is one in which the individual possesses innate tendencies towards certain styles of being and that within each individual's situation certain freedoms present themselves. He says that while 'development follows certain lines all the same; the possibilities of aberrations are not infinite' (2010: 407) and that our innate tendencies anticipate but do not determine the future. Because development is cumulative, all the different modes of being and ways of making sense of experience that are characteristic of different ages, times and places, exist simultaneously and enhance and underpin all subsequent modes of being. Nothing is ever lost.

His view of human development is therefore one in which the growth of consciousness and hence self-consciousness parallels physiological development. We are born with the ability to make sense of experience, and interpreting and anticipating the world begins from the moment of birth or before, and we gradually and cumulatively come to understand our ambiguous, embodied, intersubjective nature. This allows us to understand how the state of childhood can be distinct from the adult state at the same time as enriching and informing adulthood.

It is our intersubjectivity that leads us to know that both ourselves and others are separate and connected embodied consciousnesses, and it is through understanding this that we gain the resilience that comes with having a sense of continuity in space and time.

Early experience: primary undifferentiation

His developmental sequence begins with pre-communication, or primary undifferentiation 'in which there is [...] an anonymous collectivity, an undifferentiated group life' (1964: 119).

Just as the infant does not have to be taught to breathe or suckle, it does not have to be taught to make sense of its place in the world. The newborn infant is intentionally relating, rather than communicating, because there is no distinct and perceived other to communicate with. All experience is undifferentiated experience. At birth there is no differentiation between introceptive, internally derived stimuli, and extroceptive, externally derived stimuli. All is one. This is intersubjectivity as a communal experience and in this sense all experience is introceptive experience. Merleau-Ponty says, 'The child lives in a world which he unhesitatingly believes accessible to all around him. [...] He has no knowledge of points of view' (2002: 413). The infant therefore has no idea of the nature of, or the boundaries of his own body; he has no 'corporeal schema'.

This can be seen in the phenomenon of what he calls a 'contagion of crying' (1964: 124) when if there are number of similar age babies together, if one baby cries they all start crying. This phenomenon tends to stop after about six months. Also in primary undifferentiation, if the infant cries when someone goes away, Merleau-Ponty says it is not because of loss, but because of an 'impression of incompleteness' (ibid.), and although not a response in a conventional sense, it is also this direct and active relationship that explains the smile response. The infant does not smile because he is imitating the parent, or because he already has a theory of mind of what the other's smile means, but because of the embodied introceptive experience of well-being he shares with the other. Although Gallagher and Meltzoff's (1996) research suggests that facial recognition occurs earlier than Merleau-Ponty suggested, as with Lymer (2011), it does not substantially change Merleau-Ponty's assertion or sequence.

From the beginning, the infant connects with and relates to the world via his mouth, not just through the biological necessity of feeding and breathing but that the infant gets to know what objects are like by putting them in his mouth. The infant explores and discovers spatiality, the world comes into embodied consciousness through the mouth.

To the extent that the child lacks an image of his body, he cannot separate what he lives from what others live, or from what he sees them living. He calls this 'transitivism', the absence of a division between others and myself, and in adults its most extreme form is psychosis, when boundaries between self and other and objects disappear and merge in different ways. It is also replicated in a time-limited way by some recreational drugs.

The physiological development of the nervous system parallels that of the infant's consciousness of his own body in which the different introceptive senses – touch, hearing, sight and so on – start to be integrated and differentiated (Merleau-Ponty 1964: 123). Attention is first focused on the parts of the body – mouth, feet, hands – rather than the whole body. The infant gains an ability to focus his eyes and to control the movements of his hands. First one hand, then the other, then each with the other, and then exploring his own body, other bodies and also other things and by a comparison of these introceptive qualities a sense of their connection, a sense of what is 'my body' and what is 'not my body' begins to form, as well as what a whole body is like.

Differences gradually get discovered and 'the corporeal schema becomes precise, restructured and matures little by little' (Merleau-Ponty 1964: 123) and the infant gets a better understanding of his spatiality; of space and its possibilities. From exploring his body, other bodies and other things, the infant then discovers movement. First crawling, then sitting, then standing, then walking, then running and then climbing. This progression takes place over the first year or two and radically changes the infant's relationship with space from something that is out there to something that he is a part of, something three-dimensional rather than two-dimensional. It is something that can be owned and moved through and its possibilities can be explored. The infant gains the power to change his viewpoint, laterally as well as vertically. From this time onwards we use tools and we go outside of our body for action and resources. For an infant it may be a soft toy, a rattle or a spoon, but anything in the non-human world can be made into an extension of the human world by the way we use it. Our personal world is extended spatially by the way we use our tools, whether they are building blocks, hammers, cars, the internet, nuclear weapons or space rockets. In this way, we become co-extensive with our actions.

As children we experience settings like playgrounds as large and when we return to them as adults we are surprised to find that they are not as large as we remembered. They only seemed large because we were small. People smaller than average often dislike crowds because they literally cannot see their way out. For anyone who loses their mobility, the world becomes a different place, somewhere they cannot inhabit with the same facility. The French phenomenologist Gaston Bachelard (1969) has written eloquently and poetically about the experience of space.

The mirror and the world of others

Towards the end of the first year the child starts to notice other children of a similar age differently, and 'one has the impression that here for the first time he is perceiving another' (Merleau-Ponty 1964: 125). It is not that the social world takes precedence over the personal world, or vice versa, rather that the paradox begins to be revealed that the previously indistinct experiences of self and other have a perpetually ambiguous unity. It is when consciousness starts to transform into self-consciousness.

This transformation is mediated by the child's experience of seeing the image of his body in the mirror or in another representation, like a photograph or reflection. The idea of the mirror is meant both metaphorically and literally, and there are many other ways of getting this image apart from the visual, but the fact that personal visual stimuli are so common and increasingly so only enhances this. He calls the image the child has of himself, the 'specular image' (1964: 125) and the meaning of the mirror has two dimensions – the child's experience of the other and the child's experience of himself – and the literal and metaphorical meanings he takes from these have far-reaching implications for the rest of his life. It is for this reason that early photographs and other images of ourselves can be so resonant and meaningful. Through such images in adulthood we can return in a moment of prereflective engagement as if to an earlier mode of perception and at such times, it is as if the image 'is mysteriously inhabited by me; it is something of myself' (1964: 132). The created image is in fact humankind's first permanent imaginative act and is an object of pure magic. It is where the normal rules of time and space do not apply. In the case of a photograph, materially it is just pigment on paper; it has no physical similarity to what it aims to re-present. But through our permanent embodiment it has the ability to conjure up feelings that remind of our relationship to the world and to others, to space, to time and to existence.

Initially though, the two images – the image seen directly, in person, and the image seen indirectly, in the mirror – are seen as separate and different, and both require the child to reorganise his emerging conception of lived space. Although confusing, both the direct and the indirect image of the other are relatively easy to connect up and associate, because although in different places, they not only look much the same but also the child can see the whole of the other person both directly, in person, as well as indirectly, in the mirror.

What is more difficult though, is for the child to connect the image of himself that he sees in the mirror with his own experience of himself. The general effect of the 'specular image' he says, is 'to tear us away from our immediate [experienced and embodied] reality' (1964: 137), and it will be felt as confusion: *How can I be here at the same time as being over there?* There is a conflict between the introceptive me-I-feel-myself-to-be and the specular me-as-seen-by-others. Initially and developmentally, this image is seen as if it is someone else at least in part because the child cannot see the whole of himself directly. None of us can ... ever. He can easily see his feet, or his hands, but he cannot ever see, will never be able to see, his whole body directly. The two images, the whole but indirect image, and the fragmentary but direct image, are seen in parallel; connected temporally but not visually. Because he is always looking from his body he only gradually gains a coherent sense of himself as an embodied being in the world, of what he looks like to others.

Out of the original infantile experience of undifferentiated intersubjectivity comes the realisation that the image I see of myself in the mirror is also the image that others have of me, and just as I see others as different and separate, so others must see me as different and separate. And moreover that there is a difference between the me-I-feel-myself-to-be and the me-as-seen-by-others. Just as others are objects, out there, for me, so I am an object, out there, for others.

It is also at this time that the child develops the desire and capacity for playing hide and seek. This is a game that is dependent for its success on the implicit and embodied trust that the child has in the adult, that the adult will stay hidden for neither too long nor too short a time, and take neither too long nor too short a time to find the child. Hide and seek is about experimenting with the precariousness of existence, of trust in the other and the magic of space, memory and being held in mind by the other. About the tension between completeness and incompleteness.

De-centering and re-centering

Merleau-Ponty uses the term de-centering to describe the experience of realising that world and my relationship to it is not what I thought it was. It was originally used by Piaget in the context of intellectual development but Merleau-Ponty uses it in an existential sense. He also uses the parallel term re-centering to describe 'the manner in which the child restores his relations with others' (1964: 111).

The initial dilemma between the introceptively derived me-as-I-feel-myself-to-be and the extroceptively derived me-as-seen-by-others constitutes the first significant de-centering and re-centering of existence because it simultaneously affects the child's sense of being in space and time, their being with others and their being with themselves. But it will never be restored to what it was, because the feelings evoked by such a situation derive from the meaning of spatial and temporal change: that what was, is no more (1964: 110). This is a turning point and what is now known about the sheer otherness of others and the world can never be unknown. In future cases where re-centering is resisted, temporal change is also denied, and it will be as if time, development, has stopped at that point. The initial de-centering and re-centering of existence mediated by the mirror is only the first of many because life in fact is constant de-centering and re-centering. Nevertheless the dilemma gradually settles into a uniquely personal and habituated equilibrium which constitutes of all our lived relations with others and the world.

Language acquisition

Developmentally, all the senses are present from birth. They are followed only later by language that is a refinement of the ability to translate experiences into discrete sounds. For this reason the senses have a stronger and more direct connection with embodied memory than language, which is strongly mediated by the intellect. Eugene Gendlin (1996) calls this stronger more direct connection the 'felt-sense' and regards it as primary and essentially non- or pre-verbal. Consequently many aspects of it are so ineffable that they probably cannot ever be put into words, they are literally beyond words, but it is these that are the foundations of our most profound experiences. This goes for all emotions, which are fundamentally embodied experiences, and the reason why experiences as profound as love, or actions such as making love, are so hard to describe in words is because they cannot be put into words. The words we use to represent experiences are simply that, words. They are not the experiences. Often the nearest we get to the experiences is when the words are used in a poetic, ambiguous sense rather than a linear, defined sense.

Perception of sound begins from birth, if not before (Mehler et al. 1988; DeCasper et al. 1994; Lymer 2011), and while biological maturation, socialisation and intellect play their part, Merleau-Ponty is keen to show that neither one is the cause of the other. He says, 'At the same time that the child is assuming and forming his family relations, an entire form of thinking arises in him. It is a whole usage of language as well as a way of perceiving the world' (1964: 113).

The process of language acquisition is significant because a spoken verbal language becomes a medium to create and share we-meanings, not simply I-meanings. The parent–child unit relies for its functionality on the parent and child understanding each other. As such, they begin by relating non-verbally, intersubjectively, by developing an entirely embodied language and they implicitly understand each other by the mutual generation of an idiolect, a language invented for a single person by another single person (Roustang 1986: 72), and in this way they become known to each other. The paradox of the idiolect is that it is as personal as it is universal and our personal embodied language never gets entirely forgotten and comes to play an important part later on in our adult intimate relationships. We can get glimpses of the universality of the idiolect in our adult lives when we find we share a sense of humour with someone. It happens in therapy also at moments of mutual understanding that are beyond words. Another adult example of the importance of almost magical quality of the idiolect is in flirting.

For a child though, the personal embodied language gets overlaid by a language characterised by linearity and lack of ambiguity. This common verbal language makes it possible to exchange ideas and experiences and to create shared socially sanctioned meanings. The child discovers that they exist out there in the world not just in their imagination but in other people's imaginations too. It appears in parallel with the awareness of self-consciousness and with it comes an understanding of and use of names, pronouns, and gender and the emergence of temporality, of memory and of hope and in this way an autobiography starts to be written. Using the word 'I' comes after the child's use of his own name, when the child has become conscious of himself distinct from others.

But language acquisition can also fragment self-experience by causing a split between the verbal more social self and the embodied sense, and the authority of the lived body can not only be doubted but also lost.

Consequently, experiences that are resistant or invisible to verbal representation in the original familial culture, which will always be a refraction of the wider culture, may become split off and uncoded. The embodied experience will remain, but will not be able to be expressed because the person does not have the words for it, and even if they did there is no guarantee that others will recognise it, understand it, or want to hear it. In this way we all develop an idiosyncratic, reduced and thus distorted emotional vocabulary. Although inevitable to a certain extent, generally it is not too disabling and we show this by our ability to survive everyday de-centering relational shocks and failures of empathy that remind us that the other is another person with their own perceptions. In fact, these failures are necessary in order to introduce the existential dilemma of relationality that is the tension between our need for individuality and our need for intimacy.

However, if the empathic failures whether through language or action, are consistent, whether through passive indifference or active abuse, then the child will be ill-equipped to deal with the dilemma and will find re-centering difficult. We know extreme examples as trauma (Stolorow 2007).

A child under about three is therefore absorbed in discovering the interplay between the introceptive and the extroceptive world, and in what possibilities of ways of being it can offer. At the beginning the boundaries of its possibilities are limited and narrow and a child's impotent rage and frustration at this age – 'the terrible twos' – is often expressed as it's *not fair* because the world is not the way they imagined to be. This reaction though is by no means limited to this age. Realising the world is not the way it was imagined to be also marks the beginnings of a personal system of ethics.

Embodiment and imagination

In general a child will show more interest in other people than in things, but will only show an interest in another child if the other child is of a similar age, and it is not until later that children become interested in children of a different age. The ability of children to play together develops gradually and parallels the ability to see the person as another person rather than as an object.

Nevertheless, people are recognised at least initially in the context of a particular place. When somebody familiar is seen in a different place, it can be unsettling. This can be true for adults too. It can be unsettling for both therapists and clients when they meet unexpectedly outside the consulting room. It is also unsettling and sometimes unethical when the therapist acts out of role. Our perceptions form into unique, individual and often rigid patterns that come to constitute our identity, and we easily forget, or would rather not know about, the more unsettling option that there are far more alternatives that are possible.

Our embodiment enables us to understand others and the child understands the world through his body. This explains the ease with which children, who tend to have a stronger embodied sense than adults, can understand non-linear, abstracted paintings and sculptures that have multiple perspectives like those done by the likes of Picasso, Henry Moore and Anthony Gormley. It is this capacity that makes the child a natural phenomenologist (Welsh 2014). Not having technical ability or natural scientific notions of linearity or photographic accuracy to constrain their imagination, children are the original abstract expressionists. Merleau-Ponty says, 'The painter takes his body with him [...] it is by lending his body to the world that the artist changes the world into paintings' (1964a: 162).

Imagination, the ability to think of something that is not present, is a product of being able to suspend one's assumptions about what is, and to project oneself into other ways of being. Husserl formalised this suspension as bracketing and the projection as the process of Imaginative Variation (Langdridge 2007). Children can use their imagination easier than adults because they do not have so many assumptions to suspend. Everything is new and can be wondered at and imaginative conclusions arrived at. For the child though it not a surprise or special; it is the way they perceive. When we as adults are sometimes surprised or even shocked at children's imagination, the surprise should not be that children have imagination, but that we do not have it. It is we as adults that have lost it, and then have lost touch with the fact that we had it in the first place. At worst, imagination can be pathologised and this in itself can lead to what could be called neurotic behaviour, or alternatively it can be thought of as being a special quality that only some people, e.g. artists, have, when it is in fact a natural human quality. It also explains why such ways of understanding are more difficult for adults because although they have not lost their embodied perceptivity; they have learnt to overlay it with a more linear, disembodied, less ambiguous, more technical, culturally sanctioned way of apprehension which they give greater value to.

Incompleteness and loss

Whereas at an earlier age, deprivation was felt as incompleteness, with increased understanding of the dilemma of relationality, incompleteness can now be felt as loss. This by no means implies that it will come about easily or will ever be complete, far from it. For a small child though, love is not seen in terms of freedom and sharing, but in terms of the precarious balance between completeness and incompleteness.

Jealousy, which is about the feelings that follow from the experience of completeness and incompleteness being controlled by a third party, has its origins in infancy. As does sulking, which is about the expectation that the other person should know my needs without me needing to say what they are. In sulking there is a sudden failure of the idiolect and the consequence is de-centering and a feeling of incompleteness and despair. Both jealousy and sulking can be expressed as much by adults as children. In adults though, they have become sedimented elements of identity rather than being transient. The origins also explain why jealousy is so hard to work with in psychotherapy.

With respect to jealousy, Merleau-Ponty notes that in adulthood, situations are often manufactured to create an expression of intimacy, of completeness. For example, if we have doubts about our partner's love that give rise to our own feelings of incompleteness, we may arrange for a situation whereby our partner feels incompleteness because of our relationship with a third person, such that our partner expresses his or her attachment to us in a stronger way than usual, thus evoking feelings of completeness. Both love and anger are equally effective here since they both evoke completeness and intimacy. Indifference or being ignored is the worst alternative. Merleau-Ponty says there is an understanding, an expectation, a hope, that the other will be hurt, in the same way as oneself hurts. The jealous person will also often find a satisfaction in suffering by ruminations, investigations and hypotheses whose end result will be to heighten passions that often manifest as sexual passions but sometimes as violence. For this reason, groups of three are always unstable and anxiety producing because they frequently divide into two and one.

Acquisition of a sense of perspective

As said, the infant is born in a state of primary undifferentiation and mediated by the coherence of embodiment, and the metaphor of the mirror gradually begins to differentiate in from out, self from other, reality from imagination. There is a gradual reduction in the child's equation of himself with the situation he is in, and the child discovers both his separateness and his connectedness. This process brings about another radical de-centering and re-centering of existence.

To draw is to represent spatiality, and Merleau-Ponty uses the metaphor of the acquisition of perspective in drawing and this can be seen in children's drawings of the period (Simms 2008). The more we 'see' phenomenologically, the more we become aware that we are doing the looking, and the more we gain perspective and a sense of horizon the more we realise that our understanding is always relative to our viewpoint and also that we will always only ever have one viewpoint even though we may remember or imagine others.

We also realise that our view is not necessarily any more wrong or right than anyone else's. It is not just different and relative, but also utterly personal. A complete view is never possible. Reality is unknown, unknowable and ambiguous. The acquisition of perspective is an acknowledgement not only that I see things from my own viewpoint but also that there are other viewpoints as well. Time is to writers as space is to artists, and artists who work in two dimensions have a different sense of spatiality than those like sculptors and architects who work in three dimensions.

Realising that I have a viewpoint is the same as realising my own integrity and also the integrity of others. This leads very quickly on to the realisation that other people are both similar and different, they are not only like me, but they are also not like me. This leads on to the possibility of understanding relationships, of discovering that relationships are dynamic and ambiguous, not fixed and clear.

The psychoanalytic Oedipal conflict is a dilemma that can be reframed as a major de-centering of perspective. While it may take particular gendered and cultural forms, it is also universal. It is when there is a realisation that a relationship, the mother–infant relationship, that was thought to be completely exclusive is discovered not just as not exclusive now, but also that in one very important sense it never was exclusive. In another sense of course, the development of the mother–child idiolect is, was and always will be exclusive and special. The following sort of conversation between my son when he was about four years old and his mother is not uncommon:

Son: *I love you.*

Mother: *I love you too.*

Son: *When two people love each other they get married. Let us get married. I want to marry you.*

Mother: *How will we get married?*

Son: *I don't know. When you got married how did you?*

Mother: *A man married us. You know I am married to Daddy.*

Son: *But that's an old marriage. We will find someone to marry us.*

The changing effect of the look

Whereas up to the age of about three the look of the other is encouraging and helping, after three it can become an annoyance, a distraction, objectifying. But like the Medusa, it is both desired and feared. There is a need not just to assert separateness, but for this separateness to be freely given by the caregiver. This is most noticeable when a child is immersed in play and the adult's job is to notice but not interfere. Since the child's imagination provides the boundaries, unstructured materials like boxes, string, paper and fabric will allow the greatest flexibility without restricting their actions. A cardboard box can be a racing car as easily as it can be a fairy palace. This state of mind can be got into at any age and with any activity that involves attention, concentration and imagination and such states where time and space collapse are much sought after. At such times, 'My body takes possession of time; it brings into existence a past and a future for a present; it is not a thing, but creates time instead of submitting to it' (Merleau-Ponty 2002: 279).

But if the child is inhibited by the carer's look, if the carer interferes or directs too much, the child will feel himself to be the way others see him, as if from the outside: objectified. In adults this can manifest as shyness, or a self-consciousness that can be socially crippling. This can illuminate why it is that people can have different reactions to public speaking and performing. How some people can be enlivened by the audience and are able to feel most free, while others are paralysed by it.

This subtlety of the look is a central issue in therapy as well. Working phenomenologically demands that by attending fully the therapist grows to understand how much space each client needs in order that they are able to attend to their own process. This is how we care for each other.

It can also can lead us to an understanding of claustrophobia and agoraphobia (Adams 1998; Davidson 2000), which is not so much, or at all, about the physical space as such, but about the emotional and existential meaning of spatiality and its occupation by others who are able to objectify simply by their presence or absence.

Narcissism

Phenomenologically, narcissism is the refusal to accept that one's (current) view is only one view, that one is not the centre of the universe and is the assertion that others must support this viewpoint. In most cases the child will be cared for with the sensitivity that is his right and if this happens the child will be able to tolerate occasional unreliability and random acts of freedom and conclude that other people are generally trustworthy. The child will then learn reflexively not to be afraid of the relational consequences of his or her own freedom. In this way the ambiguity of relationships with others comes to be trusted and sought, rather than feared and dreaded.

But if the child experiences consistent unreliability and insensitivity from his carers, it can be traumatic, and development will take another course into what we can call narcissism. The child will choose to turn away from the openness and ambiguity of human relationships into the fixity and certainty of relationships that do not involve trust. This turning away from the relational world will only be chosen after the child experiences cumulative or traumatic insensitivity and decides that life is safer protected from the ambiguity of relationships. As Merleau-Ponty says, 'I leave the reality of my lived me in order to refer myself constantly to the ideal, fictitious or imaginary me, of which the specular image is the first outline' (Merleau-Ponty 1964: 137).

Since the child has experienced being treated as an object, for self-protection the child will treat both himself and others as objects. This movement from ambiguity to fixity, is what Stolorow (2007) is referring to when he talks about the sense of isolation and singularity of trauma.

Narcissism is when the image of me-as-seen-by-others, or more likely, the me-as-I-want-to-be-seen-by-others, takes priority over the me-I-feel-myself-to-be. From the myth, after looking at his image in the water, Narcissus, who had turned away from the love of others, was drawn to rejoin his (specular) image in the water. Some narcissists can be extremely attractive and charismatic because of their total lack of self-doubt. But they are also dangerous because they wish to control freedom and reduce human ambiguity and openness. Ovid elaborated the original myth of Narcissus by adding the character of Echo whose function is to agree with everything Narcissus says and does. Their intimacy is not love but co-dependency.

Later development

While the crisis at about three years brings about a restructuring such that differentiation arises out of undifferentiation, Merleau-Ponty does not see the disappearance of undifferentiation as a feature of future life. We can see this in later phenomena such as falling in love, which is a feeling of trust in undifferentiated merging. This evokes a wide variety of feelings in people. It is also a feature of some recreational drugs.

Sympathy and empathy

He makes a distinction between the initial sympathy of the pre-communication period, which rests on 'the absence of a distinction between self and the other' (Merleau-Ponty 1964: 146) and which can also be called identification, and what he calls 'adult sympathy' (1964: 120) which knows its own limits yet possesses the power to cross them without abolishing the difference between self and other. We know this as empathy. This way of seeing intersubjectivity is as two interlocking subjectivities rather than two merged subjectivities.

The possibility of empathy coming out of sympathy will increase as the person learns that a resilient sense-of-self emerges out of a constant fluctuation between lived de-centering and lived re-centering and that hope and disappointment are two sides of the same coin.

Love

The paradox of the unity of connectedness and separateness raises the question for Merleau-Ponty of whether 'one could one conceive of a love that would not be an encroachment on the freedom of the other' (Merleau-Ponty 1964: 154). He clearly sees it as possible because he says that the paradox of love is that while exerting an influence on another is likely to decrease trust and increase distance, not wishing to exerting an influence on another is likely to increase trust and decrease distance. And we simultaneously find our own freedom and the other's freedom 'precisely in the act of loving, and not in vain autonomy' (1964: 154).

But this situation is never completely comfortable because it is never static, there will 'always be the occasion for doubt' (1964: 154) because the reality of the other person's feelings can never be proved once and for all. This uncertainty evokes a range of responses. Some people refuse to trust, while others get drawn into controlling. It also has relevance for the therapeutic relationship that after all is a transient relationship founded on trust.

The alternative consists of bypassing these doubts by means of the generosity of an action that proves itself in being carried out, and in realising that love is not a commodity that can be owned or accumulated but an action that creates its own truth.

We are all interconnecting and interpenetrating bodies in space and it is precisely our experience of undifferentiation in infancy that stops us from feeling total isolation in adulthood. '[We] arrive at the universal not by abandoning our particularity but by turning it into a way of reaching others, by virtue of that mysterious affinity which makes situations mutually understandable' (Merleau-Ponty 1968: 92).

For Merleau-Ponty, an implication of acknowledging our difference from each other is the beginning of a human ethics in which we have responsibility both for each other and for ourselves together, and it is at this point that his philosophy and his politics meet.

Masculinity, femininity and the development of difference

Although Beauvoir wrote far more explicitly on the development of gender identity, it is on this issue that Merleau-Ponty and Beauvoir intersect and Merleau-Ponty's work has been read and applied from a feminist perspective.

Merleau-Ponty has been criticised by some (e.g., Sullivan 1997; Fisher 2000) for treating his universalist approach as gender neutral on the grounds that since gender is constitutive of our being, there can be no viable gender-neutral approach. But while it is true that he gives few descriptions or comparisons of gendered experience, Welsh (2013) along with Weiss (2002) and Stoller (2000) consider that his method of phenomenological enquiry is appropriate for examining gendered experience and that Merleau-Ponty's method does provide room for a consideration of gender, as well as culture and class. Consequently it has been left to Merleau-Ponty's successors to continue the work.

He echoes Beauvoir in her criticism of the idea of fixed gender roles and identities, seeing such divisions as examples of psychological rigidity: the tendency to see the world in black and white terms 'that do not allow for ambiguity or contradiction' (Merleau-Ponty 1964: 103) noting as she does that each society has its own way of defining and treating (gender) difference. He sees psychological rigidity as a metaphor for the person's relationship with the world. While acknowledging that there may well be psychological differences between men and women that arise from biological differences, he says that 'the only way to know whether such differences exist is to get rid of notions of a "feminine nature" and of a "masculine nature"' (2010: 377). In order to do this we must bracket our assumptions, but in a society that is so profoundly gendered and organises gender roles along established lines of patriarchy this is clearly difficult. Not only are we culturally determined to privilege certain values over others but our methods of accessing the truth is influenced by our situation.

On a number of occasions Merleau-Ponty is keen to insist that although psychological development parallels physiological development, neither one causes the other. This is where the individual's freedom comes in because gender development will not occur until the individual takes up and owns the personal meanings that physiological development brings. He says, 'the individual must take up again what the present bodily state has rendered possible' (2010: 407). With respect to the position a woman finds herself in, Welsh says that in an ideal society she 'might very well experience a harmonious interaction between her individual embodiment and the social allowances for individual lifestyle choices. It might also be the case that in an unhealthy society, no woman can ever feel entirely at ease with her body' (2013: 132). It is in the area of gender identity that culturally agreed meanings exert enormous pressure and this means that the space in which the individual man or woman has the freedom to take up their own meaning is correspondingly small and that this leads almost inevitably to rigid gender roles.

He also sees a parallel between the way society sees the male/female difference and the way it sees the adult/child difference, with one (male/adult) being seen as dominant and the other (female/child) as secondary. This can be extended to include any oppressed, disenfranchised group such as the old, with the adult person as the dominant one and the aged person as subsidiary.

Pregnancy

Concerning the experience of pregnancy, Merleau-Ponty suggests that the developing body in pregnancy carries with it a tie to a primordial pre-subjective existence that both undermines the sense-of-self as well as underpins it. He says, 'on the one hand the infant's body escapes her but on the other the infant who will be born is truly an extension of her own body. During the entirety of her pregnancy, she lives this major mystery which is not of the order of matter [...] but rather of the order of life' (2010: 78). When pregnant the woman becomes part of the eternal cycle of life in a unique way because she becomes aware that the life she gives birth to will in all likelihood extend past her own. She acquires a new awareness and sensitivity both to her predecessors and to her successors. It is an entirely different view of life. Using the image of the chiasm, Young says pregnancy 'challenges the integration of my body experience by rendering fluid the boundary between what is within, myself, and what is outside, separate. I experience my insides as the space of another [...] In pregnancy, I lose the sense of where my body ends and the world begins' (1985: 30). Pregnancy thus offers a more complex understanding of the relationship between freedom and determinism. In contrast, while fatherhood will have many of these resonances the one it lacks is the most obvious, that of the profound embodied phenomenon of pregnancy and birth itself.

Gendered space

Because of the cultural dominance of the nature model, there have been few extended pieces of work that talk about how gender roles and characteristics are acquired. One such is by Young (2005) in which, drawing on Beauvoir (1997), she looks at the way boys and girls grow up to use and occupy space. Beauvoir (1997) notes that the boy will learn to be outwardly directed, and even before the physiological changes of puberty, the way boys and girls are encouraged to be physical and thus to gain an understanding of how to take up, use and occupy space will be different. Activities like climbing trees, getting dirty, making noise and adventurous anarchic playing are gendered and considered to be boys' activities, and if girls do them they are thought to be boyish, 'tomboys'. Girls are encouraged to be physical in a more constrained way. Dancing and gymnastics have more formal moves and are indoor activities whereas football is freer and takes place out of doors. This constraint affects girls proportionally more after puberty than before. It also affects boys in a comparable way, where boys who are not interested in e.g. football but are interested in e.g. dance find it more difficult to be accepted by their peers. In this way, gender identity is tied up with a gendered spatial experience (Beauvoir 1997: 313). In using the everyday example of learning to throw a ball, Young (2005) says the difference between the way a boy throws a ball compared with the way a girl throws a ball is neither insignificant nor to do with biology, but is related to the way girls and boys learn to use space. This argument begins with the assertion that the dominant experience of a woman is of constant self-consciousness in the sense of watching herself as others watch her. She is objectified and her experience of her body is as a thing for herself as well as for others. The dominant experience of a man is of being embodied as free and transcendent. As such his consciousness is not on himself, but on how he can make use of the world's possibilities.

Because of this objectification girls grow to lack the trust in their bodies that boys have and this leads girls to approach physical movement with timidity, uncertainty and hesitancy based on a lack of confidence and also a fear of getting hurt, neither of which boys have so much. Girls are more likely to view a ball as coming towards them, and then passively wait for it to arrive, whereas men will see it as something they will move towards, meet and actively redirect.

In throwing, the physical difference is that girls do not involve their whole bodies as much as boys. Instead of reaching out and back, twisting, moving backward and then leaning forward, they tend to remain relatively immobile except for their arms, and even the arms are not extended as far as they could be. This does just apply to throwing; there is more general reluctance to make full use of the body's spatial and lateral potentialities as seen in sitting, standing, walking and carrying.

In committing to physical action, this hesitancy sets up a struggle between a desire for the action and a reluctance to carry it through and often gets translated into lack of confidence and inferiority.

In this way, women's experience of spatiality is one of constriction and lack of possibility. And that of men's is of openness and possibility, and as with psychological rigidity comes to be a gendered metaphor for the relationship between one person and another and for the person's relationship with the world. It also gets sedimented into gendered and socially sanctioned dress codes which are taken as being reflections of women's (and men's) true nature that reinforce and emphasise women's difficulty with negotiating and owning space; of being spatial. These are shown from puberty onwards in the physical constraints of clothing such as high heels and restrictive clothing and so on which are required for women to be seen as desirable to men. Accessing these dress codes symbolises a rite of passage from asexual girlhood, which has many similarities to asexual boyhood, to a more sexual gendered restricted womanhood.

8

Simone de Beauvoir (1908–1986)

Living with others

A review of existential philosophy's contribution to human development would not be complete without reference to Simone de Beauvoir. It is also instructive to consider why her work is rarely considered alongside other philosophers.

The eldest of two sisters by two years, she was born in Montparnasse in Paris into a bourgeois world of 'propriety and cultivated distinction' (Bair 1990: 22) in which the use of the particule 'de' showed aristocratic pretension rather than genuine membership of the aristocracy. There was very little money available to keep up the necessary appearances partly because her mother's dowry was never paid and partly because her father, an unenthusiastic lawyer, put most of his energy into amateur dramatics. He was something of a '*flâneur*'. While her mother was a strict Catholic, her father was a right-wing atheist – he was convinced of Dreyfus' guilt – who encouraged her learning and she went to a prestigious convent school. As well as introducing her to philosophy – philosophy has been a part of the school curriculum in France since the Napoleonic era – she also became an atheist at school and became intensely aware of freedom, through her lack of it. This led to an awareness of how political ideology and personal value systems shaped people's sense of identity, actions and relationships. In the final volume of her autobiography she says of her youth: 'Among my pieces of good fortune I count the fact that my parents' different views on morality drove me into consternation. I made up my mind to be answerable to myself alone' (1977: 20).

From her teenage years she was keenly aware of her gender and also that the models of womanhood she was exposed to all involved, she felt, sacrificing freedom and independence with little in return. This, combined with her family being able to offer few assets to offer a future husband, led to her parents agreeing to her becoming a philosophy teacher, although she was so determined to gain her autonomy the impression she gives in her autobiographies is that she would have done it anyway. Talking as a fifteen-year-old about the kind of relationship she wanted as an adult she says,

> I could not have accepted a man whose thoughts and work were an enigma to me; love would have to be a justification not a limitation. The man destined to be mine would be neither inferior nor different, nor outrageously superior; someone who would guarantee my existence without taking away my powers of self-determination.
>
> (1963: 146)

That man was Sartre who she met in 1929 and her work is even more entwined with her life than Sartre's. She had already become friends with Merleau-Ponty when they were at the Sorbonne together in 1927 and Sartre was one of the same group of talented friends some of whom were at the prestigious École normale supérieure. After Sartre was called up in 1939 she stayed in Paris and became politicised by the Nazi occupation and after the war ended in 1945, founded *Les Temps modernes* with Sartre and Merleau-Ponty and remained an active part of the editorial board until just prior to her death. From the beginning, Sartre and Beauvoir saw each other as equals and with a few exceptions in the latter years they were always the first to read and to criticise each other's work. There was only one book of hers that he did not read and that was about Sartre himself and published after his death (1985). They constantly influenced but never took over each other's work and it was because they were both independent thinkers that they were able to exchange ideas and also produce separate though connected bodies of work. As serious as Sartre but without his charm or sense of humour, she often came across as being rather brusque or even rude.

While neither was ever in any doubt about their commitment to each other, they were also in no doubt about the kind of relationship they wanted from each other. Ever unconventional they addressed each other throughout their lives by the more formal *'vous'* rather than the more conventional *'tu'*. Much has been made of this relationship (e.g., Rowley 2006) in which while they both considered they were 'necessary' to each other, they also considered that monogamous commitment – they never married, lived together, or had children – would restrict their freedom too much. Therefore they had what is now known as an open relationship and both had concurrent 'contingent' relationships. There are two important points to be made here. One is not so much that each had other relationships; this in itself is not and was not that unusual. What is unusual is that they made a lifelong commitment of honesty to each other not just about these relationships but about everything they did and thought. The other point is that they both tried deliberately to live the values of their philosophy. She would be the first to say that if they fell short in any way, then this was evidence of their humanity and that they regretted if any harm came from it (1968: 134). She had always lived in Montparnasse and in her twenties had taught herself to ride a bike on the paths of the Montparnasse Cemetery and the success of her novel *The Mandarins* (1960), which won the *Prix Goncourt*, allowed her at the age of forty-seven to move out of crumbling hotels and to buy a small apartment overlooking the cemetery. She died when she was seventy-eight, six years after Sartre and is buried beside him in the Montparnasse Cemetery where theirs are the plainest and the most visited graves.

Philosophy

Although just as concerned as Sartre with the concrete, the everyday, she took it in a more personal direction. Her concern was with the ethical dimension of life: how people treated each other. Her writing, which also introduces an explicit political dimension, analysed questions of power and freedom not only interpersonally and culturally but also developmentally.

One reason why her work is rarely considered alongside other philosophers is that while she wrote some explicit philosophy she did not see herself as a philosopher so much as a writer who embedded philosophical arguments in her works. Taken as a whole her work crosses the boundaries between the personal, the political and the philosophical in a way that had rarely been done in such an accessible way. In philosophy, as in many other academic fields, applied studies have always been given lesser value than pure studies. She has been largely ignored by existential philosophers and particularly by psychotherapists.

Another reason is not only that she was a woman, but she is most well known for having written about women. This had led to her most influential book, *The Second Sex*, not being thought of as philosophy. Nevertheless, although her status as a philosopher is now established, she is still hard to categorise; in bookshops and libraries she is more likely to be found under fiction, or women's studies, than under philosophy. It is hard not to put these reasons down to everyday sexism, and it is why particular attention is given to her here.

Beauvoir herself made a distinction between her philosophical writing, which she felt reflected her 'practical choices and intellectual certitudes', and her fiction, which explored the 'nuances and ambiguity' of existence (1968: 332), and different literary forms enabled her to say things in different ways. Her fiction reflects her desire to describe how individuals struggle with the philosophical themes of freedom, ambiguity and reciprocity, and her autobiographies (1963, 1966, 1968, 1969, 1977, 1985), which are entirely different in style and purpose from Sartre's, do this as well as giving us a valuable and gendered chronicle of European cultural and political life of a major part of the twentieth century, and are literary forms in their own right.

In general terms, while philosophy can talk about the abstract principles behind everyday life – what life is about – and the novel can represent lived experience – what life is like – autobiography can represent the facticity and contingency of that experience with an intensified sense of contemporaneity. Moreover, while an autobiography can incorporate apparently meaningless trivia of everyday life that lead up to usually retrospectively determined significant events, the novel rarely does. An autobiography can therefore give a sense of a life as lived, but if it is presented chronologically, as it usually is, the life can appear rather episodic and will need a universal dimension to retain the reader. It takes a writer of Vladimir Nabokov's skill to write an autobiography that manages to describe the minutiae of life without becoming determinist or episodic (1999). Hence, as Beauvoir was only too aware, the meaning of lived experience and the reality of that experience can never be captured in a single genre of writing.

The issue here, as before, is what is the best way to describe a life? Each of her autobiographies, being written with progressively less time between the events and the writing, therefore has a different character. The nearest she gets to the diary form is what is effectively a sixth volume of her autobiography, *Adieux to Sartre* (1985).

Freedom, ethics and ambiguity

Her first published work was the novel *She Came to Stay* in 1943. It was semi-autobiographical and explored the issue of commitment in intimate relationships, and the sexual and moral dilemmas that follow; it appeared in English in 1949 and it was after its success that she was able to give up teaching and support herself solely through her writing. Her philosophical work, *The Ethics of Ambiguity*, which came out in 1947 and which appeared in English one year later, begins with an epigraph by Montaigne, 'Life in itself is neither good nor evil. It is the place of good and evil, according to what you make it', and in it she develops philosophically the same ideas she explored in *She Came to Stay*. *The Ethics of Ambiguity* also anticipates the rest of her work by placing freedom at the centre of everyday life. In both these works she took up Sartre's unanswered question at the end of *Being and Nothingness* about the need for an existentialist ethics.

For Beauvoir the object of life is not to prepare for our death, for death is unknowable, 'unrealisable' (1972: 292), and therefore not a part of life. It is to use our projects to challenge necessity and strive for transcendence. This is not to deny death; she was certainly not immune to death anxiety (Moi 1994: 236–242), there are frequent references to it in her autobiographies; it is to accept it. What she means by transcendence is that only by our personal projects are we able to live our freedom, to transform essence into existence. Since we have no recourse to God for direction, all options are open to us. Freedom for Beauvoir is always situated and she uses the word 'situation' as Sartre does, existentially, to refer to the relationship between our freedom to choose a project and facticity, which is all the aspects of the world that we have not chosen. In this way a person's situation is not something outside or around them, it is the glue that binds their freedom and their facticity together.

She challenged the idea that reality is absurd and therefore without meaning, saying instead that it is ambiguous: 'its meaning is never fixed, [and] it must be constantly won' (2015: 129). By being open to ambiguity we retain a way of being in tune with the world and its randomness, and being able to take responsibility for the consequences of our actions. She says, 'to will freedom and to will to disclose being are one and the same choice' (2015: 78) and in this she is closer to Heidegger (Gothlin 2003). We can never know for certain what is the right thing to do; we only ever discover it in hindsight. But even this is uncertain, ambiguous, because what may seem right at one point in time may seem wrong from another, and vice versa. Our individual life task is to assume the responsibility for our freedom and create meaning through our choices. She says, 'let us therefore try to look the truth in the face. Let us try to assume our fundamental ambiguity. It is in the knowledge of the genuine conditions of our life that we must draw our strength to live and our reason for acting' (2015: 8). This is how we learn to live ethically.

Freedom, violence and other people

Freedom therefore is not an object or even a possession and definitely not a commodity to be bought or sold, but an action to be realised by actively engaging in the world and is demonstrated in our relationships with other people. Freedom is both an individual and also a collective undertaking and, drawing on Hegel, she addresses the question of what is the most ethical way to acknowledge the freedom, the otherness, of the other person. Hegel argued that self-consciousness couldn't exist without a corresponding sense of the other person's self-consciousness, which is always seen as a threat to one's own. *She Came to Stay* begins with an epigraph from Hegel: 'Each consciousness seeks the death of the other.'

Hegel suggested that all relationships enact a master/slave dynamic where one person, the master, the owner, is in the more powerful position, and the slave, the owned, is in the weaker position. Although the master's aim is to possess the slave's freedom this is doomed to failure because the master always knows the freedom of another can never be possessed. Beauvoir prefers the terms Subject and Other and says that whereas for Hegel this is a universal conflict, she argues that it is only a preliminary reaction to the difference of the Other and moreover is ultimately self-destructive because since I am permanently bound up with other people, the death of the Other means the death of myself. She suggests that the only way through this ontological dilemma is by acknowledging the fundamental freedom of the Other. If this does not happen, then both parties are existentially diminished and are complicit in the tyranny that follows. This is how freedom becomes a collective responsibility.

Where Beauvoir went in *The Ethics of Ambiguity* and where Sartre went later on in his work with Marxism, was in the way she acknowledged how everyday, ontic power differences between people inevitably limit both individuals' capacity for free action. The difference between them was that, whereas Sartre favoured political action, Beauvoir favoured social action. Whereas Sartre wanted to link his philosophy to his activism, Beauvoir used philosophy to examine her place in society. Freedom is both ontological and situational, and therefore there can be no true equality between individuals if there is inequality in society. This is the basis of the statement 'the personal is political' and of the way she chose to be *engagée*, beginning with her involvement with that began by her involvement with *Les Temps modernes* and found its way into her work via *The Second Sex* and later in *The Coming of Age*. She contrasts this with the aesthetic attitude that attempts to find objective truth, much as natural science does. She is clearly using the word aesthetic differently from Kierkegaard.

For Beauvoir, existentially, a violent act is committed whenever one person restricts another's freedom, and given the nature of relationships and the consequences of personal and political power imbalances, the option of violence has to be reserved in some cases in order to preserve what is the most fundamental of all human characteristics: freedom. Because freedom was perpetually in question, life in occupied Paris was one such special case. People's actions in one situation cannot be judged by the standards of another situation. This was the theme of her novel *The Blood of Others* that she published in 1945. In this way there can be no absolute ethics, only an ethics based on ambiguity and the primacy of freedom.

Her legacy is that she developed what we may think of as a set of tools for philosophical analysis and that in a more explicit way than even Sartre she made existentialism a practical philosophy.

Beauvoir and human development

For Beauvoir, human development is about the primacy of freedom and the possibility of transcendence. It is a process of coming to acknowledge the existential realities of situated freedom, relationality, responsibility and the ambiguity of values. She is also interested in how this can be interrupted, constrained or distorted.

By talking about the body phenomenologically she is able to consider biology as an aspect of our facticity that we have the freedom to take a stand on and make something personal out of. For Heinämaa (2003), this brings her closer to Merleau-Ponty. Another aspect of our facticity is our situation, and she notes that while we are all complicit in promoting the values of our culture, we also have the freedom to question them. Evading this responsibility is not an option.

Taking care not to match her process of development to chronology, she considers the categories of child, adolescent and adult more as existential rather than biological categories. Having said that, she says that we develop with and because of our understanding of time, but it is a conception of time that is both personal and universal. For our own life story, our own history, to be understood it has to be seen in the context of a time span far greater than a single life.

Using Sartre's idea of the original project, Beauvoir reminds us that the world reflects our earlier choices back to us and makes them seem fixed, rather than consequences of free action. In this way, the past appears to determine the future. In another sense though, since all choices are free, their outcome is always unforeseeable. We never really know what will happen or what it may mean, but we must nevertheless take responsibility for it. And directly contradicting Wordsworth's 1807 poem, referred to earlier, she says, 'The child does not contain the man he will become' (2015: 43).

She describes a process of existential development where at birth, the infant is 'cast into a universe which he has not helped to establish, which has been fashioned without him, and which appears to him as an absolute to which he can only submit' (2015: 35) and we move through life to a position of existential maturity where a person can 'become conscious of the real requirements of his own freedom, which can will itself only by destining itself to an open future, by seeking to extend itself by means of the freedom of others' (2015: 60). For her, although in one sense death brings our projects to an end, in another sense our projects are eternal because they are ways of establishing something that continues beyond death not for self-aggrandisement, we will quickly be forgotten, but to promote freedom and transcendence in future generations.

The development of freedom and morality

Beauvoir begins her philosophical analysis of childhood in *The Ethics of Ambiguity* and returns to it thirty years later in the final volume of her formal autobiography (1977). As with Merleau-Ponty, it is frequently ignored in reviews of her work. In this latter work she looks back on her life and considers ways the themes of chance, freedom and necessity impacted on her at different times. She reflects, for example, that apart from the pure chance of being born female her childhood world was relatively free of chance because it was largely prescribed by her parents (1977: 15). Nevertheless she was able to exercise her freedom within it and this was central to the person she became.

Childhood

She argues that children have an innate desire to explore and shape the world and it is through this that they get to understand the temporal meaning of their actions: how their past understandings translate into their present actions and into consequences that they then have to take responsibility for. She calls this desire their natural freedom. It is as much of a given as the facticity of the world; it is a part of the child's situation and she distinguishes it from the later moral freedom, which is freedom grounded by a personally chosen project and which acknowledges ambiguity and the freedom of others.

Initially, the child is dependent for his survival on the care and attention of others and comes to think of the world as essential – necessary – and of himself as non-essential – contingent. Beauvoir calls this the 'serious' attitude (2015: 37), but this is another unfortunate translation. The French word '*serieux*' as used here means something more like steady and reliable – which describes the way children take the values of their world as fixed and caused, when they are actually constructed and ambiguous. Being contingent in a necessary world, the child lives in a comfortable present, and under normal circumstances the child is oblivious of the ways that randomness and chance shape his life, or as she puts it, is 'metaphysically privileged' (2015: 39). The child is protected from having to take responsibility for any life-changing decisions. Board games like ludo and snakes and ladders are valuable relational ways of introducing the child to the way the given of the rules of the game and the randomness of the throw of the die interact to make the game what it is. No prior skill is involved, but what is learnt is the skill of understanding this interaction. Like in life, cheating is pointless. Games like draughts and chess introduce another variable: the freedom of the other person. A freedom which is nevertheless constrained by the known rules of the game.

Crying is our first sound-based language and through the way it is received the child comes to an understanding of its effectiveness. Assuming the carer is consistently attentive, the child will feel not just that he is freely loved but also that his love is freely received and a sense of mutuality will develop. Children, she says, need to experience the joys of freedom before they meet the anxieties of freedom.

By virtue of his accepted natural freedom, the child will learn to play according to his own interests and will not need direction. In play, the world can be explored with no costs, only the benefits of discovering the limits of possibility. In a reflection on the meaning of freely chosen projects that anticipates Beauvoir's move into the political arena, she says, 'There is no more obnoxious way to punish a man than to force him to perform acts which make no sense to him, as when one empties and fills the same ditch indefinitely, [or] when one forces a schoolboy to copy lines' (2015: 31). An education system that values order and planning over imagination, and premature fixing of the future in terms of career choices and the possible variety of adult projects will be saving up psychological alienation for later in life when the need to overcome accumulated bad faith will emerge.

Subjectivity is also discovered through the inevitable inconsistencies between what people say they will do and what they actually do, and between what the child hopes will happen and what actually happens. Initially the questions that arise take the form of natural freedom in a language characteristic of the time and place. For small children this can include temper tantrums, refusing to share toys, or a reluctance to eat what is provided and so on. These communications need to be understood existentially.

However, not yet able to understand the parameters of responsibility, the child can imagine himself to be responsible for things that are important for his survival but that he is not responsible for, e.g. the carer's well-being. In the case of e.g. divorce, it is all too easy for a child to feel that he may have caused it in some way and, as we know, this misattribution of responsibility can reverberate through the rest of the child's life.

If he is treated with care, the child will grow to value ambiguity and see himself as active, as a source of autonomy, to respect the freedom of others and engage in the world with excitement, creativity and openness. In later life this will translate into the ability to be both autonomous and truly present with another person.

But if the child is treated functionally, simply as a producer of actions, or senses that approval is conditional or is as she puts it, 'ill-loved' (1977: 47), the child will grow to see himself as passive, and grow to be alienated from his existence and either agree with the valuation and sacrifice his freedom, or reactively use his freedom against the valuation. In either case the child will come to define himself by what he is not, rather than by what he is. In later life opportunities will go past either untaken or unnoticed and the person will favour activities that give control and predictability: technique. Embodying passivity, he will feel unable to influence and shape the world, as often seen in chronic depression, and the person's stance towards their natural freedom will be played out in the dynamics of the therapeutic relationship.

Without realising it, the child forms his own identity, his ongoing life story, through what it means to take responsibility for his choices and actions, and sensitive carers will be able to match the amount of responsibility they give to a child to the amount he is able to take. Not giving a child enough responsibility or giving a child too much responsibility is an act of violence on the child's autonomy and is therefore immoral and evil (Bergoffen 2015). The child becomes uncared for both interpersonally and existentially.

Two apparently opposite processes lead to a child gaining an understanding of the nature of freedom and responsibility. Through autonomy the child is able to shape the given world, and through mystification the child is protected from responsibility for the given world. Therefore the paradox of the child's metaphysical privilege is that he needs to feel that the world is predictable and caring in order that he may engage with the ambiguity of his personal world and later on the wider world. She says, 'That is where the wonder of childhood lies ... for the child the world possesses a fascinating strangeness – always providing that he is lucky enough to be able to gaze upon it and explore it' (1977: 3).

The correct balance of autonomy and mystification at every moment is crucial for the discovery of resilience in the face of disappointment, and it is the carer's existential responsibility to make this assessment. This is the nature of love.

Adolescence

For Beauvoir, what we call adolescence marks the end of the metaphysically privileged era of childhood. It is when the contradictions, inconsistencies and weaknesses of adults are increasingly noticed and parents are seen for the first time as fallible. She says, 'Men stop appearing as if they were gods, and at the same time the adolescent discovers the human character of the reality about him' (2015: 41). As such it is transitional.

At the same time, and prompted by this, the adolescent begins to get a sense of his temporality as having a past behind and a future ahead. She says,

> An existence would be unable to found itself if moment by moment it crumbled into nothingness. That is why no moral question presents itself to the child as long as he is still incapable of recognizing himself in the past or seeing himself in the future. It is only when the moments of his life begin to be organized into behaviour that he can decide and choose. The value of the

> chosen end is confirmed and, reciprocally, the genuineness of the choice is manifested concretely through patience, courage, and fidelity.
>
> (2015: 27)

The serious world of childhood collapses and brings with it the moral imperative to decide and choose. This is double-edged: on the one hand it is a release from the constraints of the serious world, but on the other hand the adolescent finds himself in a world in which responsibility has to be taken. She says,

> But whatever the joy of this liberation may be, it is not without great confusion. The adolescent finds himself cast into a world which is no longer ready-made, which has to be made; he is abandoned, unjustified, the prey of a freedom that is no longer chained up by anything. What will he do in the face of this new situation?
>
> (2015: 42)

In Heideggerian terms, the adolescent is engaged in the existential task of converting the world from 'present-at-hand' to 'ready-to-hand'.

Some adolescents look forward to this and are able to embrace it, but others dread it and avoid it and the diversity of adolescent behaviour reflects this (1977: 24). Whichever is the predominant choice, she argues that nostalgia for a simpler, trouble-free past is about the wish to return to an imagined time of freedom without responsibility and the passivity of the hope that others will serve as a protection from the vicissitudes of existence. This is the myth of specialness. Nevertheless, nostalgia can be a powerful influence and can often reverberate through the whole of life gaining more importance at times of personal or cultural change. It is often influential in deciding the outcome of elections.

In Beauvoir's case, she says she was able to embrace the opportunity presented by adolescence, she says, in hindsight, 'I tore myself away from the safe comfort of certainties through my love for truth – and truth rewarded me' (1977: 24).

In circumstances where it can be embraced, the adolescent is able to choose the joy of fulfilling his existence by transforming his original childhood irresponsibility into a mature ethical responsibility that enables not only his own freedom but also that of others. This is no small task, and neither is it ever completed.

Adulthood

Given that the irresponsibility of childhood can never be returned to except in bad faith, the dilemma between freedom and necessity is present throughout life in different forms (2015: 45) and since it is a dilemma it cannot be solved; it can only be faced with courage. She says there are a number of common attempts at solutions, the more frequent of which is the serious man who chooses to deny his freedom by adopting the values he was exposed to in childhood (2015: 49). Such an adult is reluctant to take on adult responsibilities and uses nostalgia to try to remain existentially a child and is the most prevalent form of bad faith. It is present in a transient and non-pathological form when we go on holiday, and in a pathological form in addiction.

Beauvoir's own solution to the dilemma is one that combines the free action of the 'adventurer' (2015: 45) with the commitment of the 'passionate man' (2015: 68). She says,

> To will oneself free and to will that there be being are one and the same choice, the choice that man makes of himself as a presence in the world. [...] These are two aspects of a single reality. And whichever be the one under consideration, they both imply the bond of each man with all others.
>
> (2015: 70)

This is existential maturity.

Becoming a woman

Originally suggested by her friend the sculptor Alberto Giacometti and encouraged by Sartre, *The Second Sex* was first published in two volumes in 1949 and it came to grab the international public imagination in a more dramatic way than any other work by a twentieth-century philosopher. In writing it, her guiding principle was that growing up female made a bigger difference than most people, including herself when she started to write it, realised. As passionate as it is encyclopaedic, the first more academic volume about the historical origins of how women have become and continue to be the 'second' sex, i.e. secondary to men, was well received, but the second volume about how an infant born as female becomes an adult woman and the roles available to her within patriarchy caused an outrage; it was regarded more as an affront to sexual decency than as a critique of patriarchy or a phenomenological analysis of gender. Because of the influence of the Catholic Church in France, the issue of women's rights had never become political in the same way it did in the UK; there was no suffragette movement, and in general, French culture lagged behind the rest of Europe, e.g. women did not get the vote until 1945. In an echo of the French government's reaction to Rousseau's *Émile*, *The Second Sex* was placed on the Vatican's list of banned books in 1956, eight years after all Sartre's work, until the practice was discontinued in 1966. The ban only increased its sales and reputation. Albert Camus accused her of having made the French male look ridiculous (Beauvoir 1968: 200) and the established political left in France, still sedimented in the primacy of class conflict, was scarcely more encouraging.

A single-volume English edition came out in 1953, three years before *Being and Nothingness* and nine years before Heidegger's *Being and Time*. This version had some of its content cut by its American publisher on commercial grounds, and perhaps because of this it is more accessible than the more complete translation that followed in 2009 although this too is not without its critics (Moi 2010). It is interesting to note that French readers read a rather different book from English readers and perhaps because of its accessibility it had if anything an even greater impact in the English-speaking world than in France. It also began to be read by a new generation in the late 1960s (Forster and Sutton 1989) and gave rise to a much broader debate such that much of the current discourse about sex, sexuality and gender would be unthinkable without her work. Ironically the influence of *The Second Sex* across the rest of the century and into the twenty-first has contributed to her being typecast solely as a women's writer and some books on her rarely mention anything else (e.g., Grosholz 2004; and Stoller 2014).

Her analysis involves a dialectical synthesis of the biological, the social and the ontological but this has not always been fully understood, the most frequent simplification being that the ontological dimension, that of the universality of human freedom and therefore of the nature of the complicity of both men and women in prolonging the status quo has been sidelined in favour of the damaging effects of the quasi-givenness of the socially constructed ethic of patriarchy underpinned by capitalism.

In the late 1960s, particularly after the events of 1968, her stock began to rise independently of Sartre's and in 1973, her continuing and increasing belief in the necessity of the project led to her starting a column in *Les Temps modernes* called 'Le sexism ordinaire' (Everyday sexism) and in 1977 she became one of the editors of *Questions Féministes* (later Nouvelles Questions Féministes). She supported the election of the Mitterrand government because of its stance towards women and became the chair of its Commission Femme et Culture. She supported the election of the Mitterrand government because of its stance towards women and became the chair of its Commission Femme et Culture.

She opens the second part with the now well known, 'One is not born, but rather becomes, a woman', and continues, 'No biological, psychological, or economic fate determines the figure that the human female presents in society; it is civilization as a whole that produces this creature, intermediate between male and eunuch, which is described as feminine. Only the intervention of someone else can establish an individual as an Other' (1997: 295). In the 2009 translation the word 'a' is omitted in the first sentence. Until *The Second Sex,* sex and gender were considered one and the same, and the possibility that gender was socially constructed was hardly considered. She changed this.

By talking phenomenologically rather than biologically about the body, she is also able to consider gender as distinct from sex. She asks provocatively, 'Is [femininity] something secreted by the ovaries?' (1997: 13). Clearly not, and as we shall see, although she is always keen to acknowledge that biological differences make a difference, in no way do they cause either the differences between the genders or the differences in status, although they are frequently used to justify them. Femininity is instead a set of structures and conditions that describe 'the typical situation of being a woman in a particular society, as well as the typical way in which this situation is lived by the women themselves' (Young 2005: 30).

For this reason she says that for as long as patriarchy exists, it is not possible to define in any detail what the characteristics of women, or men, really are (Tidd 2004: 74), and this is why she is far more interested in analysing the ways patriarchy distorts identity than in defining it, if that was ever possible. We learn how to be from how we make sense of what we are exposed to, and it is by acting in gendered ways that we create our gendered existence, and in this way men are just as likely to have 'feminine' characteristics as women are to have 'masculine' characteristics. Since all ways of being are possibilities for all it is just as restrictive for a woman to confine herself to 'feminine' ways of being as it is for a man to confine himself to 'masculine' ways of being.

She is also keen to reinforce that equality does not mean sameness. Hers is an existential meaning of equality: every person has the same freedom to define his or her own identity and personal projects.

While *The Second Sex* can be read as a personal and gendered analysis of the position of women in post-war French society and some issues may seem specific to that time and place, her argument is that across cultures there are variations that biology alone cannot account for. She notes for example that in Catholic countries girls are more passive than girls in Protestant countries (1997: 317) and she puts this down to the way the genders are distinguished in Roman Catholicism and then how this is embedded in the values of the culture.

A constructionist approach to gender not only makes these variations intelligible but also suggests that there is a common basis to the distortion of women's freedom and transcendence.

Objectification and the development of gender identity

She sees Hegel's master/slave dynamic reflected in the relations between the sexes such that men are the Subject and women are the Other.

The overarching myth is that women, as Other, come to see themselves as defined by, and in relation to, the male Subject, as objects of desire for men, as mothers to their heirs, or as their carers and so on.

For freedom to be reclaimed, it is therefore not a solution for women to try to become more like men, or vice versa; this is just to reverse the same alienating and reductionist Subject/Other dynamic. One person's freedom and transcendence can never be achieved at the expense of another's freedom and transcendence.

As objectified beings from an early age, women learn to see themselves as relative and contingent, as immanent, in contrast to men who they see, and who see themselves, as free, necessary and transcendent.

An additional layer of mystification has been the growth in recent years of every aspect of life being subject to photographic record and comment; selfies, social media and so on, have turned everyone, both men and women, into an object for others in ways that Beauvoir did not foresee and that we are only discovering for ourselves.

A crucially important part of the myth is that in fact both men and women have their freedom constrained but in different ways. Indeed it could be said that the slave owner is more trapped by his position than the slave because he (and it is usually a 'he') has more to lose, and it is a part of the power of the myth that neither can recognise it, both are complicit in its continuation and both are necessary for it to change. The epigraph at the start of the second part of *The Second Sex* is a line from Sartre's (1955) play, *Dirty Hands*: 'Half victims, half accomplices, like everyone else.'

Beauvoir too has an underlying belief that loving relationships between women and men are possible, but they depend on both recognising each other as morally equal and free subjects for the ultimate benefit of all humanity. She says,

> Genuine love ought to be founded on the mutual recognition of two liberties; the lovers would then experience themselves both as self and as other: neither would give up transcendence, neither would be mutilated; together they would manifest values and aims in the world [...] Love would be revelation of self by the gift of self and enrichment of the world.
>
> (1997: 677)

It was this value that was behind her relationship with Sartre.

In her earliest writings she saw capitalism as responsible for promoting and reinforcing gender inequality and that a more egalitarian socialist form of politico-economic organisation would promote gender equality. While gender inequality certainly serves capitalism very well, at the end of *The Second Sex* she modified this purely social constructionist position placing importance on ontology and individual action and argues instead that equality is more likely to be promoted by women understanding their situation such that they can actively challenge patriarchy and pursue economic independence in whatever ways they choose. While different modes of social organisation and technology may offer new possibilities for emancipation, the powerful rarely concede power willingly, and self-determination still has to be fought for. Looking at her own biography shows how she did this in her own life.

Infancy and childhood

The child's immersion in and dependence on the world of others influences how the child views his or her subjectivity and natural freedom. From the beginning, for girls, just as for boys, the body is 'the radiation of subjectivity' (1997: 295) and it is through the hands and eyes that the child starts to explore and make sense of the world.

In the first few years physical differences start to be noticed and wondered about. For boys, the penis is visible, it is outside and obvious. In contrast, what girls have is not visible; it is inside and mysterious. Initially the significance is solely to do with ease in urinating and for a boy it represents freedom and control, and is simultaneously a part of him and outside him. It is also something to play with and show off. Gradually this comes to symbolise the gendered distinction that masculinity comes to be identified with exteriority, and femininity with interiority.

Psychotherapy, thinking about oneself, can be thought of as an activity of interiority and it is certainly true that women are likely to be overrepresented both as therapists and as clients. Self-harm is frequently presented in therapy and it can take many forms, with food and drugs being only two of the many options. There is increasing evidence that there is not so much a gender difference in the prevalence of self-harm, as a difference in the way different genders express it. Men are more likely to be involved in self-harm through getting into fights than women, and concerns about appearance are more likely to be managed with fitness regimes. These phenomena reinforce Beauvoir's insight about interiority and exteriority.

She suggests that almost from birth, promoted by carers, gender starts to be conflated with sex; boys and girls start to be treated differently and one way is the way they are introduced to freedom and separation. While it is always problematic, different genders have different ways of managing freedom and separation. She says that the avoidance of the problem is the origin of the fantasy in later life of merging with another person. It is also the origin of narcissism and of the expectation that one's partner should know what one needs without having to tell them.

Whereas a boy will be expected not to be upset by separation – 'boys don't cry' – and will gain approval by being independent, a girl will be protected from such separation and will gain approval by being dependent and this will have far-reaching consequences for gender relations in adult life. Enhanced by his training in managing separation, the boy will find it easier to assert the freedom of his subjectivity.

For the first few years the world is matriarchal and the father usually has less influence, but after an initial identification a boy will have to acknowledge a difference between himself and his mother. A girl on the other hand will identify with her mother for longer.

Another early way gender comes to be equated with sex is by colour coding. Blue for a boy and pink for a girl. This is soon widened to hard objects, e.g. cars, for a boy and soft objects, e.g. flowers and animals, for a girl. That this happens so early and so comprehensively is shown in this conversation I had with my granddaughter when she was five and a half years old. On setting out a board game she wanted to play with me she said,

Granddaughter: *You can have the blue counter because it's a boy colour.*

Me: *Why is blue a boy colour?*

Granddaughter: (looks puzzled) *Because it just is.*

It is also reinforced by clothing. Girls are encouraged to wear clothes that emphasise appearance and are to be looked at, either by the girl herself or by others, and be kept pretty and clean, boys wear clothes that are more functional. If girls want to do the same things as boys they will be expected to change their clothes. In this way clothing constrains and distorts movement and starts to prevent girls from competing even though they are physically just as capable. The differences between boys and girls with respect to learning to throw have been dealt with in the previous chapter.

While both girls and boys will see what their mother does, they will rarely see what their father does. The mother's activities are likely to be simple, obvious, and also in the house, and to do with caring and looking after: internal. Fathers on the other hand have activities that take them out of the house and are unknown and mysterious: external (Kraemer 1995). This can be reinforced in conventional families, and even more so by single-parent families, or by the father 'giving the mother a break' by doing interesting things with the children at weekends to the annoyance of the mother, leading to resentment.

The values of a society are passed on by the institutions of the society and also in the stories told in the society and it is common to hear assertions about how much more equal contemporary society is, compared with when Beauvoir was writing. That the nature of women's role in society has not changed that much, if at all, since Beauvoir's time, is demonstrated by the fact that when the child first goes to school he or she finds not only that most of the teachers are women but also that the stories in the books the child is exposed to have very restricted plotlines. Adams (2010) looked at a large number of books aimed at early years children and found that fathers were significantly less likely to appear in almost every way than mothers. The father's function was much more ambiguous, if not invisible.

From the beginning therefore, a girl's autonomy is problematic and 'a vicious circle is formed; for the less she exercises her freedom to understand, to grasp and discover the world about her, the less resources she will find within herself, the less she will dare to affirm herself as a subject' (1997: 308).

Puberty and adolescence

In the years just prior to the teenage years the child begins to realise that the world is not matriarchal but patriarchal. For the girl this is a disappointment and leads to the mother losing her prestige. For the boy it is the opposite; it is proof that separation has been worth it.

Although in the years up until puberty, gender distinctions are lived every day, there are few, if any, physical differences between girls and boys. This changes with puberty. The female child has grown but has not been aware of her growth, but now she is aware: 'the child's body is becoming the body of a woman' (1997: 332). Puberty is not simply biological; it is existential. Girls are more likely to react with embarrassment and shame to their physical changes, and boys with pride. For a girl, menstruation signifies interiority and passivity, it happens to her and stops her doing things she used to do, whereas for a boy, the physical changes signify exteriority and activity. In a sexually equal society Beauvoir says that menstruation would be associated with pride and not shame, and would be the girl's special way of reaching adulthood (1997: 340).

Adolescent girls' interiority is also shown in that girls are more likely to keep personal diaries than boys. But interiority and diary use also brings the possibility of psychological insight.

Nevertheless, both girls and boys will be aware of the different futures and responsibilities in store and anxiety about this can be responded to by not wanting to grow up. Denial of sexuality and wishing to retain a child-like body is a characteristic of anorexia. The increasing separation of gender roles will lead to the girl having progressively less mastery over the external world (1997: 355).

A mother who has adopted the traditional role will find it difficult if her daughter (1997: 358) wants to retain her former equality with boys because it will mean that she will have less influence over her daughter. This will feel to the mother like a 'mark of hateful ingratitude'

(1997: 534), an abandonment, and will be resisted by the mother because the only opportunity to feel superior to others, which men feel on a regular basis, is enjoyed by women only with respect to their children, especially their daughters.

The body takes on different meanings for boys and for girls and touch starts to mean something different. Building on the way touch is understood in earlier years, a touch which is sexual comes to be differentiated from other sorts of touch and many future relationship difficulties will result from different sorts of touch not being sufficiently differentiated or understood. Also at this time, the awareness that a girl is there not to look, but to be looked at, comes into sharp relief as she becomes aware for the first time of being looked at and noticed in sexualised ways by men. In addition, there is a confusion that has been set up by objectification such that masculine desire is both seen as an offence and also as a compliment, and this is echoed in dress codes (1997: 329). This is no less true today. The ways of using space that were learnt in the earlier years and got identified as feminine, from puberty onwards, are manifested in the physical constraints of clothing that women need to wear to be seen as sexually attractive and available to men. For girls, the body and sexuality is their life and attached to beauty, attracting and keeping a man, to home and children. For boys, it is adventure (1997: 319).

Adolescence is pivotal for a girl because the ever-present tension between freedom and immanence can no longer be ignored, and the dominant option that is presented is the desirability of passivity, of falling in love, of marriage and motherhood (1997: 325). In most cases this will be seamlessly adopted and the girl will come to realise that she will gain value not by increasing her worth as a human being, or in her own eyes, but by gaining value in a man's eyes. By being objectified, the woman is able to gain an identity by being associated with a Subject, a man, for example in changing their name and title on marriage.

But the desire for freedom can never be extinguished, and the characteristics we often associate with femininity are not characteristics of femininity so much as characteristics of the passive agent. This, Beauvoir says, is the myth of happiness that is in store for the adult woman.

Adulthood

The lie that the growing woman is condemned to is that she must pretend to be a fascinating object, when she senses herself to be an uncertain, dissociated being (1997: 380). Make-up and so on reinforces the objectified status of women and is a socially sanctioned attempt to swop a natural appearance for an artificial appearance, which is then asserted to be more real because it is more desired by a man. But what is desired is the woman as Other rather than as Subject, and what follows is always, will always be, a disappointment to both parties.

Sexual preference, she says, may well be biologically given but is always a matter of existential choice, arrived at in a complex total situation and she says that all intimate relationships will have a tendency to take on the culturally dominant models of gender distinction regardless of biology or sexual preference.

Falling in love and finding a permanent partner forms a large part of most people's adult life plan, and she says that marriage, formal or otherwise, is sustained by the happiness myth and that the problems usually associated with marriage are not faults of the individuals so much as the institution of marriage itself and attributing it to the individuals is a mystification. We need to remember this when working with relationship issues in psychotherapy.

The myth is perpetuated by the assumptions both women and men have about what makes for a worthwhile relationship. For the man, being in love is a means to an end, for the woman it is the end in itself; it 'becomes a religion' (1997: 653) in which the woman imagines that the only way to transcend the immanence which is in store for her is to inauthentically lose herself in the subjectivity of a man and get him to fall in love with her. In this way her status increases by being associated with him (1997: 664). The man will often become an accomplice, but this kind of love makes each necessary to the other, and this is not just the death of love, it was never love to start with.

Echoing Nietzsche's concept of *ressentiment*, an everyday adult consequence is that what passes for love between men and women is more often characterised by possession, resentment, distance, control and disappointment that neither person feels able to resolve because both are complicit. What keeps them going is the hope that things could be different and that love could be characterised by freedom, honesty, openness and trust. She notes that if sexual attraction fades in marriage, it is because the magic of eroticism needs freedom and spontaneity, and she says the myths and obligations built into marriage will automatically lead to a loss of freedom and spontaneity. A relationship that began with two subjectivities interacting dynamically leads to two objectivities interacting repetitively. If it happens at all, they will be having sex, not making love. It also dies if all that binds the couple together is friendship, or convenience (1997: 465). They need a wider joint project based on mutual freedom.

She observes three common alternatives. One is that the relationship continues with undisguised hostility. Another is that the couple live side by side without many difficulties but also without much excitement. They sacrifice their independence without escaping their loneliness (1997: 489) and this is borne out by the frequency we hear variants of the phrase 'my other half'. This is closest to the happiness myth and is most common. She leaves us in no doubt what she thinks of this option by describing it as a 'A gilded mediocrity, lacking ambition and passion, aimless days endlessly repeated, life that slips away gently towards death without questioning its purpose' (1997: 466). She decided very early that she did not want this for herself.

The third, which is possible but is as hard to get as it is worth having, is that the marriage becomes a dialectical combination of two independent existences (1997: 497). It is one in which each must 'accept the contingence of the other with all his [*sic*] idiosyncrasies, his limitations, and his basic gratuitousness' (1997: 664). When this happens 'love would be revelation of self by the gift of self and the enrichment of the world' (1997: 677). This implies that although such a relationship will necessarily involve some disagreement and conflict, disputes will be resolved and not repeated. Love is trusted because it is freely given and not a duty or extracted as a condition of continuity. She is undoubtedly drawing here on the kind of relationship she dreamt of when an adolescent and which she got in her relationship with Sartre.

Summarising Beauvoir, Cleary (2015) lists five necessary qualities of a loving monogamous relationship. The first is that it must be a free choice to love another person, the love must not feel extracted or conditional. Another is that the anxiety, the uncertainty of love must be accepted, that 'till death us do part' can be a hope, but not a condition. The next is that each person must respect the other's freedom. It is only the other's freedom that can make love real because in order to be completely true, a love must be shared. The fourth is about the need for transparency, for no secrets to be wilfully kept from the other, and the last is that the two people must treat each other as the most important person in their life. These five qualities are present throughout her writings but more importantly are the principles that Sartre and Simone de Beauvoir tried to keep to in their own relationship.

It is inevitable that the world of mid-twentieth-century Europe would not be the same as that of the early twenty-first century, and it is often said that we live in a more liberated society. One of the costs of this liberation is that while access to fields of achievement that were previously denied are now more open to women, there has not been a corresponding loosening of the stereotypes of femininity. Women are therefore expected to be passive and feminine as well as active, but still in a patriarchal world.

Motherhood

Motherhood features strongly in many women's life plans and it is clear that Beauvoir does not consider it a wholly positive experience for women and although she never wanted to be a mother herself, she also notes that the period she is writing in is in transition. Her view on motherhood is also undoubtedly influenced by her own experience of her own mother that she writes about in *Memoirs of a Dutiful Daughter* but this earlier position has to be read alongside the sensitivity she later shows in *A Very Easy Death*. It is impossible when talking about something like motherhood not to be influenced by one's own experience of it.

In an echo of Sartre's adoption of Arlette Elkaïm, the nearest Beauvoir got to motherhood was in adopting Sylvie le Bon after Sartre's death. They met in 1960 when Sylvie le Bon was a philosophy student and became close friends. After Sartre's death Beauvoir did not want what happened to Sartre's literary legacy to happen to hers, and for her part Sylvie did not want to be compared to Arlette, but nevertheless, on Sartre's death in 1980 she became Beauvoir's adopted daughter. In contrast to Arlette though, on Beauvoir's death, she facilitated the publishing of Beauvoir's remaining works and letters.

In *The Second Sex* she rejects the idea of a maternal instinct in a biological sense citing, as with gender, the variability of women's wishes for, and experience of, motherhood. She says that 'no maternal "instinct" exists [...] the mother's attitude depends on her total situation and her reaction to it' (1997: 526). Her position is that the maternal instinct is a patriarchal fabrication that promotes female objectification, thus reducing the possibility of transcendence and instilling maternal guilt. This point about the maternal instinct has been challenged by Gennari (1958) and Lilar (1969) among others with the debate hinging around the definition of instinct.

Motherhood brings a further twist to the happiness myth, in that the chosen man has to be the father of her children. While she sees that motherhood creates a different set of life choices in which sexuality takes a back seat to maternity, she acknowledges that it affects women differently and that a loss of freedom is not always inevitable. What is inevitable though is the qualitative change in the woman as she becomes a mother (Stern and Bruschweiler-Stern 1998; Stadlen 2004, 2011).

Those women who find this a particular challenge, she notes, will be those whose identity as a woman is tied up with youthfulness and their sexual attractiveness to men. Such women will be 'distressed to see themselves deformed, disfigured, incapable of arousing desire' (1997: 520).

For the little girl, identifying with her mother, maternity seems like a miracle that is her destiny, and the doll 'represents a future baby to possess and domineer over' (1997: 510) but for the adolescent girl, maternity can be, in turns, a threat to her emerging autonomy and integrity, or embraced and longed for. If the former, later on in adulthood, (1997: 512) the pregnant woman will feel the immanence of her body; she will feel taken over just at the time when she is feeling at her most transcendent. If the latter, the mother will be delighted to feel herself necessary, and her maternity can feel almost saintly. But this is not all there is, she says the mother is 'almost always a discontented woman' (1997: 528) and consequently maternity is 'a strange mixture of narcissism, altruism, idle daydreaming, sincerity, bad faith, devotion and cynicism' (1997: 528) and the negatives among this list are likely to result in the mother seeking to compensate for her frustrations through her child, and 'seek to make herself a slave of her offspring to compensate for the emptiness of her heart to punish herself for her unavowed hostility [...] thus assuming the role of victim' (1997: 529).

For this reason Beauvoir says that motherhood is too important a task to entrust to a sector of the population who are denied full autonomy. She says,

> it is outrageously paradoxical to deny women all activity in public affairs, to shut her out of masculine careers, to assess her incapacity in all fields of effort and then to entrust the most delicate and most serious undertaking of all; the molding of a human being.
>
> (1997: 538)

And later that,

> In a properly organized society, where children will be largely taken in charge by the community another cared for and helped, maternity would not be wholly incompatible with careers for women.
>
> (1997: 540)

Growing old(er)

To review Beauvoir's writings on age and ageing is to review her whole work; she was always preoccupied with the relationship between freedom and temporality. Autobiographies at any age are ways we have of taking stock of our lives, and it is not without significance that she started to write her own in her early fifties around the time that her ageing was becoming more apparent to her (1977: 43).

In *The Second Sex,* written in her late thirties, she devoted just a single chapter to the second half of life, and it is fair to say the picture she painted was overwhelmingly negative and characterised by loss and atrophy. It is not hard to put this down to the views that she had then not just of ageing in general, but also of her own ageing in particular. It was her own ageism and in this she was adopting something of the natural cultural attitude to ageing and old age.

She wrote her work on ageing, which is often sidelined or even ignored in reviews of her work, in her early sixties, and although there is only one translation, it has been given two titles: *Old Age,* for the UK market, and *The Coming of Age,* for the US market. Of these, the former is closest to the original French, *La Vieillese,* although the ambiguity of the latter better describes the content. It is not without significance that grammatically the title in French is feminine.

But her main reasons for writing about old age were, as always, personal and one was the response she got from readers (1977: 146) when she wrote about her own ageing (1968). Another reason was that her mother's death brought home to her the reality of the experience of the ill and ageing body and the ethical issues to do with freedom that surrounded the ending of life (1969). Another was witnessing Sartre's slow decline. She knew she had touched a raw nerve, both in herself and in others. Of her readers' reaction she says, 'Tired worn out clichés have been tossed at me and I wanted to rip [the myths of ageing] to pieces. [...] I was on the threshold of old age and I wished to know the bounds of the nature of the aged state' (1977: 146–147). She wrote, as usual, so she could understand. That attitudes have not changed in the intervening 40 years is shown by a recent study by the Royal Society for Public Health (2018).

The reception of the book was, as always, mixed, she said some things that some people clearly did not want to hear – she had never courted popularity anyway – but it was commended by politicians of both sides in France and it was also welcomed by gerontologists who praised Beauvoir for breaking the conspiracy of silence surrounding old age (1977: 150).

As with *The Second Sex, The Coming of Age* is a passionate and encyclopaedic work that is both singular and also universal, both of its time and place, and also general. Although she talks from time to time about differences between male and female experiences of ageing, her concern in this book is always on the human experience of ageing.

Following the same analytic model as she used in *The Second Sex,* she says that old people as a whole are seen as the immanent Other incapable of change, only passive deterioration, and distinct from adults who are seen as transcendent and active Subjects, and in talking about something that was previously taboo, she changed old people from Others into Subjects. From infancy, she says, the myths of ageing are reinforced at the level of individual subjectivity by immersion in a culture that denies the significance of embodied temporality and sees time as more important than temporality.

The Coming of Age starts with the singular universal of Prince Siddartha, and his realisation of the significance of ageing in the life cycle. Having left the palace, Siddartha saw an old man walking slowly with a stick and says, 'It is the world's pity that weak and ignorant beings, drunk with the vanity of youth, do not behold old age! What is the use of pleasures and delights, since I myself am the dwelling house of old age' (1972: 1).

The realisation that old age is here, now, and cannot be ducked was not particularly sudden for Beauvoir, although it was a shock. She is unequivocal about the necessity of this shock for our development as beings. She says, 'If we do not know what we are going to be, we cannot know what we are: let us recognize ourselves in this old man or this old woman. It must be done if we are to take on the entirety of the human state' (1972: 5). She means that we need to be able to reflect on our whole life and the inevitability of our ageing if we are to become fully human.

As with gender, old age is biological and cultural as well as existential and while the biological and the cultural contribute to how we view ageing they do not determine it. We all have personal responsibility to choose how we are going to fill our time usefully, however long or short it may be. Two common solutions to the dilemma of ageing are either to become old too early or to try to stay young for too long. Both are based on denial but whichever is chosen, 'our attitude towards ageing will express our relationship with the world in general' (Tidd 2004: 106).

The overarching myth of ageing is that adulthood is the norm and old people are different, they are other. Actually, old people are not different; ageing is universal, they are simply people for whom less time remains than has been lived. The marginalised and homogenised existence allotted to the old, she says, is not just unjust and false, it is 'downright criminal' (1972: 2), and the myths of ageing conspire to conceal and mystify its heterogeneity and make it virtually impossible to say anything definitive about its characteristics (1972: 218).

Whereas society projects its future hopes on to the child, the old person is seen as 'no more than a corpse under suspended sentence' (1972: 217) and time simply carries the person 'towards an end – death – which is not his or laid down by any project' (1972: 217). The myths of ageing are not, she says, driven by a fear of physical death as much as existential death, by a fear of the ending of freedom and the ending of change; of the start of a permanent inertia.

Ageing is in fact a continuous process of temporal embodiment from the moment of birth to the moment of death and we experience our temporality differently as we go through life. Learning to distinguish time from temporality is lifelong. One simple example of this is that the older we get, the more sense we get of it and the faster it seems to run. This is because each time period, week, month, year, is proportionally smaller than the one before. We have simply lived longer. She says, 'life is an unstable system in which balance is continually lost and continually recovered [...] Change is the law of life. And it is a particular kind of change that distinguishes ageing – an irreversible, unfavourable change; a decline' (1972: 11) and the fear of loss of freedom and possibility that ageing evokes in younger people contributes to the myths of ageing that presents itself in ageism.

As with *The Second Sex* she notes capitalism's complicity with the marginalisation of the old: the old are no longer instrumental in the production of profits; indeed they deplete profits by living longer and continuing to take their pensions. Moreover old people are complicit in the maintenance of the myths if only because they were once not-old and hence grew up believing it. But they are also implicated in it changing.

The converse of the myth of ageing as passive deterioration is the myth that old age brings serenity. She says that 'the adult world has done its best to see mankind's condition in a hopeful light; it has attributed to ages that are not its own, virtues that they do not possess: innocence to childhood, serenity to old-age. It has deliberately chosen to look upon the end of life as a time when all the conflicts that tear it apart are resolved' (1972: 485). While seductive, she says this is a convenient illusion simply legitimises the ageist stereotypes that the old are happy and therefore in no need of ongoing attention. In fact, she says, 'they are hagridden by anxiety' (1972: 485). An extension of the serenity myth is that the old are 'required to be standing examples of all the virtues' (1972: 3). She goes on, 'if old people show the same desires, the same feelings and the same requirements of the young, the world looks upon them with disgust: in them love and jealousy seem revolting or absurd, sexuality repulsive and violence ludicrous' (1972: 3).

The myth of sexuality is one she takes particular issue with because sexuality is a form of relation to the world and is a part of our embodied existence as beings and only disappears with death. Younger people may find it uncomfortable to acknowledge that an active sexual life is as meaningful to older people as it is to younger people, though will take on different meanings corresponding to the person's life situation (Neto 2012; Lee 2017). For example, an emphasis on achieving orgasm may be replaced with a pleasure in the other's body and an extended merging of selves, of which orgasm is only a part, that comes out of an intimacy and trust that can only be built up over a number of years. Also, the old will retain an embodied memory of their active sexuality even when they have become comparatively inactive and men and women will show this in different ways. Having said that, the wish to extend one's active sexual life will only apply to those who have found it rewarding earlier on and this can apply to any age, not just to old people and certainly not across the board to old people. It is more true to say that those for whom sex was unsatisfactory or problematic will use age as an excuse to withdraw from it (1972: 320).

There is always a split, a tension, between how we see ourselves and how we are seen by others, and while this tension is constitutive of our being, in ageing it takes on an additional temporal significance. The dilemma is that on the one hand we maintain an internal and relatively constant sense-of-self, and on the other hand we become aware, in part from feedback from others, of our changing appearance. By keeping these separate, we can attempt to evade the existential fact of our embodied temporality and to maintain a personal myth of agelessness and relative youthfulness (Miller 2001). Most old people can vividly remember with quite some ambivalence the first time they were offered a seat on public transport, imagining that it was being offered to someone else, not them, who unlike them, looked old. It is always a shock to find that Chronos, age, has registered its inevitable mark on our body that reminds us that we are not eternal.

A contemporary example of this is The Rolling Stones, who it is often said are doing very well for their age (average age seventy-four in October 2018) and while their set list is largely the same as it was some forty or fifty years ago they are also playing the songs in much the same way as they did then. This can be read either as a celebration of perpetual youthfulness, as an invocation of nostalgia, or as a denial of temporality. As we see, it is usually praised and aspired to, but it is also an example of the myth how the old are good when they are not-old. The issue does, however, illuminate the question of what the characteristics of ageing actually are, and what we mean by age-appropriate. A different stance is taken by, e.g., Bob Dylan or Leonard Cohen who perform(ed) both new and old songs, except that they perform(ed) the old songs differently. For them, the songs change as the singer changes.

When the internal evidence and the external evidence become more and more difficult to keep apart, the possibility that they may join becomes terrifying. This can constitute something of an identity crisis, *Can I have become a different being while I still remain myself?,* and can give rise to despair, loss of hope and an increase in denial by maintaining the split between the ageing external view and the non-ageing internal view. It can also lead to a reliance on nostalgia and looking back, rather than forward for personal meaning. This (re)discovery of temporality can be something of a trauma, but as Stolorow (2007) says, trauma is not something that happens to other people; it is a part of life, and the seeds of recovery from trauma are sown within the nature of the trauma itself in the sense that it can force us to re-evaluate our lives and our values, and change our stance towards the future. The existential trauma brought on by old age can weaken adult defences and bring the conflicts of childhood and adolescence to life once more.

This transition from adulthood into old age therefore constitutes an important developmental milestone because it has the potential to prompt us to approach the end of our days realistically. This, however, is not automatic and will depend largely on the degree to which the person is prepared to question the myths of old age and embrace their temporality.

Accordingly, many people live their old age in the same way they lived the rest of the life. Those who in their adult life found freedom to be more frightening than exciting, will be likely to carry on much as before and 'there will be not much difference between the futile activities of [...] middle age and the inactivity of [the] later years' (1972: 305). Such people have 'a fine old-age' (1972: 305), with few challenges. This is because habit and the accumulation of experience, knowledge and conclusions over the years of adulthood can 'provide the person with a kind of ontological security. Because of habit he knows who he is. It protects him from his generalised anxieties by assuring him that tomorrow will be a repetition of today' (1972: 469). But it is a security based on a denial not only of freedom but also of temporality.

But decluttering and downsizing does not have to be an altruistic action that makes life easier for one's descendants, or a way of reducing the horizons of existence preparatory to death, it can be a re-evaluation of what is important and needed such that the rest of life can be lived free of unneeded ties and unnecessary demands; free, as Sartre says, of the viscosity of the past. Looking back can certainly bring regret and nostalgia but Beauvoir notes how old age can also bring a renewed appreciation of the present and quotes the poet Paul Claudel who says, 'you must reach old age before you can understand the meaning [...] of the word "today"' (1972: 448). In this context Beauvoir observes the paradox that on some occasions the doubts a person has in old age about his entire life's work and purpose can lead to the highest achievement. She wonders if '[having] these doubts themselves help to enrich it. [Or it may be that] age brings technical mastery and freedom and a challenging questioning state of mind. This sweeping away of fetishes and illusions is the truest most worthwhile of all the contributions brought by age' (1972: 492). This can be seen in the work of artists like Rembrandt and Poussin as well as Monet, Matisse and Turner who produced their most innovative and revolutionary work in their final years (King 2017: 304).

Nevertheless it is important to note that for some people ageing does not have this effect; it is a reminder of the past mistakes and regrets. For some though, this joy can be felt by grandparents in their relationships with their grandchildren. Freed up from the complications of parenthood like identification, guilt and frustration they can 'love the children in a [...] wholly generous manner because they have neither rights nor responsibilities' (1972: 475). And this love can be returned because the children can look on them 'as a refuge against their parents' severity' (1972: 475). The grandparents' contact with their grandchildren makes them feel younger and is able to carry them along into 'the infinity of the future' (1972: 475). Nevertheless, it is rather short-lived and can be a defence against temporality, and the joy of the contact can be mixed with sadness, because of the certainty that they will not be around to see their grandchildren grown up.

Another point is that marginalisation and disenfranchisement can paradoxically give rise to a freedom that was previously lacking. No longer feeling it necessary to please other people, and no longer dependent on others' approval, older people can start to please themselves; 'they no longer have to practice hypocrisy' (1972: 488). Losing standing in the world means that the older person is forced to find standing in himself. But this too is not automatic. She suggests that women can find this easier to do than men because when they were adults they had less invested in the maintenance of the status quo. Women who did not have any, may find it easier to use freedom when presented with it. Men are likely find it harder to give up exercising the skills they took a life of work to refine, or may hanker, nostalgically and pointlessly, after reinstating their lost authority.

When old age became a reality for Beauvoir she did not look forward to it, regretting in advance the loss of the activities of youth and adulthood like mountain hiking and new love affairs, and the realisation that there would be fewer and fewer first times. She saw only decline, loss of freedom and repetition. She realised that whereas at forty being around younger people made her feel young, at fifty they made her feel old. What was previously an absent presence, became a distinct presence, and when it did enter her thoughts, it was, in the words of Prospero in Shakespeare's final play *The Tempest* (5: 1), the content of 'every third thought'. The third volume of her autobiography (1968) ends on this note.

While it is certainly true that similar experiences can be seen as repeats, and that this can lead to passivity and to a withdrawal from life, in her sixties Beauvoir began to see repetition rather differently. Although in one sense her days did resemble each other, paradoxically this repetition was the very thing that enabled her to see that in fact nothing can be repeated, ever. The second time is the first and only second time, not the first time again. One sunrise, sunset or night sky is not like any other sunrise, sunset or night sky and all are equally and differently awesome and mysterious. Embodying temporality, she realised that life is finite and growing ever more so, and that this 'alters one's focus so as to find the novel at the heart of repetition, rather than in a life of external change' (quoted in Deutscher 2003: 291). She was able to see the new in the old and the old in the new.

This is a radical change indeed and is enlivening rather than numbing, and by attending fully, the familiar can become more, rather than less, intense. She was able to substitute the either/or options of either constant or changing, for the dialectical both/and options of both constant and changing.

She rediscovered that simply being alive can bring its own reward and that all the explanations and answers to the question *Why?* that she asked throughout her adult years, although seductive and useful, did not allow, indeed detracted from, an appreciation of the mystery and presence of existence, things that can only be got by asking the phenomenological question What?

Similarly, looking back did not automatically bring regrets; it brought the possibility of understanding, but this is not an understanding where all becomes clear, it is an understanding of the mystery and unknowability of life. She says, 'the nearer I come towards the end of my days, the more I am enabled to see that strange thing, a life, and to see it whole' (1977: 7) and that 'one of the advantages of age is that it allows one to see the progress of certain lives in their continuity and their unexpected developments' (1977: 45). She acknowledges the limits of her knowledge, of anyone's knowledge, when she says, 'the meaning of my period is uncertain and that helps to pursue the meaning of my own personal existence. I have to confess that the coming generations have a great advantage over me, they will understand my period. Whereas my period does not understand itself' (1977: 49).

This led her on to a new understanding of ageing, old age and death. If the tension between the internal and the external can be seen and accepted in its temporal context, both the past, the present and the future can become apparent at the same time and one by means of the other. But it is not until we approach the end of life that this is revealed.

And what is revealed is that 'life is a long preparation for something that never happens' (1977: 491). This is what Sartre meant when he said that life is a useless passion. The thing that never happens is the completion of our personal projects. Unless we make the decision to have no more projects, in which case we commit existential suicide, there will always be projects we never complete. Life is an incomplete project and it is only death that brings completeness, for with death comes the end of freedom and the final ending of our projects, and in death our fate is given over to those still living. We come to realise that the point of life is not to complete projects but to strive to complete projects and it is the striving that makes for a meaningful life. She says, 'The truth of the human state is accomplished only at the end of our becoming' (1977: 492).

Old age can be a blow to our narcissism by reminding us of our transience: that we were not just alive in our own time but that there was life before and there will be life after. And that,

> There is only one solution if old age is not to be an absurd parody of our former life and that is to go on pursuing ends that give our existence a meaning – devotion to individuals, to groups or to causes, social, political, intellectual, or creative work [...] one's life has value so long as one contributes value to the life of others by means of love, friendship, indignation, compassion.
>
> (1977: 540–541)

Indignation may seem like a curious addition to this list, but it makes sense because a certain amount of dissatisfaction with the human world is necessary in order that we may generate projects that we hope will contribute to an increase in the sum total of human freedom, even if we are not around when they come to fruition. The alternative is passivity and despair. The paradox is that while in one sense it is death that brings our projects to an end, in another sense our projects are eternal.

In this way we fulfil our existential commitment to future generations. When she said, 'To will oneself free is also to will others free' (2015: 73), she was not just talking about present known others, but also future unknown others.

While this is clearly a legitimate philosophical position it is important to remember that she is writing autobiographically and for a particular purpose: public consumption. Also, and more importantly, it is written at a particular time, from a particular perspective. She is writing just a few years after the death of her mother, which affected her greatly, and also when she was in her early sixties and still able and productive. Death was close, but not very close, not yet personal enough. During the next few years *The Second Sex* was discovered by a new generation of women and she consequently became well known and feted in her own right.

In recent years old age has been subdivided into the third age and the fourth age, the first and second being childhood and adulthood. The term third age, which originated in France, refers to people who no longer work, who have good health and the financial means to enjoy it and who fill their time with self-defined projects. The fourth age refers to people whose health issues, whether chronic or terminal, mean that their lives are considerably constrained and even if they have the financial means, they will probably not be self-supporting; they will need carers. Just a few years after Merleau-Ponty died suddenly at fifty-three, thus avoiding the third and fourth ages, in her late fifties Beauvoir found that the experience of seeing her mother go from the third age to the fourth age radically changed her view of old age and also of her own temporality.

It led firstly to *A Very Easy Death* and then to *The Coming of Age*. This latter book was also influenced by Sartre's slower transition from the third to the fourth age. They were times of great change for her personally which she did not record except obliquely in *Adieux: A Farewell to Sartre* (Bair 1990). This work, whose story begins in 1970 and spans the final ten years of Sartre's life, includes a number of conversations between herself and Sartre from 1974 and she proves herself to be a tenacious if rather leading interviewer. Another reason for the book was also that she did not feel as close to Sartre because of the presence in his life of Arlette Elkaïm, whose influence was personal, and his secretary Benny Lévy whose influence was political (Cohen-Solal 1987; Bair 1990). She wanted to preserve Sartre's legacy against the influence of these two figures. As such it can be considered as autobiography, but as different from the other four volumes as they are from one another. Not surprisingly, she was greatly affected by Sartre's death; immediately after the funeral she was admitted to hospital with pneumonia and was not expected to survive, but although she did survive she drew increasingly on the support of Sylvie le Bon, which may well have been an ulterior motive for adopting her in the first place. Along with issues of inheritance, another reason for adoption was that in French law doctors are only allowed to discuss the patient with the patient's family. Beauvoir's sister, Hélène, and her politically moderate husband lived on the other side of France and if and increasingly when she became infirm she did not want them to be responsible for her. In any case Hélène was only two years younger than her, so this alone made it impractical. She was not prepared to become dependent on someone else against her will and against her choosing (Bair 1990).

After recovering from Sartre's death she returned to feminism, being more actively involved than she had been before and made full use of the celebrity status she had in her own right before her own health began to fade, and without Sylvie's support would probably have died earlier.

She eventually died in hospital of pulmonary oedema, the same as Sartre, just eight hours short of the anniversary of Sartre's death six years earlier. On Sartre's death, their close friend and her former lover, the film-maker Claude Lanzmann, the current chief editor of *Les Temps modernes*, had unbeknown to her bought the plot next to Sartre in the Montparnasse Cemetery because, like Sartre, she did not wish to be buried in the family plot in the Père Lachaise Cemetery (Bair 1990). As with Sartre's, the funeral was attended by many thousands, from all walks of life and from all over the world, and those present were just a very small fraction of the millions who had been influenced, inspired and had their lives changed by her writings. She was, and continues to be, the most influential but the most underrated of all the writers mentioned in this book.

PART III

9

Implications for Therapeutic Practice

Having looked at what Kierkegaard, Nietzsche, Heidegger, Sartre, Merleau-Ponty and Beauvoir have to say about human development, it is obvious that they all have distinct ideas about the issues we face as we live between birth and death, as we struggle to understand the difference between time and temporality. But it is also apparent that there are considerable overlaps between them. They are, after all, talking about the same thing, you and me. Some of these overlaps are more obvious, some less, some more compatible with each other, some less.

Although I have referred from time to time to issues that relate to both everyday life and also to therapeutic practice, it is my intention in this chapter to relate the common issues addressed by all the philosophers more directly to therapeutic practice. I consider these to be the general, ontological principles that we all meet and choose our stance towards, moment by moment, as we go through life. The way we do this comes to be the way we live and who we are. In this way we demonstrate our skills of living.

Some of these relate directly to particular ages; most are present throughout life but manifest in different ways according to age and circumstance. All relate directly to an existential understanding of development.

Whenever we attempt to answer the only important question of life, *How shall I live?*, the answers we find are not simple and permanent, but complex and dynamic. We find the question cannot be answered rhetorically with an either/or answer but has to be answered dialectically with a both/and answer. Most problem-solving techniques formalise rhetorical either/or solutions. Rhetoric is useful where certainty is possible, facts are clear-cut and solutions are likely to be permanent. This is a technological approach to life. Dialectic is more appropriate with respect to human issues, which are not mechanical but are about understanding and personally chosen values. For Socrates, overcoming opposites dialectically was a way to get closer to truth, always remembering that like authenticity, truth never lasts beyond the present moment. In doing this we also discover paradox and dilemma in which the solution, such as it is, is not one of fact but one of commitment to a course of action. Life questions can never be solved by asking someone else what to do; they can only ever be solved by living them and clients come to psychotherapy when the answers they have tried up until then have either not worked, or are not working as well as they used do.

The basic paradox of human existence is that we have to live as if there is certainty while knowing that there is none, and the basic dilemma is that we have to make our choices with no guarantee of success. This is the existential nature of our freedom and as Sartre says, it is what we are condemned to (2003: 129). We are thrown into it, and it is our life task to make something of it in whichever way we choose and it is this that evokes anxiety that is present for as long as we are alive.

Like life, existential therapy is a dialectical process of learning the skills of facing up to conflict, polarity, ambiguity and the unexpected in order to arrive at a solution which is always temporary and provisional. Life in fact is given its excitement by this ambiguity and if we are able to take the paradoxes of existence in our stride and tolerate the anxiety that comes with the freedom of the both/and, we are more likely to live a satisfying life.

When considering human development existentially the question becomes,

> *How do we get from birth, when the paradoxes and dilemmas of existence are not understood, to existential maturity – which is by no means automatic – when they are understood?*

Working with age

We are born, we live and then we die, and always in that order and there is no doubt that people at different ages define life issues in different ways. There are both ontological and biological as well as socially constructed issues at play here and because they intertwine, on many occasions it is hard but not impossible to tell them apart. This means that we must take care not to apply norms from one life context onto another life context. For example, when we use the concepts of age-appropriate behaviour and age-appropriate treatment, we need to understand on what basis these judgements are being made. Philosophically, a person's behaviour, etc. is always meaningful and appropriate to them in some way, and we have to remember to bracket our assumptions because the meaning is always yet to be discovered. It may be that the client's behaviour is not usual in comparison with their peers, but that is different. Existentially it is more accurate to use the concept of person-appropriate rather than age-appropriate because it addresses the meaning of this particular action, behaviour, etc. to this particular person, now. To minimise the effect of our assumptions this means that regardless of the age of the client, as psychotherapists we need to reflect on the impact of our own age on the way we are, what impact our age may have on the client, and the biases and prejudices we have about different ages.

But as we have seen from the work of the philosophers, to limit a consideration of human development simply to age, as stage theory does, gives rise to the artefact of the difference between different ages when what is more important is the similarity between ages. At every age we are all doing the same thing: trying to live with meaning and purpose as temporal beings.

Working with young(er) people

In counselling and psychotherapy training, the tradition has developed that working with children and young people requires specialist knowledge and skills that are in addition to or different from those needed to work with adults, and that this need is met by specialist courses.

Consequently most therapists feel ill-equipped to work with children and may claim not to know anything about children, in spite of having been a child themselves and therefore having had direct experience of childhood, and in many cases being parents themselves. We can speculate on what has conspired to make many adults lose touch with the authority of their own experience of childhood but children are somehow thought of being in some way Other, in the sense that Hegel and Beauvoir meant, and this leads to the temptation to standardise and objectify them by age, maturity, academic ability, medical diagnosis, behaviour and so on.

Existentially though, children are no more and no less human beings than adults. Which is to say that, regardless of the amount of time since birth, we are all actively trying to understand our place in the world and striving towards the future with varying degrees of success. This is not to say that there is no difference between a child's and an adult's experience, but Briod (1989) notes, the lived experience of the child cannot be deduced either by subtraction – the child is lesser than the adult – or by equation – the child is the same as the adult.

One way childhood is objectified is in terms of the cultural dominance of the idea that the child should go through fixed stages through in order to reach maturity. But looking at human development existentially reveals something far more complex and dynamic. It is that human development is a gradual, fluid but permanently cumulative and meaning-based process from the moment of birth to the uncertain moment of death.

Existentially, we are born as pure existence and with no essence except for our facticity and our thrownness. In a relentless search for coherence our sense-of-self coalesces round the sense of an original project which epitomises our fundamental relationship to others and to the world. Because of its existential rather than cognitive nature, the original project is more likely to be embodied and is about our place in the world – our stance to dilemma, paradox and uncertainty.

One obvious difference between children and adults is that adults have simply had longer to sediment their original project into the so-called facts of their personality in order to avoid the anxiety of freedom and choice.

A child is involved in this as much if not more than an adult. Adults believe they have understood it, children know they have not. Children have an immediacy of experience that is forgotten and often pathologised and standardised by adults. Maybe adults are afraid of children's flexibility, imagination and passion.

Dialogue is central to existential practice and the principles that guide our understanding of adult behaviour are the same as those that guide our understanding of child behaviour. These are that our sense of identity and understanding of life are drawn from our relationships and the way we use language is intimately bound up with these relationships.

In our work with adults we use language without really thinking about it. We think of dialogue and language as being almost synonymous. But they are not and it is in working with children that we realise this because our adult grasp of language is so different, not necessarily more, than theirs. This can be difficult in a verbal culture and as adults we can find it difficult to use language differently. But the use of a common spoken language is not the only way that dialogue can develop, and the first task of the therapist working with children is to establish a language they can both use and this will frequently not be a verbal, cognitive language, it will be a language of play, of drawing, of enactment (Scalzo 2010). As such it will not need to be interpreted, to do this is to misunderstand the nature of language. It will simply need to be understood as a communication from one person to another and that on many occasions by interpreting we will be attempting to put something it into words that need not and importantly cannot be put into words. The dialogue that follows from immersion and enactment in play will inevitably result in a freeing of the emerging sedimentation and the child rediscovering choice.

The issue of responsibility is if anything even more important to acknowledge in working with children and young people than it is with adults. Struggling with the nature of autonomy and responsibility is an issue for children and adolescents just as much of as it is for adults. Therapists must be even more aware of the ways they subtly guide and use suggestion in their work with this age group so as not to leap in and take over the child's emergent autonomy.

But there is another dimension to the issue of responsibility that impacts on our work with children, and that is the legal dimension. A cornerstone of work with adults is that they freely consent to the therapy contract. It is an ethical *sine qua non* that work cannot start without it. The alternative is coercion or dishonesty. Adults are assumed to be able to know what they are consenting to. Perhaps existentially, but certainly legally, children do not have the ability to consent, so work with children will always involve working with those, most often the parent(s) or carer(s), who will need to give their consent on the child's behalf. This means that unlike working with an adult who we can meet for the first session without knowing anything more about them than their name, we will always know a great deal about the child's history and relationships from the point of view of other people. We have to try to bracket this at the same time as understanding the child as a relational product of their very particular context. Quite apart from the child's understanding of the concept of confidentiality almost certainly being different from an adult's understanding, the reality of who is entitled to know what about our work with the child will also be different and will need to be negotiated. This makes our work with children that much more complex as we are never just working with the child although our allegiance should always be with the child in the context of their life at present (Scalzo 2010). The existential principle of being-in-the-world is even more true for the child as the child is the product of their relationships. The child is the messenger bringing news of what is going on in the family. This makes the tendency towards the objectification and standardisation of childhood even more important to resist.

Working with old(er) people

Children are seen as beginning life, and old people as ending life, with adults as somewhere between and separate from both, and therapeutic work with people at the end of life makes an interesting contrast with those at the beginning. Not only do other therapeutic perspectives have even less to say about old age but it does not have a status of a specialism either. It is so sidelined therapeutically that practitioners are able to maintain an active and institutionalised bias against working with the old (Schaie 1993; Woolfe and Biggs 1997; Nelson 2011). If anything, old people are more stereotyped, objectified and standardised than young people and this support the perception that working with older people is a poor investment of time and that they would be unlikely to benefit from psychotherapy (Collins 2014). In fact the opposite is true. Research from the NHS Improving Access to Psychological Therapies (IAPT) programme has also shown that while older people in therapy had the highest recovery rate of all age groups (HSCIC 2015) they also had the lowest referral rate. Recent research (BACP 2017) has shown that 68 per cent of over 55s would have taken up counselling if they had been referred.

Contradicting directly the prejudice that the old are unlikely to benefit from psychotherapy, Quinodoz (2004), Barnett (2008) and Yalom (2008, 2015) all say that probably at no other time in life is there as potent a force towards self-awareness operating as in old age. Psychotherapists will not, unfortunately, usually encounter fourth-age clients, except in specialist settings.

In contrast to the 'young', the 'old' are hard to define. There is for example no legal definition. Age brings no extra cultural privileges, only exemption from societal obligation and this leads to a gradual disenfranchisement. In the UK one marker is having a bus pass but this is not exclusive to chronologically old people and is also invisible. There is even ambiguity about how to refer to them. They are variously described as 'old', 'elderly', 'senior', 'pensioner', 'granny', usually pejoratively or patronisingly. Old people are complimented on how not-old, how young they look and this translates into socially acceptable ageism. (RSPH: 2018)

That researchers cannot agree when old age begins (e.g., Hill and Brettle 2006) is hardly surprising because 'old' as an identity that is either given or owned is only tenuously connected to chronological age. Instead one thing it is connected to is health, and regardless of actual age those people who have health concerns are seen, and see themselves, as old; for this group death is more likely to be less than every third thought, and people whose health is good are seen, and see themselves, as not-old or even as middle-aged, and for this group death is less likely to feature in their thoughts. But the most influential measure is whether they are economically productive or self-supporting, but this too can be health linked (Thane 2005). The determining point here is whether or not they contribute to the financial wealth of the nation, and although the view of old age in Europe has always been negative and remains so (RSPH: 2018). (Thane 2005), in times when government policy is of fiscal austerity, socially acceptable ageism will be reinforced. In any case what is considered as retirement and/or pensionable age has been a largely twentieth-century occupation-linked political decision anyway and the qualifying age has been moved up and down for economic reasons. In twenty-first century UK it is currently being pushed later. This links the identity of old to retirement, whenever this comes (e.g. Malette and Oliver 2006; Gee 2011; Edwards and Milton 2014). Hazel Barnes (1997), one of Sartre's main translators and interpreters, talks eloquently about this issue.

It is easy for younger therapists to adopt the wider cultural myths of ageing and see the old as homogeneous, when in fact they are an extraordinarily heterogeneous group, in terms of health, wealth, ability and aspirations, and as policy makers realise, it is not an issue that will go away; by 2035 more than a third of the population of the UK will be over sixty-five. If as some say, old age starts at fifty then the age span can be up to forty or more years, nearly two generations. In the UK in 2015 the average age expectation for women is eighty-two and seventy-eight for men and rising. There are also enormous individual and socio-economic differences between individuals, with some older people being well and high functioning, while others twenty or thirty years younger may be showing signs of frailty (Munk 2010). Some old people are some of the fittest, richest and most powerful in society while some are the most decrepit, poorest and powerless. Retirement is almost the first time since childhood when we can decide what to do and when to do it ... or not. Because of social conditioning, men who are more likely to have worked consistently throughout their lives will have greater problems using the freedom of retirement. Women on the other hand who have been carers will find there is always someone else to care for, children, then parents, then grandchildren, then partners. Also personal appearance will be less of an issue for men than for women.

While it is true that in later life gains may be outweighed by losses, suggesting that ageing is a process of decay or decline is neither a helpful way of viewing the final part of life nor consistent with the experience of older people.

Existentialism challenges the assumption that ageing equals loss but we must also acknowledge that the opposite counter-myth that over emphasises the positive elements of getting old may be fuelled by the therapist's own death denial. This is a young person's prejudice (RSPH: 2018). Neither is a useful or helpful basis on which to construct therapeutic interventions.

As said, older people are an underrepresented client group. Most work is with people who are of the same generation or younger than the therapist. It is hard not to put this down to a wider cultural and existential avoidance of death and endings. Research by the RSPH (2018) has found that nearly two in three people (64%) don't have a single friendship with an age gap of 30 years or more. And on a personal level, it has shown (Woolfe and Biggs 1997, Lee et al. 2003, Collins 2014) that therapists' reluctance to work with old people reflects their personal fears about their own ageing and mortality. Nevertheless, having exposure to and knowledge about working with older adults will give them the opportunity to confront their own anxieties and fears about ageing and mortality.

Rather than stereotyping the issues that older people bring to therapy as always being to do with loss, death and dying, we need to reframe them as issues associated with the everyday challenges of a life being lived in a context in which less time remains than has been lived. Phenomenologically the natural attitude is overcome by the acquisition of a sense of perspective: horizon. As a person gets older they at least have the possibility of seeing life more clearly, because they have experienced a greater variety of perspectives. The work then becomes about how the individual is able to understand the many experiences they have had in their lives and how they are making sense of it now that the end is in sight.

In one sense though, the work is no different from that with any other client group. Phenomenologically we work with every individual as they are, regardless of their chronological age. Having said that, it is inevitable that there will be some differences. For a start, some older people might just not know what therapy is. This will mean that there will be a need for a less formal and consequently a more active engagement to gain an understanding of what the client wants to achieve. What may start as an ordinary therapeutic relationship may become more like a friendship that both enjoy and benefit from (Collins 2014; Kewell 2017) and issues of health and mobility may mean that the therapist visits the client rather than vice versa.

Existential change is always related to humility in the face of the givens, and the skill and confidence of the therapist is correlated with their capacity for humility in the face of the unknown, and the experience of people older than oneself is always unknown.

A major issue will be the assumptions the therapist and client have of each other with respect to their relative ages. The therapist may be uneasy talking to someone the same age as their parents, and the client may be uneasy talking to someone the same age as their children. For the therapist this will inevitably bring up thoughts about their own and their parents' ageing and death, and for the client it will bring up thoughts of when they were a generation younger with more years ahead. It is important for the therapist to be ready to learn from their clients about their experience of a different generation. This is one of the biggest obstacles in working with older people: the fact that the work will impact deeply on the therapist. Paradoxically the old are more able to address ageing than the young, and if they are open to it the young have a great deal to learn about ageing from the old. Not only should the therapist aiming to work with older adults be aware of their own beliefs and biases towards older people, but they must also take the time to gain an understanding of the existential reality of old age.

The most important thing that young(er) therapists will learn from old(er) clients is the simple fact that everyone, including the therapist, not just other people, gets old and dies.

Working with truth, narrative and the sense-of-self

Making and exchanging stories is a uniquely human quality and the history of humanity is the history of storytelling, from cave paintings about 40,000 years ago to the emergence of writing about 6,000 years ago up to the way we use social media in the present day.

Some of our stories are to entertain, some are to get insight, some are to remember, but telling and listening to stories is how we relate to each other and thus gain a sense-of-self; they are how we write our autobiography (McLean 2015).

Telling stories, if only by ourselves, enables us to reflect on past choices and future possibilities and our place between the two, and in this way our sense-of-self is tied up with our temporality and the questioning implicit in authenticity about whether we are facing or avoiding the givens of existence and the givens of our particular existence. We cannot help wondering, *Am I writing my own life or am I letting someone else write it for me?*

In this way, the question *Why now?* and its derivatives, *Why this?*, *Why me?* and *Why here?*, when seen in the context of human development take on a greater importance and relevance. We always need to consider what is going on for this particular client at this particular time of life and circumstances that has given them the gift of despair that brings them to therapy.

But there are paradoxes at the heart of making an autobiography, and one is that we always know that our knowledge is partial, reality is ambiguous, and our story can only be up to the present day. Another is that we gain a resilient and coherent sense-of-self because of, and not in spite of, our ability to be different in different circumstances: by being open to change. In a similar way that I changed 'self' to 'selve' earlier, it becomes necessary to change the noun 'story' into the verb 'to story'. Storying is active, made and fluid, not passive, given and fixed.

We start to write our autobiography from birth and through our need for meaning and purpose we look for a narrative template we can use to bring some coherence to all our random experiences and because of our vulnerability we take the lead from our context, from the expectations and judgements of our parents, from other formative people and significant experiences.

These gradually coalesce into a small number of similar themes that lead us to a conclusion about how to be. In this sense our life seems to be given to us, embodied.

Our Sartrean original choice operates as a self-fulfilling prophecy in that it leads us to choose opportunities that coincide with it and reject opportunities that do not, and these largely unreflected-on choices become our projects. They are how we construct our sense-of-self and while we get some security from this, we also cannot help but wonder, *What if things were different?*, *What if I was like that, instead of this?*, and this is the point at which clients often come to therapy. We always know that what we thought was determined was actually chosen. And the fact that it was chosen means it can be unchosen and it is this that allows development in an existential sense to take place.

When we revisit our original choice and discover it as something that is not fixed for all time but flexible and context-dependent we also realise that the future is not determined, but can be chosen. This is when we become existentially born, and it can happen at any time. When we become complacent we start dying existentially.

On the simplest level, therapist and client are just two people sitting together in a room, telling stories to each other. To be of any use to our clients, as therapists we need to have reflected on our own life story – this is one of the purposes of personal therapy in training – and the influences on it. But more importantly we need to know how we constructed it and continue to construct it. This is how we develop existentially. The client tells a story of how they came to be the person they are now and what it is like for them. Often the stories has gaps, either of time, so that some periods of their lives appear to have been forgotten, or of meaning, where significant events appear to have gone unnoticed and the way they tell their story is a clue to the resilience of their sense-of-self (Holmes 2001). The therapist tells stories based on her understanding of the client's world. Some stories are coherent and the client needs little from us except our attention for them to ask themselves and answer questions. Others are harder to follow and require more from us so that some coherence can be introduced. This always involves challenging, in various ways (Holmes 2001: 86).

Many people come to a therapist with the idea that when they find out what really happened in their past, their present and future will become clear. But, existentially, psychotherapy is not about the search for what really happened, or even for an interpretation that fits better.

Since the past is a matter of interpretation and is presently being acted out, the task of therapy is to find out how past choices led to current actions and then to future intentions. When the client is able to identify the current meaning of their original project, they will be able to re-own it so that the choice can be revisited and remade.

Existentially, well-being does not depend upon the search for the key memory and its correct interpretation, rather than a fluid dialectic between story-making and story-breaking. A task of the existential therapist is to assist with this story-making and story-breaking. It is about being able to update autobiography in line with current experience and realising that there is no guarantee that the current meaning will last beyond the present moment. In this sense then the therapist is an assistant autobiographer who assists the person with writing their autobiography, rather than being a biographer (Holmes 2001).

From the moment of birth, parents and babies are telling each other stories about what it's like to be in each other's company, and in this way as Laing says, both start becoming existentially born, but in different ways: the woman gets born as a mother (Stern and Bruschweiler-Stern 1998). Elements of everyday conversation like, *Do you remember when ...?* or *Daddy will be here in an hour*, or *Are we nearly there yet?*, all contribute towards an understanding of time and temporality.

Research has shown how life stories change with age. By around two or three, children can tell and share stories and appreciate having stories read to them, and while they will not have a coherent life story at eight years old, there will begin to be one by twelve and this will increase in complexity thereafter (Bertstein and Rubin 2012: 238).

In adolescence a qualitatively different sense of the personal meaning of events starts to emerge (Habermas and Paha 2001). It is also the time of personal diary writing and late adolescents are more likely to tell stories to gain insight into their motives than early adolescents (McLean 2005). Also, peers become more significant for late adolescents as people to tell stories to rather than their parents. This is important when considering the development of children who are isolated either from parents and carers or from their peers. Also in adolescence, temporality opens out in a much more personal way than before to include not just the future but also the past; questions like, *How did I get here?* and *What am I going to do?*, become relevant. It is when people start to ask questions about how to live. Temporality brings thoughts not only of death but also responsibility for life.

However, Randall and McKim (2008), concentrating on the stories we tell ourselves, note that ageing beyond mid-life is not for the faint-hearted because the changes directly impact our acquired sense-of-self. They suggest that we need a strong, i.e. flexible and resilient, story that we can use to meet these changes. Disputing as an ageist myth that the old are incapable of learning new things, these changes can inspire either narrative elaboration in which our lives become richer and thicker with age, or narrative foreclosure in which we become smaller and we start to fade away existentially. The same events, depending on our openness to them, have the capacity to re-story or to de-story.

The idea of transformational moments and episodes is embedded in all cultures in terms of the formal rituals that we use to mark the end of one way of being and the beginning of another. Birthdays: the distance from the date we were thrown into the world – those birthdays with a zero at the end have a special meaning, *Can I really be 10 years older!?* New Year: with an expectation of resolutions to make the next year different from the last. The first day at school: symbolic of a separation from parents and the ability to have secrets and to know things that parents do not. Leaving home: independence. Religious ceremonies: symbolising the time when the person is deemed capable of faith. Graduation, the first sexual experience, engagement, marriage, parenthood, mid-life, funerals, retirement, death of a parent, birth of grandchildren, death of a contemporary, death of someone younger, etc., etc., and anniversaries of all these. They are how we mark our lives and all lead us to reflect on our temporality (Adams 2018). Some of them we prepare for and look forward to, and others we do not. At the right time they will, in Laing's words, enhance the feeling of being 'real and alive' and having 'a sense of being an entity with continuity in time and a location in space' (1965: 41). At the wrong time they will fracture this sense. As therapists, we need to be alert to their resonance and we can start doing this by acknowledging what such landmarks mean to us. Each echo is different because it happens at a different time.

All therapists are expected to write case studies if only as a part of their training, and the case study is a research method, but it is also a story written by one person, the therapist, of how two people who previously knew nothing of each other's lives, come together, meet and then part; and the knowledge of what happened before is patchy and unreliable. It is usually written as a story with an artificially imposed ending; neither knows what will happen after and even if the work has finished neither the life of the client nor that of the therapist has. All we really know is what happens in the meeting – and we don't know much about that, as Yalom (1974) shows. The case study has to find a way to honestly and ethically represent, or rather re-present, in words, the spirit of the richness and ambiguity of this experience. And to do this a narrative magnet has to be found for the story to revolve around, but every piece of therapeutic work can have any number of narrative magnets, and as many different ways of talking about them, each one as relevant as the next. Briod (1989) is critical of the value of deriving theories of human development from psychotherapy from the case study for two reasons. Firstly, the sample is skewed, and secondly, there is too great an entanglement with pre-existing theory and this is especially true of case studies written on training courses. This is another way of saying that the filters of pre-existing theory distort and determine the findings. If we use the case study method we need to remember that we cannot use it to prove the theory in a natural scientific sense. Both the client and the therapeutic relationship have to be regarded as singular universals to be investigated phenomenologically in the way that a research method like Interpretative Phenomenological Analysis (IPA) does (Smith et al. 2009). This question about the use of the written word to describe something as ambiguous as a life is not related simply to the case study; it applies to all uses of the written word.

Working with beginnings and endings

Yalom (1980) suggests that our avoidance and mystification of death in everyday life is paralleled in psychotherapeutic theory by sex standing in for death. It seems that it is less mysterious and somehow less problematic to consider where we come from biologically than either where we came from or where we are going to, existentially. I referred to this earlier as the tension between natality and mortality.

In a similar way, just as there is an emphasis in therapeutic theory on the beginning of life and that this is translated into practice as an emphasis on the beginning and the maintenance of the work, therapeutic theory largely ignores the end of life and this is translated into practice by there being little written on endings and it is hard not to put this down to a universal avoidance of the issue of death and endings.

A common mistake when considering beginnings and endings is to see them as events rather than as processes, like a race when the beginning is the moment of getting off the starting blocks, and ending is the moment of crossing the finish line. But by emphasising not the start of the word, but the end of the word, the *'–ing'*, we realise that beginnings and endings are just different ways of looking at the same process: life. Another mistake is to conflate the biological with the existential, such that birth only refers to biological birth and death only refers to biological death.

But as I have said, and as Laing reminds us, they are not the same and remembering the difference recalls Heidegger's distinction between demise – our being-at-an-end – and temporality – our being-towards-death (1962: 293). When we see beginnings and endings as processes we realise that everything in life is beginning and ending simultaneously and also involves both gains and losses, choices and sacrifices, and that by trying to stand still, we go backwards.

A fuller understanding of temporality is that each new moment is therefore potentially a new beginning and simultaneously a new ending, and the client's presence in psychotherapy suggests that they are dissatisfied with the way their life has gone up until referral, and that they hope that somehow there could be a way of approaching the rest of life differently from the old way. That they could be reborn, existentially.

As life is beginnings and endings, our natural condition is one of change. Change is ontological. It follows that, existentially, many problems in living are the consequence of denial and evasion of change. In existential therapy we do not work on change; we work on stopping stopping. We work on resistance to change. We work on reintroducing the client to change and therefore to responsibility. This inevitably evokes anxiety that is there to be met, not soothed, explained, evaded or denied.

But the certainty of the familiar is hard to give up and it contributes to our evasion and denial of change, and its origins and purposes have to be examined thoroughly before it can be unchosen, and new options chosen and the uncertain future embraced. Although Peter Pan, a boy who rejected his temporality, thought that death would be 'an awfully big adventure', in fact biological death is different because it is the only ending which is not followed by a beginning that we do not take part in personally, though we know that life for others will go on after we are gone.

Nevertheless, while as we get older we can get to see the new in the old, as Beauvoir did, we also realise that last times start to outweigh first times and that each ending, each loss, whether of a thing, event, relationship or a person, is a preparation for our own final ending. Our personal history of loss therefore at least has the possibility of teaching us what makes life actually worth living. This is a key lesson because when we learn that we also learn when life is no longer worth living – and then we can die, as Nietzsche says, happy.

Confrontation with death and dying will invariably evoke a reassessment of life's achievements and values for both therapist and client on a par with the most effective therapy. In this sense dying people, of whatever age, have an uncanny way of exposing a central existential dilemma of life. Therapists will get to understand that talking about death can never be theoretical, it will always be about 'my death' (Cooper and Adams 2005). Having exposure to and knowledge about working with dying people will give therapists the opportunity to confront their own anxieties and fears not just about ageing and mortality but also about life and living (RSPH: 2018).

The way individuals deal with the final loss is directly related to how they have understood their earlier experiences of loss, and this principle applies equally to client and therapist. If the therapist is reluctant to ask herself questions like, *When am I going to retire?*, or *What would I do if I had only six months left to live?*, their avoidance will only compound the client's sense of inner isolation. Also the more anxious the therapist is about their own death, the more likely they will be to stereotype and pathologise those clients who are closer to death.

On the retirement issue, the fact that many therapists are not bound by conventional retirement dates enables them to maintain their denial of temporality and to link their occupation too closely with their identity. It also enables them to avoid changing what started as an open-ended contract to a fixed-term contract and working through the consequences of this. In an analogous way to Stolorow's (2007: 13) absolutisms, a paradox of therapy is that like life, no contract can ever be open-ended. It will always come to an end; the question is not if, but when and how. The therapist's reluctance to stop working means that when the end comes, as it surely will, it runs the risk of coming because of the therapist's own reducing competence through age-related loss of hearing or memory, or even sudden death. The implications of the latter are movingly and comprehensively discussed by Jeffries (2000) and Barnett (2008).

Frequently the issue of loss of a parent, partner or even a child will be the presenting issue and although this can happen at any time of life, it begins to happen more frequently in mid-life. In cases of bereavement, Yalom (1980) says that by thinking of the work as solely about loss is to miss the point. Death is personal, and our reluctance to acknowledge this may lead us to conclude, incorrectly, that the client 'is already too overwhelmed to accept the added risk of dealing with his or her own finiteness' (ibid.: 167). It is not the client that does not want to look at it but ourselves (Cooper and Adams 2005) and if we persist we do a disservice to our clients who are certainly thinking about it. Although the client's attitude may be mixed, overall though, they will be grateful for the opportunity to talk about it and we can use the immediacy of the relationship to focus on their ability to choose how they want to be.

On many occasions when dealing with these issues there is very little that needs to be said, very little that can be said. It is enough to attend fully and be with the client's questions. Yalom says that 'One can offer no greater service to someone facing death [...] than to offer him or her your sheer presence' (2008: 130). This is a good example of a dialogue when no words need to be spoken. We can communicate that the client's thoughts and feelings are natural human responses that can be understood simply by being tolerated and shared with another person. It is inevitable that it will be challenging for us as therapists too, because if we are giving our full attention we will start to think about our own death and how we want to live the rest of our lives.

Strasser and Strasser (1997) and Ioannou (2017) note that brief existential work closely echoes the human condition because the end is in sight from the beginning. As therapists, although we clearly know this intellectually, we can easily forget its existential impact. Paradoxically, the more experience a therapist has, the less she or he may be able to remember what it was like when they stopped seeing their own therapist. While it may be the first time a particular client has been to a therapist, for that therapist it may be the 200th time they see a client for the first time, and similarly with the ending. And for the therapist there is always another client, but not so for the client. Experienced therapists need to remember this.

The beginning of the work is a process where the two people get to know each other and find out by trial and error how much each can be trusted, and by learning about each other's use of language, both verbal and non-verbal, they start to develop an idiolect. It is the start of a process of discovery for both. The client is there to find out something they do not yet know, and neither knows how long it will take, and it is inevitable that this uncertainty will evoke anxiety in both. We need to remember from the very start of the work that it will end at some point and this awareness of the end will prompt both therapist and client to make the best use of the time. In the wider world this after all is the purpose of what we rather appropriately call deadlines, and deadlines evoke a range of responses in people: action, panic, denial, incompetence, etc. Many clients come to therapy with issues about unsatisfactory endings or losses, and it is important that the client does not experience the end of the therapy as something else that ended unsatisfactorily. It is the therapist's responsibility to know how to model the ending of the work so that they get to the end of the work at the end of the available time. We cannot model a good ending if we do not know what one is like ourselves. We also need to know how to make a bad ending into a good ending.

Given that endings are universally difficult and frequently avoided, with an open-ended contract the issue for both the therapist and the client is to arrive at an ending which is at the right time for both of them. The termination of therapy is not just a cessation of activity; it is a process to be worked through. This can only be known by the two people on the basis of their work together, but in assessing the end it is useful to bear in mind the risks and signs of poorly managed endings, like the client leaving before the work has had a chance to start, or ending after a specific goal has only been partially met, or the client leaving without notice, or leaving suddenly because they do not understand that ending is a process and not a cessation of action. But there is another way of avoiding the ending: by not ending at all, by staying too long to avoid the pain of ending. It is not the job of the existential therapist to advise the client to stay or to go but to ensure that the reasons for staying or for going are sufficiently examined. Whether it is an appropriate decision or not cannot be known unless the issue is discussed. To this end, if a client is reluctant to discuss a sudden departure, the likelihood is that the ending will not be well managed, but if they will discuss it, the likelihood is that it will be well managed. The therapist has to be able to face endings with openness and to know when they either prolong or shorten the ending for their own reasons. Supervision is very important in throwing light on these blind spots.

Whatever the contract, it is often found that no less than, and in many cases more than, one-sixth of the total time together is spent considering the ending. With a fixed-term contract the decision of when to stop is taken away, but what remains is to work out how to evaluate and end the work. Therefore, clients who have a particular sensitivity to loss and endings will need more time and care in working through the implications of the ending so they can move on to the next part of their lives knowing something more about beginnings and endings. In these cases the whole time may be spent considering the ending. Placing an emphasis on the number of sessions left and monitoring its meaning will reduce the likelihood of premature termination.

The end of therapy is not like the end of life and as therapy is about relationship as well as task, the client will probably wish to know that the therapist will remember them in the future. This is less likely to come about simply by saying so and is more likely to be reinforced by the quality of the therapist's attention over the whole time and especially at the end. Often the way the client remembers the therapy, its effectiveness and the therapists' attentiveness will be correlated with how well the ending is managed. The better the ending, the more the work will be remembered as valuable and the gains sustainable. But a good ending does not mean that all loose ends have been tied up and that the problems of life have been solved. On the contrary, it means that both therapist and client can have faith that the client has learnt enough to be equal to any further challenges that life will inevitably throw their way.

Working with embodiment

Existentialists dispute the traditional distinction between the mind and the body, preferring the term embodiment. We perceive the world, as Merleau-Ponty said, from and in terms of the body. While in one way we know this in everyday phrases like when we describe someone we do not get on with as a 'pain in the neck' or after a personal disappointment we say we are 'gutted', in another way language conspires against it with the ease that we can distinguish between 'my mind' and 'my body', with the body being in some way mistrusted and other, and of emotions as being disruptive of our equilibrium. In this way, we are not at home in our body, and this distinction is embedded in the way illnesses are thought of, with some being described as psychosomatic. As the work of Oliver Sacks shows, whether or not the condition has an identifiable biological cause, it has a dramatic existential impact that has to be acknowledged. The person is not mind or body; the person is mind and body and they are together the total situation and are functionally inseparable.

In this way our sense of being embodied is the foundation of our entire existence. Our emotions are the way we feel in the our body; they are embodied sensations that change the meaning of the world and our place in it. When we feel objects in the world, we feel them with our body, and when we act on the world, we act on it with our body. But neither are we separate and isolated bodies; as Merleau-Ponty again says, our consciousness is turned towards the world and finds meaning, both similarity and difference, in the world. This is what is meant by intersubjectivity.

Human development can be seen as being about understanding the changing meaning of our embodiment, and in therapeutic practice, if we only consider the biological, the psychological, the cognitive or the social dimensions of our clients lives, we are likely to miss embodiment.

We live in a verbal culture and to a certain extent psychotherapy is a product of that: Freud did after all call it the talking cure. But this is not all it is; indeed it could be said that talking is only a small part of it. We are instead interconnected bodies in space and our bodies are lived through meanings. We know this by the different feelings that are evoked in us when we are in the bodily presence of different people. Some we want to get closer to, some the opposite, and so on.

Prior to the acquisition of language, around age three, a child's being will be entirely embodied and because of the child's immersion and absorption in a particular social setting, as the child's facility with language increases, some experiences will get translated into a verbal language, but it is inevitable that some will not. But all will be embodied.

This is recognised by Sartre in the way that our original choice is sensed or embodied and then acted. Consequently, if questioned at all, it will feel as if it has always been there. We think of it as our essence, as who we are. It is unreflected experience.

This ties in with the practice of focusing, which was developed by Gendlin from researching into what made psychotherapy effective. He found that success invariably came about when the client was able to gain an intuitive awareness of a subtle quality of their bodily awareness that he called the 'felt sense' and he regarded this as primary and essentially non- or pre-verbal (1996). Focusing is a way of becoming aware of what Heidegger called our 'mood' by trying to suspend our natural attitude, the linguistic interpretations we make about it, and instead being open to it.

It is a therapeutic practice that centres on the body's awareness and connectedness to other bodies. Unlike mindfulness it is therefore not a practice someone can do on their own. The value of the listener's attention is ontologically crucial and the listener keeps the focuser company while they both try to make sense of and see if the *'felt-sense'* can be put into words, be reflected on, in ways that they have never been able to, to dare to do, before.

Having said that, focusing acknowledges that many aspects of the 'felt sense' are so profound, so ineffable, that they probably cannot ever be put into words, but also that it is these experiences that we have lost touch with and that we need to tune into in order to regain some balance in our lives. The therapist must therefore take care not to impose an order, but to allow it to emerge. In this sense, the aim of focusing is not to be detached from, but to be passionately curious about, the embodied and problematic aspects of existence. Being less dependent on the use of language as communication it is particularly appropriate for use with children (Verliefd and Stapert 2008). The phenomenological intervention, *What's that like?*, is particularly valuable here (Deurzen and Adams 2016).

Scalzo (2010), talking about working with children, considers play as an important communication between two people, and that while children may have a smaller emotional vocabulary and certainly have a smaller linguistic vocabulary they can readily express themselves in play. He also notes that many adults have forgotten the poetic, ambiguous language of play, and only value the linearity of defined verbal language. This can be seen in the way play is judged to be frivolous or not as valuable as more structured activities. But play is anything but frivolous. It is the way we exercise our natural freedom throughout life and discover for ourselves the mysteries of the world and our place in it. What is discovered through play can never be learnt from books. Play is central to human development and has its own 'sacred seriousness' (ibid.: 37). Entering into play with a child requires a commitment to lose ourselves in the narrative and to suspend our adult natural attitude and appreciate that it is a privilege to be invited into the child's play world. Interpretations are not needed, indeed they will most likely fracture the relationship; all that is needed is pure attention and a phenomenological curiosity. At these times something more profound than simply working on the specific issue is happening. The two people are engaging together as open and embodied beings, both trusting their own and the other's natural freedom with no 'irritable reaching after fact or reason', as Keats put it. He was echoing the medieval mystical work *The Cloud of Unknowing* and also anticipating what Kierkegaard was to mean later by faith.

Extrapolating from the idea that we are always in relation with the other through our postural schema and that this is crucial in understanding human development, Langdridge (2005) suggests that psychotherapists can usefully extend their practice with adults by incorporating more active non-language-based embodied practices. He says that talking may just not work for some clients and that in these cases enactment, or role-play of some sort, may be more effective in reinforcing the embodied nature of existence. The primary function of therapeutic homework whether formal or informal, therapist directed or client directed, is after all to get the client to practice, to enact, what has merely been talked about. This is equivalent to translating what is 'present-at-hand' into the 'ready-to-hand', and as such introduces us to ownership, to life skills, and to temporality.

It allows the person to recognise aspects of their embodied intersubjectivity that were previously obscured, like the inadequacy of language to describe the entirely of experience, and acknowledging that the factors such as posture and gesture constitute fundamental aspects of their being-in-the-world. In this way the therapeutic encounter 'becomes a dance where therapist and client form a unity, a synchronous back and forth of embodied mutuality' (ibid.: 96).

Simone de Beauvoir's work has allowed us to understand not just the distinction between sexuality and gender but also how these embodied distinctions come about and what they mean throughout the life cycle. This is that being impressionable and searching for coherence, we absorb and come to embody the meanings of the world we are thrown into and then accept these, with all their inconsistencies, tensions and power differentials as normal. In this way our views about gender and sexuality start to become fixed, embodied, from infancy and boys and girls are raised to have a different understanding of their agency and the way they occupy space and this had been summed up by the art critic John Berger who says, '... men act and women appear. Men look at women. Women watch themselves being looked at' (emphasis in original) (1972: 47).

Adolescence is when we start to be more aware of our responsibility, temporality and sexuality and is when these tensions usually begin to make themselves felt and we can then choose to either question them in various ways or go along with them and enact them. Either way has consequences, but when they become problematic they can frequently present as genderised physical issues like vaginismus (Barker 2011), eating disorders, self-harm, extreme fitness regimes, body dysmorphic disorder and so on. In working with these issues, understanding that gender identity and sexuality is socially constructed allows us to respect the assumptions that lead to the presenting issues but also to challenge them in terms of how valuable or useful they are.

The desire to be wanted by the other, to be seen as sexually desirable is common to both men and women, it is ontological, and sexuality is a fundamental facet of our intersubjectivity. But socially constructed inconsistencies, tensions and power differentials can manifest in different ways throughout the life cycle, for example the middle years can bring a fading of sexual attractiveness bringing a premonition of temporality reinforced by competition with a more energetic younger generation. We know this as the mid-life crisis in which e.g. depression in women has been linked to their identities being tied to caring for others and being deprived of this role by the departure of their children (Johnstone 2000).

Because our assumptions about gender and sexuality are both embodied and problematic it means that therapists must be especially careful to examine and challenge their own assumptions so that they do not continue to mystify and reinforce attitudes and beliefs that constrain their clients' freedom (Richards et al. 2013). Regardless of therapists' aspirations to equality, the tension within the therapeutic relationship will be added to by sexual preference that cannot help but reflect the ideology of the culture outside the consulting room. This is a tension that will be so deeply familiar that it may not have been reflected on. Nevertheless it will need to be understood so that its constraints can be transcended and the two people see each other as free agents who are also sexual men or women.

Beauvoir's work has also allowed us to understand not only the embodied nature of the ageing process in general and that of older people in particular but the impact that working with ageing or even dying people has on the therapist and the therapeutic process.

Working with randomness and chance

While randomness and chance are considered to be givens of existence, we can gain a distinctive and valuable insight into their significance when we consider their relationship with trauma, how we work with it and its connection with human development.

Although trauma is addressed in other therapeutic perspectives it is not often made clear what it is that is traumatised. The focus is usually on the specific event and it is often used as a synonym for a very large shock of some sort and while having some truth to it, this is not the whole story.

Stolorow says that existentially, trauma is 'a catastrophic loss of innocence that permanently alters one's sense of being-in-the-world' (2007: 16) by exposing the universe as random and unpredictable. For the metaphysically privileged child, such a shock, especially if it is repeated, will be traumatic and the response may well be the protectionism of narcissism. One way this can come about was described by Bateson's (1972) idea of the double bind. What is traumatised, then, is our belief in a benign predictable universe; it is when we find that everything we took to be so, is not so.

As Heidegger says, every moment both preserves the past and anticipates the future and this continuity forms the foundation of our sense-of-self. In trauma this ability of the moment to establish continuity is shattered. 'Everyday familiarity collapses' (Heidegger 1962: 233), and experience 'becomes freeze-framed into an eternal present' (Stolorow 2007: 20) and becomes isolated from human dialogue. Such experiences are beyond words. We stop becoming existentially born and start existentially dying. We stop developing.

Whenever something random happens, whether good or bad, we ask, *Why me?*, to which the only answer is, *No reason, why not you?* Unexpected and selfless acts of kindness can have a similarly disorientating effect. We habitually defend ourselves with ideas of divine or diabolic intervention, of personal specialness, of good or bad luck, of determinism, or of narcissism. We can generally take minor reminders of randomness in our stride; life is after all about coming to terms with our insignificance and powerlessness in the grand scheme of things, and many of these events will be salutary and will help us to develop our resilience and sense of perspective. But major or cumulative reminders will shatter our trust in continuity and when this happens we become protectively enclosed and separated not just from everyday life in general but also from the possibility of an encounter with another person in particular.

In trauma we are opened to ontological anxiety and in an instant the world goes from being 'present-at-hand', owned and personally meaningful, to being 'ready-to-hand', separate and meaningless. We become not just interpersonally alone, but existentially alone.

This profound sense of singularity, as Stolorow calls it, is built into the experience of trauma itself and it also means that even if attunement is subsequently present it cannot be readily felt.

Being ontological therefore means that trauma is not unusual and special; it is ordinary and everyday and can potentially arise out of anything that reminds us that the universe is random and that no continuity of being can be assured. As Stolorow says, 'at any moment those you love can be struck down by a senseless random event. Not many people know that' (2007: 16).

The ordinariness of trauma illuminates a central paradox that, for example, when we say to a friend, *See you tomorrow*, we implicitly assume that we will both be alive tomorrow in order to meet. And when we add, *God willing*, thereby invoking divine intervention, we acknowledge that whether the meeting takes place will be largely down to factors outside our control. The paradox is that we need the protection of the delusion of a benign predictable universe to carry on with everyday life. Stolorow calls these sort of injunctions the 'absolutisms of everyday life'.

Realising that our world is random is so difficult to tolerate that we would rather take responsibility instead, even when it is nothing to do with us. It is somehow more comforting to think it was in some way our own fault, that maybe we deserved it. But this comfort is a dead-end. Our sense of self, our autonomy, however shaky, has to be preserved at all costs and what usually happens, as we know from our clinical work, is that traumatised people frequently blame themselves in some way. They feel victimised. This makes the events seem a bit less random and at least provides a rationale through the belief that one was the author, in some unknown way, of one's own misfortune. The existential reality is that the relational element of the trauma is more than likely not due to what we like to call deliberate malice, evil, diabolic intervention, but human frailty, and that understanding this will enable us to forgive the perpetrators, bearing in mind that forgiveness does not mean agreeing that they were right to do it. It is a way of being released from the victim narrative and re-engaging with life (Kampusch 2010).

Trauma can apply just as much to interpersonal events like domestic violence as it can to events that have no rhyme or reason like car crashes or life-threatening illnesses. And if those close to us are the perpetrators of the violence and supposed to be our carers, the trauma will feel as if multiplied. It is bad enough for the event to have happened but even worse when its effect is carried out by and/or not acknowledged by others.

Therefore, what defines whether something becomes traumatic or not, is not the event as such but the way its effect is treated by those close to us. Whatever the origin, trauma becomes a relational event.

Stolorow uses the experience of trauma to dispute Heidegger's general principle about the unrelationality of death – that we die alone – and says that the key to recovery from trauma is Heidegger's notion of solicitude He says,

> just as finitude is fundamental to our existential constitution, so too is it constitutive of our existence, that we meet each other as brothers and sisters in the same dark night. Thus although the possibility of emotional trauma is ever present, so too is the possibility of forming bonds of deep emotional attachment within which devastating emotional pain can be held, rendered more tolerable, and, eventually integrated.
>
> (1994: 97)

This brings to light another paradox about trauma: that just as trauma is part of life then so is recovery from trauma.

This understanding of trauma has some clear implications for therapeutic practice. One is that if the therapist's attunement is not accurate enough it will create a model for subsequent retraumatisation within the therapy. Reluctance and resistance can then be seen as legitimate protections against retraumatisation. By acknowledging this, the therapist will be able to be sensitive to the client's attempts to reconnect to being. It follows therefore that in order to work with trauma the therapist needs to have reflected on the way randomness and chance have impacted on their own lives, and how they managed the traumatic events that followed.

A sense of belonging and coming to terms with the randomness of existence is much more likely to be re-established and trusted through the concentrated attention and accurate attunement of a therapist who can tolerate the anxiety of living in a universe where events may have no rhyme or reason, than it will by interpretation and explanation.

Working with adversity

Happiness is a part of everyone's life plan, but it is also elusive and a part of the problem is that we tend to think of it as the absence of anxiety and of having a future free from adversity and struggle. We want it to last. Another problem is that when we try to achieve it technologically with drugs, whether prescribed, recreational or behavioural, or with other shortcuts, it is always at a cost to our humanity.

All these options invoke our nostalgia for our metaphysically privileged childhood, and while such anxiety-free moments are valuable and can enable us to reflect, like when we go on an all-inclusive holiday, we also know they are transient, and that as Heidegger says, we will soon be drawn back to the reality of existence by the 'call of conscience'.

Existentially, genuine lasting tranquility can only come with completeness, but since we are only complete on death it is hard to be permanently happy with this option. Happiness is therefore neither a birthright nor something that can be given or taken, nor, as with authenticity and the self, something we can save up. As Beauvoir said, 'I've always wished for happiness without wishing I had any right to it: I thought of it as being constructed by me [...] You had to win your happiness, as I saw it, amid conditions some of which were burdensome, others favourable' (1991: 170). These 'conditions' manifest throughout life as our everyday paradoxes and dilemmas, and it is the fact that they are unsolvable that evokes the anxiety that makes us want to continually explore their possibilities.

For Nietzsche, life is struggle, and the paradox is that it is our struggle against adversity, not freedom from adversity, that makes life worth living. Being able to set ourselves successive challenges and meet them on our own terms, again and again, leads to us to become existentially alive, and by not setting ourselves challenges we existentially die. We are the challenges we set ourselves. The path of least resistance leads to the place of least existence.

Happiness, then, is the transient satisfaction, joy or relief that we get from knowing that we have persevered against adversity and succeeded. And while we can never be sure what may bring it about, we know that when we persevere against adversity especially in difficult conditions, we do generate meaning and purpose and have moments of genuine happiness, and that when we do not persevere we neither generate it nor develop lasting personal resilience.

Ultimately though, there is one overarching adversity: the absurdity of finding a reason to live in the face of death, and although Nietzsche mentioned it in TOI, this idea is best encapsulated in Viktor Frankl's translation: 'He who has a *why to* live for can bear almost any *how*' (2004: 109; emphasis in original).

The need to persevere against adversity is universal to all humanity and whether I am stacking wooden bricks or playing a game like snakes and ladders with my granddaughter, or working with a client on a difficult issue, or supervising a student's research project, or making a new stone carving, the process is always the same. I need to acknowledge the context-specific characteristics of the task, and work such that there is an optimum amount of anxiety, for I know from experience that the right amount of anxiety will promote learning. I know that too much, or too little, will hinder it. This is, as we know, not easy to get right. We benefit from persevering against adversity. In psychotherapy this balance is maintained through concentrated attention, but because of human fallibility it is inevitable that there will be some occasions when mistakes are made: the task will be too easy or too difficult, or the support will be too abandoning or too intrusive. This balance was described by Heidegger as the difference between 'leaping-in solicitude' and 'leaping-ahead solicitude' and it will be monitored by the therapist's reflexivity.

Perseverance, our ability to learn through making mistakes in our interactions with the world and to continue, is in fact our most transferable skill. The word 'mistake' here is perhaps inaccurate because existentially the only true mistake is one we do not recognise as such and therefore do not learn from. A more accurate word is opportunity.

All this is directly relevant to our work as psychotherapists because while it means that our focus should always be on the search for meaning and purpose rather than the search for symptom relief or transient happiness, it also means that meaning and purpose will only arise from challenge and from struggling against adversity. It also means that since meaning and purpose are always personally defined, the psychotherapist will need to know personally what it means to struggle against adversity and succeed. This knowledge will give them the sensitivity, the humility and the faith in the human spirit to accompany the client in their struggles.

Researching into the process of how we move from having no meaning and purpose, to having meaning and purpose, Denne and Thompson talk about the importance of what they call 'decisional turning points' (1991: 122). The significance of these moments for human development was noted by Sartre as 'presence to being' (2003: 121), when we turn fixed essence into free existence; by Cannon as the 'psychological instant' (1999: 51); by Kierkegaard, Nietzsche and Heidegger as the 'glance of the eye'; and by Merleau-Ponty (1964: 111) as de-centering and re-centering. Decisional turning points have a number of components: decision, risk, acceptance of possible negatives and experiential validation of the decision.

The process begins when we decide that something about our current situation is unsustainable, when our life has lost meaning because the way we are living is inconsistent with our values. It happens because we close ourselves to the continuity of change, and that while we do not know what to do, we know that the only way forward is to risk the unknown and that this will involve a sacrifice. Risk in this sense means opening to ambiguity, opening both to our own freedom and also to others, as well as the randomness of the world. To risk is to embrace, with faith, the freedom of creating oneself.

It is important to note that even though we may feel that the unknown future is preferable to the familiar present and that because of this we have no choice or that we may feel pushed into a particular action, what Denne and Thompson mean by decision is not about selecting between options, rather than committing to a course of action. Often, even though we may feel we have no options, we still have the existential choice of committing or not committing to a course of action.

Any change always involves a risk that it could all go horribly wrong. This has to be acknowledged along with the fact that no one anywhere can give any guarantees – either way. We live on our own account. Many people try to reduce the risk by trying to control the outcome, but while some planning is possible, control never is. It just shows a lack of faith.

The transition to meaning and purpose is completed by realising that the risk had been worth it, and that it didn't, after all, all go horribly wrong. Such is our fear of change, of temporality, that we find it easy to catastrophise, but actually although things rarely go horribly wrong they also rarely go wonderfully right. They usually go unexpectedly different – and continue in this way for as long as we stay open to temporality.

Moreover, Denne and Thompson conclude that meaning and purpose is not linked to any particular sorts of decisions, courses of action or consequences so much as the action of taking and owning a decision to face adversity and risk with faith, and with living and owning the consequences of that decision. It is the act of struggle that makes the difference rather than the nature of the struggle.

People come to psychotherapy when their lives are lacking in meaning and purpose and our task is to provide enough support so that they can find the courage to embrace the challenges they have avoided up to that point, and face an unknown future where they can live more honestly and more resiliently knowing that they have not shied away from adversity.

The skills learning process

Existentially, human development is a gradual but permanently cumulative learning process and a principle of all existential therapeutic work is to introduce, or re-introduce, the client to the reality that they have an active part in their learning. Learning skills is about finding what obstacles we put in our way and finding the resources to overcome them. This applies as much to therapy as it does to everyday life and as much to the therapist as to the client. But as well as learning the skills of living more resourcefully, clients also have to learn the skill of using therapy. Experienced therapists find it easier easy to forget this.

The skills learning process is marked by a characteristic sequence of thoughts, feelings and actions that can evolve backwards and forwards through a sequence of qualitatively different but interconnected phases, dependent on the nature of the adversity. Also, each phase requires something different from us as therapists (Adams 2016; Deurzen and Adams 2016).

The first challenge begins before the first meeting. For the client, it begins when they acknowledge receipt of the gift of despair and start to ask themselves questions about the way they are living. These may either be intense and clear or dull and niggling. But either way there is a sense that things are not the way they should be. That they come to therapy shows they have some hope. With every new client an entirely new relationship is created and we can never take it for granted what will work. This is the challenge for the therapist, and the client will also need to work out whether the therapist is capable of rising to the challenge they give them.

Our task is to be phenomenological. As we attend, listen and clarify, we begin to find out about their worldview and how they usually meet adversity: at what point challenges become too much and they give up. Gradually, things, people and events, start to be understood in relation to each other rather than separately. Also, the client starts to understand that she is the thread that connects everything together. This is often disorientating and can be as frightening as it can be exciting. If frightening, the client may not believe that any good can come from it and wish to leave.

Our task here is to try to understand and tolerate these feelings, and facilitate the client to understand their experience in a new way. It may mean we will be challenging and interpreting; we will be searching with our client for accurate re-descriptions that focus on ambiguity and paradoxes in the client's life, or how they repeat past patterns.

The challenge for the therapist is to stay with them as they find the courage to discover what might need to change and as such the therapist will have to fall back on their own resources. If we have not had the experience of learning from such adversity it is unlikely we will be of much help and may well do harm by seeking easy solutions. Assuming we are up to the task, gradually the client will get used to the new experience of facing adversity with a different outcome.

Our task is then to try to consolidate the changes made so they can be integrated into the client's idea of who they now are. Life is full of setbacks and we need to affirm their learning at the same time as acknowledging that the uncertainty of existence can be exciting instead of terrifying.

But as the client gets used to doing things differently, they also become more resilient. Our task here is to encourage the emerging competence and confidence while at the same time guarding against over-confidence that can means the end of learning. A challenge for the therapist, and particularly for the experienced therapist, is that their years of experience can lead them into complacency and arrogance. They have stopped learning and what were once skills have now become techniques. This is when they make a mistake and because they do not realise it is a mistake they see it as the client's mistake, responsibility or pathology. This is dangerous for both therapist and client.

Working with love

Each of us enters and leaves life alone and in between we are surrounded by other people. It is ontological, no one escapes it; even a hermit's identity is as a person-without-others. One of the great puzzles of human existence is to work out what other people are there for and how to get on with them so that our lives are enhanced rather than diminished.

Nevertheless it is the close bonds of love with other people that enable the development of the resilience we need in order to define and carry out our personal projects. It is these bonds that begin from birth that promote existential growth and it is these same bonds that form the basis of an existentialist ethics that in turn are the foundation of existential therapy.

It was some years after their first meeting that Medard Boss learned why Heidegger had replied to him so readily (Boss 1988: 3). It was that Boss took Heidegger's (1962: 158) reference to the ideal relationship between any two people to be a description of a truly therapeutic relationship. This is that if a therapist can act towards a client with leaping-ahead solicitude that acknowledges autonomy and opens out being, he or she is working with love. In contrast, if out of our personal anxiety, we seek to take over and suggest, direct, advise, fix or control the client we will not be working with love and the client's autonomy will be disabled (Karban 2017) and will be relieved of their ability to respond in their own way and given nothing in return. Leaping-in not only leads to a 'constricted Dasein' (Mills 1997: 46) but also diminishes us as therapists.

As Viktor Frankl says, 'we can see the therapist as a technician only if we have first viewed the patient as some sort of machine' (2000: 26). People are not machines. When we leap in we do it out of our own personal desire to evade and deny temporality or as a part of the legacy of our own unsatisfactory experience of being cared for. If as therapists we start to view the client as someone to be directed instead of someone whose life is just as precious and personal to them as ours is to us, we lose faith in humanity and diminish both the client and ourselves. For Sartre and Beauvoir, this is an act of violence committed against a person's freedom and for Beauvoir, 'Genuine love ought to be founded on the mutual recognition of two liberties [...] Love would be revelation of self by the gift of self and enrichment of the world' (1997: 677).

What Boss saw in the idea of leaping-ahead is also what Laing (1965: 45) meant when he said that,

> In therapy [...] the last thing there is any point in is to pretend to more 'love' or concern than one has. The more the therapist's own necessarily very complex motives for trying to 'help' a person [...] genuinely converge on a concern for him which is prepared to 'let him be' [...] the more hope there will be in the horizon.
>
> (1965: 45)

But as it is an ideal it is also always compromised, as Beauvoir reminds us, by the everyday ontic power differences in society which cannot help but be echoed within the therapeutic relationship. In therapy, these manifest in a general sense in the dynamics between the more powerful and knowledgeable therapist and the less powerful client who has come for help, and in the more specific and variable sense in the power dynamics between the therapist of one particular age and the client of another particular age. An example of this is how old people are seen as marginal and unlikely to benefit from therapy (Collins 2014).

For Sartre, love is not an emotion; it is an action. As Laing says, referring to therapy as much as to everyday life, 'The way we treat each other is the treatment' (Tougas and Shandel 1989). We grow to realise we are loved not by single dramatic acts but by what Stadlen describes as the way that individual acts of understanding, not much in themselves, act like 'grains of sand' that gradually accumulate into 'a big sand castle' (2011: 90).

The idea of leaping-ahead is translated into existential practice through operationalising the phenomenological principles of attention and reflexivity. The therapeutic relationship is started and is sustained by the kind of attention that respects and is curious about the client's life and the way they have lived it up until the present moment and the way they see the future. And the therapist uses her reflexivity to monitor any tendencies to suggest or direct that come out of her own anxiety of the uncertainty of the encounter.

Leaping-ahead is hard to maintain because the fundamental dilemma of relationships is that we wish to be separate and distinct at the same time as being connected and known, and it is better to see it as an aim rather than an objective, a journey rather than a destination. Like other existential principles, the risks are great, but so are the benefits. As the writer Blake Morrison says, in the story of his relationship with his father,

> It is an awful paradox that the more you love and are loved the more sadness you will leave behind because the people you loved and were loved by will miss you. Love brings meaning and happiness but also sadness and loss. But it is a fulfilled sort of sadness and loss. The sadness and loss that comes from never having loved and being loved is an empty hollow feeling.
>
> (2006: 235)

People fear abandonment and harassment equally and we try to solve the paradox of relationships either by merging with another, as in falling in love, which either fades or becomes more threatening, or by trying to distance themselves from intimacy. That mutuality is difficult is shown by the frequency with which people enter therapy because of relationship difficulties.

But while there is no simple either/or solution, there is a dialectical both/and solution and it is that by making a leap of faith and tolerating the inherent paradox of relationships people discover the paradoxical freedom of intimacy. This is existential maturity.

Another way of thinking about Heidegger's notion of solicitude is in terms of the difference between dialogue, duologue and monologue.

A monologue is when one person is talking and another is listening and the talker's main concern is to talk with little concern about how she or he is received. The listener's experience is often one of being talked at rather than being talked to or with. They do not feel included in the conversation.

A duologue is when two people are talking to each other and only superficially listening to each other. They may well take it in turns to talk and to listen and even to respond to what each other says, but they are not really hearing each other. They are more likely to be listening to what they want the other to say and can then respond to. Another way to think of this is as two simultaneous but interlocking monologues.

A dialogue is when the two people are genuinely attending and listening to each other in a spirit of cooperation and trust rather than competition and defensiveness, not for what they want to hear but for what is actually being said, and also to what is only being hinted at. It involves a reflexive openness to the other person and also to oneself. A true dialogue will always be characterised by a certain amount of anxiety which may be felt as excitement, but it is the anxiety of never knowing quite what will happen next. It is natural quality of a live, dynamic, present relationship. In the therapeutic relationship both the therapist and the client should be feeling some anxiety about what will happen next. If one or the other is not, then what follows will be a duologue pretending to be a dialogue. Therapist and client will be finding out things they already know. We can only discover something new and develop if we are open and ready for the possibility of finding a new perspective on the world. We have to be prepared to have our views challenged, for our stories to be broken. Dialogue is also connected to an existential understanding of empathy. Since we are connected as well as separate from other people we can never feel what they are feeling, but we can resonate with them much as the strings of a guitar will resonate when a nearby piano is played. But the sound the guitar makes is not the same as the sound the piano made. Our value to the client is our ability to be similar to them, but not the same as them; to be different from them. If we forget our difference we risk either sympathy or identification (Deurzen and Adams 2016) and risk making cooperation into competition, dialogue into duologue or monologue, leaping-ahead to leaping-in and ultimately constraining existential development.

Although dialogue is usually thought of in terms of talking, it is primarily about listening and searching for meaning. The development of dialogue is down to the therapist evaluating how to provide and maintain an optimum amount of challenge and support. Most often this means the therapist is silent, at least at the start of therapy, but it is not always so. If the client needs the therapist just to listen, it is a mistake to talk, and if the client needs the therapist to talk, it is a mistake to be silent. The route from monologue or duologue to dialogue will be different for each relationship and every dialogue simply by virtue of being dynamic and not controlled is at risk of changing from being cooperative to being competitive when one of the participants feels short-changed or disempowered.

It is also important to acknowledge that gaining and losing trust is active rather than passive. We make it happen and an existential therapist will need to know what can go wrong in relationships and what can go right, but more importantly what they can do to make one into the other. They will know that trust will not grow without risk and without being tested. We will know that our clients only trust us when they risk telling us something important and find that when it is treated with respect, interest and understanding, it creates a new sense of hope. In this way they become reconnected with their temporality and regain a sense of a future that has possibilities. If a client is able to experience cooperation and true dialogue in the therapeutic relationship she is more likely to be able to transfer this to her everyday life. All this can only be gained from personal experience and by the same token, if the therapist is unable practice cooperative relationships in their intimate daily life it is unlikely they will be able to do so in their working life. As Nietzsche says, 'You have to be sure of yourself, you have to be standing bravely on your own two feet, otherwise you simply cannot love' (EH III: 5).

Working with freedom, responsibility and choice

Existentially, all that is certain is that we are thrown into and out of life. What we do with the space in between is up to us and this is what Sartre meant when he said that, 'To be free is to be condemned to be free' (2003: 129). We have responsibility for our lives whether we like it or not and although there are many things that we can do nothing about, these are our personal givens, they constitute our facticity and we are responsible for our response to them.

In everyday life we are confronted with choices of where to go, what to buy, who to be with, what word to write next and so on and it is easy to be unduly influenced, and when we are we lose touch with our autonomy. But existentially, these are not choices at all but options, and they all leave us with the same dilemma: which one to commit to. As Kierkegaard says, 'The crucial thing is to find a truth which is truth for me, to find the idea for which I am willing to live and die.' Ultimately there is only one choice, as Hamlet knows: to embrace life or to reject life. The consequence of embracing life is openness to possibility, authenticity; and the consequence of rejecting life is existential guilt, inauthenticity. Rejection leads to despair and powerlessness and an ignorance of our complicity in our own disempowerment. Although always risky, openness leads to an enhanced sense of meaning and purpose, and it also means that we can take the credit for our successes. It is not so much that we make choices and commit to them; we are our choices and commitments. Existentially we die by denying our agency, and we become born by owning it.

Autonomy is a fundamental property of human being. Beauvoir calls it our natural freedom and when Dreyfus says the human being starts Daseining from birth he means autonomy starts from birth and from this moment on, our choices and actions are contingent on our immersion in our context and contribute to the formation of our original choice and project.

Some people, though, have greater constraints on their everyday freedom, and the legal and the familial implications for working with children have already been addressed.

Beauvoir notes that it is the child's metaphysical privilege that enables the child to own his or her natural freedom and that this leads to being an active agent in adulthood. For the child, these will be things like what and who to play with, and how to play, and whether to eat what has been given, and these all feel to the child to be of enormous importance, as all parents know from their own experience. Tantrums, to use a common but pejorative word, are only an indicator of what matters to the child. This means that the only differences between adults and children are in what matters to them (Scalzo 2010). Adults need to remember this; they often forget that children are people too.

Clearly though, when working with anyone, we need to take care not to leap in and what Boss took from Heidegger as being central to therapeutic practice in particular and to human development in general is that when we care for someone what we care for is their autonomy, regardless of their chronological or existential age. One of the questions we have to consider then is, *How much autonomy can this person take on right now?* We are not in any way different from our clients; we just temporarily have a different role with respect to them. As said, we meet each other as 'brothers and sisters in the same dark night' (Vogel 1994: 97). As therapists, we need to know how to adapt and monitor our practice such that an optimum amount of autonomy is present within the relationship, bearing in mind that mistakes will always be made. Indeed, acknowledging we are fallible and that mistakes will always be made is probably the best we can manage.

There is always a tension between acceptance of freedom and denial of freedom, and we need to remember that freedom is not a thing, it cannot be accumulated; freedom is relational being. Discovery, or rather re-discovery of freedom, is therefore always relational. It happens between us and an underlying principle of all existential work is to introduce, or re-introduce, the client to the Law of Existential Consequence (Adams 2013): that when I do something, something follows that I have responsibility for. And that this applies just as much to deliberate acts as to accidental acts.

In this way a link is reinforced between the past, the present and the future, which is to say that only when we discover the meaning of our past, can we be responsible for making our own future. As Laing says we gain a sense of 'continuity in time and a location in space' (1965: 41) and as therapists we have a responsibility to know the meaning of this in our own lives.

It begins when the client realises that, *This is my life now*, or *Anxiety is there to be risked*, or *Although in general nothing is gained by avoidance, the real skill is knowing when to act and when not to act*. The prototype existential dysfunction is when we take responsibility for things we do not have responsibility for and/or to deny responsibility for those things we do have responsibility for. A person is born, then dies and we see our clients at some point between birth and death. Most of them have no idea where. Our task is to find out as much as we can about how past choices led to current actions and future intentions. When the client is able to identify the current meaning of their original project, they will be able to re-own it so that the choice can be revisited and remade. In the process the existential realities of freedom, choice and responsibility come to replace the determinist fantasies of causation and passivity and they stop existentially dying and start existentially living. In this sense, maturity is about understanding what can be changed and what cannot, and then acting on it.

Every age, every period of life, every life-specific dilemma, will give rise to different choices, responsibilities and things to commit to. Information about ages of clients is hard to come by but a recent report on the use of IAPT services (HSCIC 2015) shows proportionally more 18–35-year-olds than 36–64-year-olds. Moreover, that referrals of those above age sixty-five are only 6 per cent of the total. There are many factors that influence this imbalance, and indeed these particular age divisions, and no information is given about what issues each age group brought, only diagnostic categories. But if my own experience over several decades as a therapist in the NHS general practice and in private practice is anything to go by, people aged 25–40 are likely to be preoccupied with issues of career, committing to a partner for life and/or parenthood, and those older will be bringing choices relating to loss and death.

It is common to suppose that the older someone is the more autonomy they have and while this may have some truth to it, we cannot take it as automatic, especially when thinking about the third and fourth ages.

Also, while we may have a faith that clients can be autonomous and self-sufficient in future – it is after all the aim of therapy – we cannot assume anything when they come to see us. Talking about the process of process of therapy, Sartre says that,

> existential psychoanalysis will have to be completely flexible and adapt itself to the slightest observable changes in the subject. Our concern here is to understand what is individual and often even instantaneous. The method which has served for one subject will not necessarily be suitable for another subject or for the same subject at a later period.
>
> (2003: 573)

Denial of freedom, responsibility and autonomy is denial of our humanity and is therefore equivalent to self-destructiveness and in everyday life there are a number of ways this can manifest. We are used to thinking of things like addiction, eating disorders, self-harm, shopping, hoarding and so on as being different but they have more similarities than differences. They are all self-destructive acts in which there is an abdication of personal responsibility in favour of the location of responsibility outside the self, in the outside world, in others, in personal history, or in the substance or action. The uncertainty and risk of the relational world is turned away from in favour of the predictability of the substance or action and even though they may be very active in getting the 'drug', the person's relationship with the 'drug' is passive rather than active. Sometimes this manifests as extreme passivity as in the assertion that *I can't help it; it's the way I am* that serves almost as a determinist justification of passivity.

There is not so much a gender and age difference in their prevalence, as a difference in the way different genders and ages express it. For example, there is much concern about alcohol abuse among young people; it is just as prevalent though less visible among older people and especially so among affluent older people.

What the substance or action does so well is to block out problematic feelings or substitute them with others, and this becomes the organising principle of everyday life. The most problematic emotions are those closest to shame, because they are nearest to a sense of identity and worth as a person. To paraphrase Laing (1965: 41), the anxiety is about feeling they do not have a sense of being an entity with continuity in time and a location in space. A sense of identity and worth starts to form from birth and the person chooses very early to be lived by-the-world, rather than to live in-the-world.

A paradox of all self-destructiveness is that since assertion of autonomy is so important, it feels more important to make what feels like an autonomous choice, even though the choice is ultimately destructive of autonomy.

This is a reason why such conditions are so difficult to treat. The starting point for all therapeutic work has to be that the client volunteers for it and it is this principle that highlights the existential nature of the condition; that in order for therapy to have a chance of success the person has to make a personal decision to enter it and take responsibility for their choice.

Recovery, development, can only start by the person owning that they are powerless to do anything about their situation on their own. This is often known as rock-bottom (Kemp 2013) and one person's rock-bottom is not like another's. It is the beginning of a process of acknowledging that they can choose or not choose their addiction as a way of life. This makes choice central to an existential understanding of addiction (Schaler 1999). Personal meaning and responsibility is also a central though paradoxical principle of twelve-step programmes.

The principal fear in this sort of self-destructiveness is that of success because success means taking personal responsibility for choices, actions and consequences. This is so challenging that an almost automatic reaction is triggered and the person is returned to their previous position of denial and failure. Until the person consistently realises how they are letting themselves down, there is no possibility of change. The emotional and existential reasons for not owning responsibility are very powerful, and evasion and denial will be returned to again and again. The need to establish a trusting relationship with firm boundaries through phenomenological practice is extremely important because without these we will not be able to challenge the evasion and denials effectively.

Another variant of self-destructiveness is when we feel that we lack the power to make our life different. We call this depression and the depressed person will frequently deny their personal power because they fear change and the ultimate fear of change is the fear of death.

Existentially, the paradox of death is that although physical death will kill me and the denial of death will destroy the time I have left, the idea of death will save me in the sense that it will prompt me to live my life more resourcefully. Of these three, the depressed person's response is denial and passivity. This is the paradox of depression, that by waiting passively for things to improve, the depressed person actively contributes to things remaining the same.

In contrast with addiction, depression is largely about a comfortable familiarity with failure. Existentially, depression can be seen as a disturbance of time and temporality, it is about a past of guilt, of lost opportunities, and of being powerless to do anything about it, of a loss of the future. Often due to an unpredicted event, which may simply be time passing, as in the arrival of a birthday with a zero at the end, the belief in the benign movement of time is shaken and substituted with a freezing of time. Time, which had been seen as an inauthentic eternal present, is discovered to be temporality, and the future is seen as beyond their grasp. There is a belief as Cohn says that, 'everything that is possible has already happened. Life is ruled by the shadow of loss – a loss which is not just anticipated but already fact' (1997: 110). One sees oneself only as having had a past. Beauvoir reminds us that nostalgia, which may happen at any age but will be prompted by a landmark of some sort, is the belief that everything good has already happened, and is about the fantasy of a return to a simpler, trouble-free time of freedom without responsibility and the hope that others will serve as a protection from the vicissitudes of existence.

Viktor Frankl (2004) sees depression arising out of the gap between where the person is now and where they want to be, with the depressed person seeing the gap as unbridgeable, whereas the non-depressed person sees it as an exciting challenge. In a sense, both see it accurately – we are never where we want to be – there is always something else to do and life is only complete on death – but their interpretations are different. Depression is therefore self-perpetuating but in a way that the person is unaware of. They do not understand the Law of Consequence, the effect of what they do on their mood. One of our tasks as therapists is to bring this to their notice. Existentially, we seek to enable clients to look at every aspect of their life but particularly the way they are living their lives now and how they regard the future.

Avoidance of responsibility is also a significant feature in close adult relationships. As Sartre says, in managing the otherness, the freedom, of other people, we either tend to dominate, submit or withdraw from relationships, imagining that these solve the fundamental dilemma of relationships; they don't. They only ever work temporarily. These three roles are known colloquially and descriptively as persecutor, victim and rescuer (Karpman 1968; Holden 2013). The person in the persecutor role seeks to persuade or control the other so that they do things 'properly'. But while it may help us to feel good about our ability to get things done, since we do it for our own benefit, the other person's freedom is actually diminished and they feel bullied. They are made into a thing.

The person in the victim role feels and presents themselves as 'done to' by the other and as powerless to stand up to them. While there is a possibility that in restricting our own freedom, a tension may be overcome, it invariably leads to defeatism and despair. We make ourselves into a thing. They look for persecutors to be controlled by and/or rescuers to be rescued by.

The person in the rescuer role makes saving other people their project. While we can feel good about our own capacity for care, since we rescue for our own benefit, the other person's freedom is restricted. In fact the rescuer's only reason for helping others is because it establishes them in a superior position, and as such the rescuer encourages dependency.

The two people often switch roles within a particular dispute and this may give rise to an impression of development and growth, but it is illusory, and any understanding is patchy and temporary. Such a process may happen many times, each exactly the same. There will be an illusion of time passing and moving on but in fact it is just repeated on an endless loop, with no meaningful memory of the other occasions. The word 'role' is used here to reinforce that the role is a choice we take up in order to protect us from the paralysing feeling of nothingness. Although superficially different, what all three roles have in common is that they are all objectifying, and all deny personal responsibility rather than acknowledge the difficulty of trust. While all three roles are all strategies of bad faith, all denials of the Nietzschean spirit, the victim role is often seen as the favoured position, to feel most 'done to', to have the least agency. They are common in most relationships to a greater or lesser extent but particularly so in situations of domestic violence (Adams and Jepson 2013).

The roles are also taken up in co-dependent relationships where one person makes it their project that their partner changes in some way. In fact if their partner did change, it would destabilise the relationship and risk something new happening: a full confrontation with the freedom of intimacy. Addiction is often a strong component in co-dependent relationships and because the person in the rescuer is addicted to helping, they will invariably actively prevent the addict's recovery at the same time as promoting it.

There is particular danger in the rescuer role for psychotherapists because the therapy situation can easily replicate the rescuer–victim relationship with the therapist as the rescuer and the client as the victim to be rescued either from specific others, themselves, or from the givens of existence.

The overall task is always that we need to find a way to live with the existential reality of other people's freedom.

The solution to the dilemma of responsibility and freedom in relationships is not an either/or/neither solution; it is a dialectical both/and solution. As Beauvoir says, 'To will oneself free and to will that there be being are one and the same choice, [and] they both imply the bond of each man with all others' (2015: 70). This is a realisation that like everything else in life, intimacy and trust are difficult but ultimately more rewarding than separation and fear.

Conclusion

One of the many threads that have woven their way through this book has been the one from Kierkegaard that I began with, that life must be lived forwards but understood backwards, because we can never find a solid enough place to look at the whole of life to be able to understand it.

While we do not know what thoughts Kierkegaard had in his last days in his hospital bed, we do know that in general he felt it was important to try to find a truth important enough to live and die for, and that before his breakdown Nietzsche valued struggle above all else, and he also exhorted us to live life as if we would be happy to repeat it, endlessly. And while we only know obliquely what Heidegger's thinking was in his latter years, we do know that Sartre said that a life cannot be assessed until death, after which time it is up to others to assess it. We lose our freedom on death. All we can do, he said, is to keep on doing what we can, knowing that in the grand scale of things it isn't much. Merleau-Ponty, we can imagine, died before he started to think of such things, but we know he was a natural optimist. For Beauvoir, not only was freedom primary, but that it necessarily involved the freedom of others, both present and future, and that for a meaningful life promoting freedom has to be at the core of our projects. She also felt that she had a place from which to understand not just life, but her own life; it was her old age. But she also acknowledged the fundamental relativity of this understanding, suggesting that while an even greater distance is probably necessary to achieve such understanding, it is also impossible to get. This is a given.

An essentialist psychotherapy is one that is based on a model of human development that relies on the principles of biological and environmental determinism, and as such, an essentialist psychotherapy is a technical process of analysis akin to any other natural scientifically based analysis.

But the fact that people are different is not due simply to biological variety – nature – or the complexity of environmental influences – nurture – though these are clearly significant. It is because people are free, have choice and hence are fundamentally unpredictable. It is human freedom that makes all creativity possible, whether in a formal art sense or an informal living sense. It is freedom that allows new things to arise out of old and for problems to be solved dialectically. This means that existentially there can be no universal normative stages of human development, and neither can it be linear or unidirectional. This also means that there will never be an existential theory of human development in the way that there is a psychoanalytic, or a cognitive, or a neurological theory of human development.

Just as the most perfect work of art will never be produced by anyone, and that no true artist thinks they have made the best work they will ever make, such questions will never be solved. It is in our nature to be unfinished projects and when we stop having projects we die, and while we can find out many fascinating things, we need to remember life is a mystery that has no end and we need to acknowledge that there are limits to our knowledge.

Stephen Hawking, who died in March 2018, knew more about time and temporality than almost anyone else. The study of time was his chosen subject area and fifty years before his death he was given two years to live, which prompted him to spend at least as long thinking about temporality as well. He said, 'Remember to look up at the stars and not down at your feet, never give up work, work gives you meaning and purpose and if you are lucky to find love, remember it is there and don't throw it away'.

Therapeutic theories divide roughly into those that aspire to a mastery over life and those that investigate the mystery of life. Also it is often said that there are as many different types of therapies as there are therapeutic relationships, and while this undoubtedly has some truth to it, it is also true that we all have our humanity in common. As Laing says, 'the way we treat each other is the treatment' (Tougas and Shandel 1989). In terms of what makes psychotherapy effective, the polarised debate is between the technical factors on the one hand and the relational factors on the other. While much valuable research is being done and certainly needs to be done, to think that there will ever be an answer to the specific/non-specific factors question is a mistake. This is a technological way of thinking, and our inability to answer the question definitively is not a measure of our incompetence. Indeed, the opposite is true, that if we think we have solved it, we haven't. The ancient Greeks called it hubris. If we were to ever find everything out, it would be a cause for profound and eternal despair and it would be the end of human existence as we know it.

The questions of psychotherapy are the same as the questions of life; people, after all, bring the questions of life to psychotherapy, and while we can delineate some general principles of life, because freedom is not just a given of existence but is also situated, there can therefore be no rules of cause and effect that govern an individual life. This cannot be the task of existential therapy.

What we can do though, and what I have tried to do in this book, is increase our understanding of the general ontological principles that constitute the parameters of human life and therefore of human striving for meaning and purpose.

We are all singular universals and the six philosophers are no exception. They lived their lives by making choices in the face of an unknown future and living with the consequences, and deciding the best thing to do next. As has been said about Kierkegaard, the particular way he chose to live his life enhances his relevance rather than detracts from it and this applies not just to all the other philosophers but to all people, ourselves included.

In increasing our understanding we come to realise we are all future-directed and actively living our lives moment by moment according to the decisions, choices and actions we make in the light of our values and aspirations, and the paradoxes and dilemmas of existence, as well as the prevailing conditions. Monitoring the effects of these decisions, choices and actions allows us to practise and refine the skills of living.

As in life and in psychotherapy then so in this book. When I began this book I had a rough title, which changed a few times in the writing. I also had a reasonably clear idea of what I wanted to say but only a rough plan of how I was going to say it. On more than one occasion the reasonably clear idea became so unclear that I wondered if the project was possible at all. The plan also changed a few times; sections have been started only to be abandoned. Life is full of dead ends that seem like a good idea at the time, and it is only later that it becomes obvious that they would never have worked. Hindsight is a wonderful thing but it can lead to notions of determinism. But, nothing is lost; I now know more than I would otherwise have known about why the other plans did not work.

The book you have just read is the one that I have written now. To apply Nietzsche's ideal of eternal recurrence to this book would suggest, firstly, that I have said everything I wanted to say, and secondly, that if I was to start again I would write exactly the same book. Nietzsche's point, of course, is that although we may aspire to this recurrence, we never achieve it because there is always something else to do, always another struggle. Accordingly, I have a more modest aspiration. Not only have I not said everything I wanted to say, but also if I was to start again I know I would almost certainly write a different book. Life, knowledge, is cumulative and involves gains, losses, sacrifices, dead ends, frustration, occasional moments of clarity, but most of all unexpected change.

I regard the book as a beginning and my hope is that others will read it and expand on it and yes, even change it.

References

Adams, M. (1998) On the Experience and Representation of Space. *Existential Analysis,* 9.1: 2–16.

Adams, M. (2006) Towards an Existential Phenomenological Theory of Human Development. *Existential Analysis,* 17.2: 261–280.

Adams, M. (2010) Where's Daddy? Researching What Parents Do in Children's Picturebooks. *Research in Education,* 3.1: 10–11.

Adams, M. (2013a) *A Concise Introduction to Existential Counselling*. London: Sage.

Adams, M. (2013b) Human Development from an Existential Phenomenological Perspective: Some Thoughts and Considerations. *Existential Analysis,* 24.1: 48–56.

Adams, M. (2014) Human Development and Existential Counselling Psychology, *Counselling Psychology Review*, 29.1: 34–42.

Adams, M. (2016) Existential Therapy as a Skills Learning Process. *Existential Analysis,* 27.1: 58–69.

Adams, M. and Jepson, M. (2013) Working with Relationship Violence and Abuse. In E. van Deurzen and S. Iacovou (eds) *Existential Perspectives on Relationship Therapy*. London: Palgrave.

Adams, M. (2018) Why Me, Why Now? On Discovering That Time Is Passing. In S. Du Plock (ed.) *Case Studies in Existential Therapy*. Ross-on-Wye: PCCS.

Allen, W. (1989) *Crimes and Misdemeanours*. USA: Orion Pictures. Film.

Andrikopoulou, A. (2004) Studying Five-Year-Olds' Understanding of the Components of Death. *Educational and Child Psychology,* 21: 41–59.

Appleyard, J. (1991) *Becoming a Reader: The Experience of Fiction from Childhood to Adulthood*. Cambridge: Cambridge University Press.

Arendt, H. (1998) *The Human Condition*. Chicago, IL: University of Chicago (First published 1958).

Ariès, P. (1962) *Centuries of Childhood: A Social History of Family Life* (trans. R. Baldick). New York: Bantam (First published 1960).

Armstrong, K. (2006) *A Short History of Myth*. London: Canongate.

Bachelard, G. (1969) *The Poetics of Space*. London: Beacon.

BACP (2017) Older People Are Not Getting the Mental Health Support They Deserve. www.bacp.co.uk/news/2017/1-october-2017-older-people-are-not-getting-the/, Accessed 13/03/2018.

Bair, D. (1990) *Simone de Beauvoir: A Biography*. New York: Simon and Schuster.

Bakewell, S. (2016) *At the Existentialist Café: Freedom, Being, and Apricot Cocktails*. London: Chatto and Windus.

Baltes, P.B. (1987) Theoretical Propositions of Life Span Developmental Psychology: On the Dynamic Between Growth and Decline. *Developmental Psychology*, 23: 611–626.

Barker, M. (2011) De Beauvoir, Bridget Jones' Pants and Vaginismus. *Existential Analysis,* 22.2: 203–217.

Barnes, H. (1974) *Sartre*. London: Quartet.

Barnes, H. (1993) Sartre's Concept of the Self. In K. Hoeller (ed.) *Studies in Existential Psychology and Psychiatry: Sartre and Psychology*. New Jersey: Humanities Press.

Barnes, H. (1997) *The Story I Tell Myself: A Venture in Existentialist Autobiography*. Chicago, IL: University of Chicago Press.

Barnett, L. (ed.) (2008) *When Death Enters the Therapeutic Space: Existential Perspectives in Psychotherapy and Counselling*. London: Routledge.

Bateson, G. (1972) *Steps to an Ecology of Mind*. New York: Ballantine.

Baumeister, R. (1992) *Meanings of Life*. New York: Guilford.

Beauvoir, S. de (1960) *The Mandarins* (trans. L. Friedman). London: Fontana and Collins (First published 1954).

Beauvoir, S. de (1963) *Memoirs of a Dutiful Daughter* (trans. J. Kirkup). Harmondsworth: Penguin.

Beauvoir, S. de (1966) *The Prime of Life* (trans. P. Green). London: Penguin.

Beauvoir, S. de (1968) *Force of Circumstance* (trans. R. Howard). Harmondsworth: Penguin.

Beauvoir, S. de (1969) *A Very Easy Death* (trans. P. O'Brian). London: Penguin (First published 1964).

Beauvoir, S. de (1972) *The Coming of Age* (trans. P. O'Brian). New York: G.P. Putnam's (First published 1958).

Beauvoir, S. de (1977) *All Said and Done* (trans. P. O'Brian). London: Penguin.

Beauvoir, S. de (1979) Interview with Simone de Beauvoir. *Signs: Journal of Women in Culture and Society* 5: 224–236.

Beauvoir, S. de (1985) *Adieux: A Farewell to Sartre* (trans. P. O'Brian). London: Penguin.

Beauvoir, S. de (1990) *The Blood of Others* (trans. R. Senhouse). London: Penguin (First published 1958).

Beauvoir, S. de (1991) *Letters to Sartre* (trans. Q. Hoare). London: Radius (First published 1990).

Beauvoir, S. de (1997) *The Second Sex* (trans. H. Parshley). London: Vintage (First published 1949).

Beauvoir, S. de (1999) *She Came to Stay* (trans. Y. Moyse and R. Senhouse). New York: Norton (First published 1943).

Beauvoir, S. de (2009) *The Second Sex* (trans. C. Borde and S. Mavany-Chevallier). London: Cape (First published 1949).

Beauvoir, S. de (2015) *The Ethics of Ambiguity* (trans. B. Frechtman). New York: Citadel (First published 1947).

Becker, C. (1992) *Living and Relating. An Introduction to Phenomenology*. London: Sage.

Becker, E. (1973) *The Denial of Death*. New York: Free Press Paperbacks.

Berger, J. (1972) *Ways of Seeing*. London: BBC and Penguin.

Bergoffen, D. (Fall 2015 Edition) Simone de Beauvoir. In Edward N. Zalta (ed.) *The Stanford Encyclopedia of Philosophy*. http://plato.stanford.edu/archives/fall2015/entries/beauvoir/, Accessed 13/03/2018.

Bertstein, D. and Rubin, D. (eds) (2012) *Understanding Autobiographical Memory: Theories and Approaches*. Cambridge: Cambridge University Press.

Binswanger, L. (1975) *Being-in-the-World: Selected Papers of Ludwig Binswanger*, edited by J. Needleman. London: Souvenir.

Blanchflower, D.G. and. Oswald, A.J. (2007) *Is Well-Being U-Shaped Over the Life Cycle?* Bonn: IZA.

Boss, M. (1988) Martin Heidegger's Zollikon Seminars (trans. B. Kenny). In K. Hoeller (ed.) *Review of Existential Psychology and Psychiatry: Heidegger & Psychology*. XVI: 7–20 (Seattle, WA).

Boss, M. (1994) *Existential Foundations of Medicine & Psychology* (trans. S. Conway and A. Cleaves). Northvale, NJ: Jason Aronson (First published 1979).

Bowlby, J. (1969) *Attachment and Loss*. Vol. 1. Harmondsworth: Pelican.

Bowlby, J. (1988) *A Secure Base*. London: Tavistock.

Boyd, W. (2003) *Any Human Heart*. London: Penguin.

Boyd, W. (2010) William Boyd on filming Any Human Heart. *The Telegraph*, 5 November, www.telegraph.co.uk/culture/tvandradio/8109938/William-Boyd-on-filming-Any-Human-Heart.html, Accessed 13/03/2018.

Brandon, S., Boakes, J., Glaser, D., Green, R., MacKeith, J. and Whewell, P. (1997) Reported Recovered Memories of Child Sexual Abuse: Recommendations for Good Practice and Implications for Training, Continuing Professional Development and Research. *Psychiatric Bulletin*, 21.10: 663–665.

Briod, M. (1989) A Phenomenological Approach to Child Development. In S. Halling and R. Valle (eds) *Existential Phenomenological Perspectives in Psychology*. New York: Plenum.

Buber, M. (1958) *I and Thou* (trans. G. Smith). Edinburgh: Clark.

Bühler, C. and Massarik, F. (1968) *The Course of the Human Life: A Study of Goals in a Humanistic Perspective*. New York: Springer.

Burman, E. (2008) *Deconstructing Developmental Psychology*, 2nd edn. London: Routledge.

Burston, D. (2003) Scheler, Nietzsche and Social Psychology. *Existential Analysis*, 14: 22–13.

Butler, R.N. (1969) Age-ism: Another Form of Bigotry. The Gerontologist, 9: 243-246.

Byock, I. (2002) The Meaning and Value of Death. *Journal of Palliative Medicine*, 5.2: 279–288.

Camus, A. (1996) *Notebooks 1935–1942* (trans. P. Thody). New York: Marlowe.

Cannon, B. (1991) *Sartre and Psychoanalysis: An Existentialist Challenge to Clinical Metatheory*. Kansas: University of Kansas.

Cannon, B. (1999) Sartre and Existential Psychoanalysis. *The Humanistic Psychologist*, 27.1: 23–50.

Carman, T. (2004) *The Cambridge Companion to Merleau-Ponty*. Cambridge: Cambridge University Press.

Carman, T. (2006) *Merleau-Ponty*. Abingdon: Routledge.

Chaplin, C. (1936) *Modern Times*. United Artists. Film.

Chessick, R.D. (1996) Heidegger's 'Authenticity' in the Psychotherapy of Adolescence. *American Journal of Psychotherapy*, 50.2: 208–216.

Cleary, S. (2015) *Existentialism and Romantic Love*. New York: Palgrave Macmillan.

Cohler, B.J. (1982) Personal Narrative and Life Course. In P. Baltes and O.G. Brim (eds) *Life Span Development and Behaviour,* 4: 206–241. New York: Haworth.
Cohen-Solal, A. (1987) *Sartre: A Life*. London: Heinemann.
Cohn, H. (1997) *Existential Thought and Therapeutic Practice*. London: Sage.
Cohn, H. (1998) John Bowlby's Concern with the Actual Phenomenological Aspects of Attachment Theory. *Existential Analysis,* 9.1: 43–51.
Cohn, H. (2002) *Heidegger and the Roots of Existential Psychotherapy*. London: Continuum.
Collins, R. (2014) The Reluctant Therapist?: The Experience of Working Therapeutically with the Older Client, PhD thesis, University of Wales. http://ethos.bl.uk/OrderDetails.do?uin=uk.bl.ethos.646081, Accessed 13/03/2018.
Cooper, D. (1967) *Psychiatry and Anti-Psychiatry*. London: Routledge.
Cooper, M. (2015) *Existential Psychotherapy and Counselling: Contributions to a Pluralistic Practice*. London: Sage.
Cooper, M. and Adams, M. (2005) Death. In E. van Deurzen and C. Arnold-Baker (eds) *Existential Perspectives on Human Issues: A Handbook for Therapeutic Practice*. Basingstoke: Palgrave Macmillan.
Cooper, M. and McLeod, J. (2010) *Pluralistic Counselling and Psychotherapy*. London: Sage.
Cox, G. (2009a) *How to Be an Existentialist or How to Get Real, Get a Grip and Stop Making Excuses*. London: Continuum.
Cox, G. (2009b) *Sartre and Fiction*. London: Continuum.
Crawford, M. (2010a) *The Case for Working with Your Hands or Why Office Work is Bad for Us and Fixing Things Feels Good*. London: Penguin.
Crawford, M. (2010b) The Limits of Neuro-Talk. In J.J. Giordano and B. Gordijn (eds) *Scientific and Philosophical Perspectives in Neuroethics*. Cambridge: Cambridge University Press.
Crawford, M. (2016) *The World Beyond Your Head: How to Flourish in an Age of Distraction*. London: Penguin.
Dante Alighieri (1308) *The Convivio*. London: Forgotten Books.
Davidson, J. (2000) A Phenomenology of Fear: Merleau-Ponty and Agoraphobic Life-Worlds. *Sociology of Health and Illness,* 22.5: 640–660.
DeCasper, A., Lecanuet, J., Maugais, R., Graniere-DeFerre, C. and Busnel, M. (1994) Fetal Reactions to Recurrent Maternal Speech. *Infant Behavior and Development,* 17: 159–164.
Denne, J.M. and Thompson, N.L. (1991) The Experience of Transition to Meaning and Purpose in Life. *Journal of Phenomenological Psychology,* 22: 109–133.
Deurzen, E. van (2008) *Psychotherapy and the Quest for Happiness*. London: Sage.
Deurzen, E. van (2010) *Everyday Mysteries: Existential Dimensions of Psychotherapy*. London: Routledge.
Deurzen, E. van (2015) *Paradox and Passion in Psychotherapy: An Existential Approach*. Chichester: Wiley.
Deurzen, E. van and Adams, M. (2016) *Skills in Existential Counselling and Psychotherapy*. London: Sage.
Deutscher, P. (2003) Beauvoir's Old Age. In C. Card (2003) *The Cambridge Companion to Simone de Beauvoir*. Cambridge: Cambridge University Press..

Dimattia, G. and Regazzo, L.D. (1995) The Sense of Death in Childhood: An Investigation Among Primary School Teachers in Padua and the Province of Veneto. *Existential Analysis,* 6.2: 141–157.

Dreyfus, H.L. (1991) *Being-in-the-World: A Commentary on Heidegger's Being and Time, Division I.* Cambridge, MA: MIT Press.

Dreyfus, H.L. and Wrathall, M. (2014) *Skillful Coping: Essays on the Phenomenology of Everyday Perception and Action.* Oxford: Oxford University Press.

Edwards, W. and Milton, M. (2014) Retirement Therapy? Older People's Experiences of Existential Therapy Relating to their Transition to Retirement, *Counselling Psychology Review,* 29.2: 43–53.

Edwards, M. and Titman, P. (2010) *Promoting Psychological Well-Being in Children with Acute and Chronic Illness.* London: JKP.

Erikson, E. (1950) *Childhood and Society.* New York: Norton.

Fairbairn, W.R.D. (1952) *Psychoanalytic Studies of the Personality.* London: Routledge.

Firestone, R.W. (2015) The Ultimate Resistance. *Journal of Humanistic Psychology,* 55: 77–101.

Fisher, L. (2000) Phenomenology and Feminism: Perspectives on their Relation. In L. Embree (ed.) *Feminist Phenomenology.* Dordrecht: Kluwer.

Fitzgerald, B. (2005) An Existential View of Adolescent Development *Adolescence,* 40.160: 793–799.

Fivush, R. (2013) *Autobiographical Memory and the Construction of a Narrative Self.* Haden, CA: Routledge.

Forster, P. and Sutton, I. (eds) (1989) *Daughters of de Beauvoir.* London: The Women's Press.

Fourcher, L. (1981) A Developmental Scheme is a 'Bad Dialectic'. *Human Development,* 24: 172–194.

Frankl, V. (2000) *Man's Search for Ultimate Meaning.* New York: Perseus.

Frankl, V. (2004) *Man's Search for Meaning.* London: Rider (First published 1946).

Freadman, R. (2001) *Threads of Life: Autobiography and the Will.* Chicago, IL: Chicago University Press.

Frears, S. (2000) *High Fidelity.* UK/USA: Dogstar Films.

Freud, S. (1911) *Two Principles of Mental Functioning.* SE12. London: Hogarth.

Freud, S. (1923) *The Ego and the Id.* SE19. London: Hogarth.

Fry, E. (1966) *Cubism.* London: Thames and Hudson.

Fukuyama, F. (1992) *The End of History and the Last Man.* London: Penguin.

Gallagher, S and Meltzoff, A.N. (1996) The Earliest Sense of Self and Others: Merleau-Ponty and Recent Developmental Studies. *Philosophical Quarterly,* 9: 211–233.

Gee, P. (2011) 'Approach and Sensibility': A Personal Reflection on Analysis and Writing using Interpretative Phenomenological Analysis. *Qualitative Methods in Psychology Bulletin,* 11: 8–22 (British Psychological Society).

Gendlin, E. (1996) *Focusing-Oriented Psychotherapy: A Manual of the Experiential Method.* New York: Guilford.

Gennari, G. (1958) *Simone de Beauvoir.* Paris: Éditions Universitaires.

Gibson, C. (2017) Authentic Love and the Mother-Child Relationship. *Sartre Studies International,* 23.1: 60–79.

Goehr, L. (2004) Understanding the Engaged Philosopher: On Politics, Philosophy, and Art. In T. Carman (ed.) *The Cambridge Companion to Merleau-Ponty*. Cambridge: Cambridge University Press.

Gothlin, E. (2003) Reading Simone de Beauvoir with Martin Heidegger. In C. Card (ed.) *The Cambridge Companion to Simone de Beauvoir*. Cambridge: Cambridge University Press.

Graves, R. (1960) *The Greek Myths*, Vol 2. London: Penguin.

Gray, J.G. (1967) The Problem of Death in Modern Philosophy. In N.A. Scott Jr. (ed.) *The Modern Vision of Death*. Richmond, VA: John Knox Press.

Grollman, E.A. (ed.) (1992) *Explaining Death to Children*. Boston, MA: Beacon Press.

Grosholz, E. (2004) *The Legacy of Simone de Beauvoir*. Oxford: Oxford University Press.

Grotstein, J.S. and Rinsley, D.B. (eds) (1994) *Fairbairn and the Origins of Object Relations*. London: Free Association.

Gould, R. (1979) *Transformations: Growth and Change in Adult Life*. New York: Simon and Schuster.

Habermas, T. and Paha, C. (2001) The Development of Coherence in Adolescents' Life Narratives. *Narrative Inquiry*, 11: 35–54.

Hagen, R.M. and Hagen, R. (2001) *15th Century Paintings*. London: Taschen.

Hare, D. (2002) 'Why Fabulate?', *The Guardian*, 2 February 2002. www.theguardian.com/education/2002/feb/02/socialsciences.highereducation1

Harrison, R.P. (2014) *Juvenescence: A Cultural History of Our Age*. London: University of Chicago Press.

Heidegger, M. (1962) *Being and Time* (trans. J. McQuarrie). Oxford: Blackwell (First published 1958).

Heidegger, M. (1971) *Poetry, Language, Thought* (trans. A. Hofstadter). London: Harper and Row.

Heidegger, M. (1977) *The Question Concerning Technology and Other Essays* (trans. W. Lovitt). New York and London: Garland Publishing (First published 1954).

Heidegger, M. (1979) *Nietzsche* (trans. D. Krell). New York: Harper and Row (First published 1961).

Heidegger, M. (1998) *Pathmarks*. W. McNeill (ed.) Cambridge: Cambridge University Press (First published 1967).

Heidegger, M. (2001) *Zollikon Seminars: Protocols – Conversations – Letters*. M. Boss (ed.) (trans. R. Askay and F. Mayr). Evanston, IL: Northwestern University Press.

Heidegger, M. (2014) *Introduction to Metaphysics* (trans. G. Fried and R. Polt). London: Yale (First published 1929).

Heinämaa, S. (2003) The Body as Instrument and as Expression. In C. Card (ed.) *The Cambridge Companion to Simone de Beauvoir*. Cambridge: Cambridge University Press.

Higgs, P. and Gilliard, C. (2015) *Rethinking Old Age: Theorising the Fourth Age*. London: Palgrave.

Hill, A. and Brettle, A. (2006) Counselling Older People: What Can We Learn from Research Evidence?, *Journal of Social Work Practice*, 20.3: 281–297.

Holden, C. (2013) *The Drama Triangle*. Kindle edition.
Hollingdale, R.J. (1999) *Nietzsche: The Man and his Philosophy*. Cambridge: Cambridge University Press.
Holmes, J. (2001) *The Search for the Secure Base: Attachment Theory and Psychotherapy*. Hove: Routledge.
HSCIC (Health & Social Care Information Centre) (2015) *Psychological Therapies, Annual Report on the Use of IAPT Services: England – 2014/15 Experimental Statistics*. London: HSCIC. www.gov.uk/government/statistics/psychological-therapies-annual-report-on-the-use-of-iapt-services-england-201415, Accessed 13/03/2018.
Huenemann, C. (2013) Nietzsche's Illness. In K. Gemes and J. Richardson (eds) *The Oxford Handbook of Nietzsche*. Oxford: Oxford University Press.
Ioannou, A. (2017) Existential Time-Limited Therapy: An Interpretative Phenomenological Analysis of the Experience of Existential Counselling Psychologists and Psychotherapists Providing Therapy in Time-Limited Contexts, DProf thesis, University of Middlesex http://eprints.mdx.ac.uk/21954/1/AIoannou thesis.pdf Accessed 07/06/2018.
Jaques, E. (1965) Death and the Mid-Life Crisis. *International Journal of Psychoanalysis*, 46: 502–505.
Jaspers, K. (1932) Boundary Situations (trans. E.B. Ashton). In *Philosophy*, Vol. 2. Chicago, IL: The University of Chicago Press.
Jeffries R. (2000) The Disappearing Counsellor. *Counselling* 11.8: 478–481
Jenkinson, M. and Adams, M. (2007) The Ontology of Change: Dilemma and Tragedy as Gateways to Deeper Meaning. *Existential Analysis,* 18.2: 230–246.
Johnson, W. (2013) Wilko Johnson: 'Terminal Cancer Has Made Me Feel Alive'. *BBC News*, 25 January, www.bbc.co.uk/news/entertainment-arts-21187740, Accessed 13/03/2018.
Johnstone, L. (2000) *Users and Abusers of Psychiatry*. London: Routledge.
Jung, C.G. (1934) *Modern Man in Search of a Soul*. London: Kegan Paul.
Kagan, J. (1984) *The Nature of the Child*. New York: Basic Books.
Kampusch, N. (2010) *3,096 Days*. London: Penguin.
Kane, B. (1979) Children's Concepts of Death. *The Journal of Genetic Psychology: Research and Theory on Human Development*, 134: 141–153.
Karban, B. (2017) Leaping-In and Leaping-Ahead: An Exploration of Heidegger's Notion of Solicitude. *Existential Analysis,* 28.2: 106–117.
Karpman, S. (1968) Fairy Tales and Script Drama Analysis. *Transactional Analysis Bulletin*. 26.7: 39–43.
Kaufmann, W. (1950) *Nietzsche: Philosopher, Psychologist, Antichrist*. Princeton, NJ: Princeton University Press.
Kearney, R. (2010) Merleau-Ponty and the Sacramentality of the Flesh. In K. Semonovitch and N. DeRoo (eds) *Merleau-Ponty at the Limits of Art, Religion, and Perception*. London: Continuum.
Keenan, T. and Evans, S. (2009) *An Introduction to Child Development*. London: Sage.
Kemp, R. (2013) Rock-Bottom as an Event of Truth. *Existential Analysis*, 24.1: 106–117.

Kenyon, B. (2001) Current Research in Children's Conceptions of Death: A Critical Review. *Omega: Journal of Death and Dying*, 43: 63–91.
Kewell, H. (2017) Waiting for the Southsea Bus. *Therapy Today*, 28.4: 20–24.
Kidd, D. and Castano, E. (2013) Reading Literary Fiction Improves Theory of Mind. *Sciencexpress*. http://science.sciencemag.org/content/sci/suppl/2013/10/03/science.1239918.DC1/1239918.Kidd.SM.revision1.pdf, Accessed 13/03/2018.
Kierkegaard, S. (1940) *Stages on Life's Way* (trans. E. Hong and H. Hong). Princeton, NJ: Princeton University Press (First published 1845).
Kierkegaard, S. (1941) *Concluding Unscientific Postscript* (trans. D. Swenson and W. Lowrie). Princeton, NJ: Princeton University Press (First published 1846).
Kierkegaard, S. (1946) *Works of Love* (trans. D. Swenson and L. Swenson). Princeton, NJ: Princeton University Press (First published 1847).
Kierkegaard, S. (1962) The *Point of View for My Work as an Author* (trans. W. Lowrie). New York: Torch (First published 1851).
Kierkegaard, S. (1976) Søren *Kierkegaard's Journals and Papers – Volume 1* (ed. and trans. H. Hong). Bloomington, IN: Indiana University Press.
Kierkegaard, S. (1980) *The Sickness unto Death* (ed. and trans. H. Hong and E. Hong). Princeton, NJ: Princeton University Press (First published 1849).
Kierkegaard, S. (1981) *The Concept of Anxiety* (trans. R. Thomte). Princeton, NJ: Princeton University Press (First published 1844).
Kierkegaard, S. (1983) *Fear and Trembling/Repetition* (ed. and trans. H. Hong and E. Hong). Princeton, NJ: Princeton University Press (First published 1843).
Kierkegaard, S. (1992) *Either/Or* (trans. A. Hannay). London: Penguin (First published 1843).
Kierkegaard, S. (1996) *Papers and Journals*. (Selected and trans. A. Hannay). Harmondsworth: Penguin.
King, R. (2017) *Mad Enchantment: Claude Monet and the Painting of the Water Lilies*. London: Bloomsbury.
Klein, M. (1946) Notes on Some Schizoid Mechanisms. In Mitchell, J. (1986) (ed.) *The Selected Melanie Klein*. London: Penguin.
Knowles, R.T. (1986) *Human Development and Human Possibility: Erikson in the Light of Heidegger*. Lanham, MD: UPA.
Kraemer, S. (1995) What are Fathers for? In C. Burck and B. Speed (1995) (eds) *Gender Power and Relationships*. London: Routledge.
La Rochefoucauld (1959) *Maxims* (trans. L. W. Tancock). Harmondsworth: Penguin.
Laing, R.D. (1965) *The Divided Self*. Harmondsworth: Penguin.
Laing, R.D. (1967) *The Politics of Experience*. Harmondsworth: Penguin.
Laing, R.D. and Esterson, D. (1964) *Sanity, Madness, and the Family*. London: Tavistock.
Laing, R.D. (1970) *Knots*. London: Penguin.
Laing, R.D. (1971) *Self and Others*. Harmondsworth: Penguin.
Langdridge, D. (2005) 'The Child's Relations with Others' – Merleau-Ponty, Embodiment and Psychotherapy. *Existential Analysis*, 16.1: 87–99.
Langdridge, D. (2007) *Phenomenological Psychology: Theory, Research and Method*. Harlow: Pearson.

Laslett, P. (1989) *Fresh Map of Life: Emergence of the Third Age*. London: Weidenfeld & Nicolson.
Lee, K., Volans, P.J. and Gregory, N. (2003) Trainee clinical psychologists' views on recruitment to work with older people. *Ageing and Society* 23.1: 83–97.
Lee, D. (2017) *'How Long Will I Love You?' – Sex and Intimacy in Later Life*. Report. University of Manchester Institute for Collaborative Research on Ageing. www.manchester.ac.uk/discover/news/sexual-health-older-people, Accessed 13/03/2018.
Leibniz, G. von (2012) The Principles of Nature and Grace, based on Reason. In *Discourse on Metaphysics and Other Writings* (ed. P. Loptson, trans. R. Latta and G.R. Montgomery). Peterborough, ON: Broadview Press (First published 1714).
Levinson, D. (1980) *The Seasons of a Man's Life*. New York: Knopf.
Levinson, D. (1996) *The Seasons of a Woman's Life*. New York: Knopf.
Lilar, S. (1969) *Le Malentendu du Deuxième Sexe*. Paris: PUF.
Lowrie, W. (1942) *A Short Life of Kierkegaard*. Princeton, NJ: Princeton University Press.
Lymer, J. (2011) Merleau-Ponty and the Affective Maternal-Foetal Relation. *Parrhesia*, 13: 126–143.
McAdams, D.P. (1993) *The Stories we Live by: Personal Myths and the Making of the Self*. New York: The Guilford Press.
McLean, K.C. (2005) Late Adolescent Identity Development: Narrative Meaning Making and Memory Telling. *Developmental Psychology,* 41.4: 683–691.
McLean, K.C. (2015) *The Co-authored Self: Family Stories and the Construction of Personal Identity*. Oxford: Oxford University Press.
Macquarrie, J. (1972) *Existentialism*. London: Penguin.
Malette, J. and Oliver, L. (2006) Retirement and Existential Meaning in the Older Adult: A Qualitative Study Using Life Review. *Counselling, Psychotherapy, and Health*, 2.1: 30–49.
Marcia. (1980) Identity in Adolescence. In J. Adelson (ed.) *Handbook of Adolescent Psychology*. New York: Wiley.
Maslow, A.H. (1962) *Towards a Psychology of Being*. Princeton, NJ: Van Nostrand.
May, R. (1950) *The Meaning of Anxiety*. New York: Ronald Press.
Mazis, G. (2016) *Merleau-Ponty and the Face of the World: Silence, Ethics, Imagination, and Poetic Ontology*. New York: SUNY Press.
Mehler, J., Juszyk, P., Lambertz, G., Halsted, N., Bertoncini, J. and Amiel-Tison, C. (1988) A Precursor of Language Acquisition in Young Infants. *Cognition,* 29: 143–178.
Mendelson, E. (2007) *The Things That Matter: What Seven Classic Novels Have to Say about the Stages of Life*. New York: Pantheon.
Merleau-Ponty, M. (1960) *Signs* (trans. R. McCleary). Evanston, IL: Northwestern University Press.
Merleau-Ponty, M. (1963) *The Structure of Behavior* (trans. A. Fisher). Boston, MA: Beacon Press (First published 1942).
Merleau-Ponty, M. (1964a) The Child's Relations with Others (trans. W. Cobb). In *The Primacy of Perception*. Evanston, IL: Northwestern University Press.

Merleau-Ponty, M. (1964b) Eye and Mind (trans. C. Dallery). In *The Primacy of Perception*. Evanston, IL: Northwestern University Press.
Merleau-Ponty, M. (1968) *The Visible and the Invisible* (Studies in Phenomenology and Existential Philosophy). Evanston, IL: Northwestern University Press.
Merleau-Ponty, M. (1973) *Adventures of the Dialectic*. Evanston, IL: Northwestern University Press (First published 1955).
Merleau-Ponty, M. (2002) *The Phenomenology of Perception* (trans. C. Smith). London: Routledge Classics (First published 1945).
Merleau-Ponty, M. (2010) *Child Psychology and Pedagogy* (trans. T. Welsh). Evanston, IL: Northwestern University Press.
Miller, S.C. (2001) The Lived Experience of Doubling: Simone de Beauvoir's Phenomenology of Old Age. In W. O'Brien and L. Embree (eds) *The Existential Phenomenology of Simone de Beauvoir*. Dordrecht: Kluwer.
Mills, J. (1997) The False Dasein: From Heidegger to Sartre and Psychoanalysis. *Journal of Phenomenological Psychology*, 28.1: 42–65.
Moi, T. (1994) *Simone de Beauvoir: The Making of an Intellectual Woman*. Oxford: Blackwell.
Moi, T. (2010) The Adulteress Wife. Review of The Second Sex by Simone de Beauvoir (trans. C. Borde and S. Mavany-Chevallier). *London Review of Books*, 32.3: 3–6.
Montaigne, Michel de. (1580) Of the Education of Children (trans. C. Cotton). https://toleratedindividuality.files.wordpress.com/2015/11/montaigne_essays.pdf, Accessed 13/03/2018.
Morrison, B. (2006) *And When Did You Last See Your Father*. London: Granta.
Munk, K.P. (2010) New Aspects of Late Life Depression. *Nordic Psychology*, 62.2: 1.
Nabokov, V. (1999) *Speak, Memory*. London: David Campbell.
Nehamas, A. (1985) *Nietzsche: Life and Literature*. Cambridge, MA: Harvard University Press.
Nelson, T.D. (2011) Ageism: The Strange Case of Prejudice Against the Older You. In R.L. Weiner (ed.) *Disability and Aging Discrimination*, 37–47. New York: Springer.
Neiman, S. (2014) *Why Grow Up?* London: Penguin.
Neto, F. (2012) Perceptions of Love and Sex Across The Adult Life Span. *Journal of Social and Personal Relationships*, 29.6: 760–775.
Nietzsche, F. (1968) *The Will to Power* (trans. W. Kaufmann and R.J. Hollingdale). London: Penguin (First published 1895).
Nietzsche, F. (1969) *On the Genealogy of Morals* (trans. W. Kaufmann and R.J. Hollingdale). London: Penguin (First published 1887).
Nietzsche, F. (1990) *Twilight of the Idols* (trans. R.J. Hollingdale). London: Penguin (First published 1888).
Nietzsche, F. (1993) *The Birth of Tragedy* (trans. S. Whiteside). London: Penguin (First published 1872).
Nietzsche, F. (1996) *Human, All Too Human: A Book for Free Spirits* (trans. R.J. Hollingdale). Cambridge: Cambridge University Press (First published 1878).
Nietzsche, F. (2001) *The Gay Science* (ed. B. Williams trans. J. Nauckhoff). Cambridge: Cambridge University Press (First published 1882).

Nietzsche, F. (2006a) *Thus Spoke Zarathustra* (ed. and trans. A. del Caro). Cambridge: Cambridge University Press (First published 1883).

Nietzsche, F. (2006b) *Beyond Good and Evil* (trans. W. Kaufmann). London: Vintage (First published 1886).

Nietzsche, F. (2007) *Ecce Homo* (trans. D. Large). Oxford: Oxford University Press (First published 1888).

Noppe, I.C. and Noppe, L.D. (2004) Adolescent Experiences with Death: Letting Go of Immortality. *Journal of Mental Health Counseling,* 26: 2.

O'Byrne, A. (2010) *Natality and Finitude*. Indiana: Indiana University Press.

ONS (Office of National Statistics). (2016) *At What Age is Personal Well-Being the Highest?* www.ons.gov.uk/peoplepopulationandcommunity/wellbeing/articles/measuringnationalwellbeing/apr2017, Accessed 13/03/2018.

Powell, A. (2005) *A Dance to the Music of Time.* (12 vols.) London: Arrow.

Putnam, H.W. (1999) *The Threefold Cord: Mind, Body, and World*. New York: Columbia University Press.

Quinodoz, D. (2004) *Growing Old: A Journey of Self-Discovery* (trans. D. Alcorn). London: Routledge.

Randall, W.L. and McKim, A.E. (2008) *Reading our Lives: The Poetics of Growing Old*. Oxford: Oxford University Press.

Reuther, B. (2014) On Our Everyday Being: Heidegger and Attachment Theory. *Journal of Theoretical and Philosophical Psychology,* 34: 101–115.

Richards, C., Barker, M. and Lenihan, P. (eds) (2013) *Sexuality and Gender for Counsellors, Psychologists and Health Professionals: A Practical Guide*. London: Sage.

Rothko, M. (1987) *Mark Rothko*. London: Tate Gallery Publications.

Rousseau, J.J. (1979) *Émile, or On Education* (trans. A. Bloom). New York: Basic Books.

Roustang, F. (1986) *Dire Mastery: Discipleship from Freud to Lacan* (trans. N. Lukacher). Arlington, VA: American Psychiatric Press.

Rowley, H. (2006) *Tête-à-Tête: The Tumultuous Lives and Loves of Simone de Beauvoir and Jean-Paul Sartre*. London: Harper.

RSPH (Royal Society for Public Health) (2018) *That Age Old Question: How Attitudes to Ageing Affect our Health and Wellbeing*. London: RSPH/Calouste Gulbenkian Foundation. www.rsph.org.uk/our-work/policy/older-people/that-age-old-question.html, Accessed 10/06/2018

Rycroft, C. (1972) *A Critical Dictionary of Psychoanalysis*. London: Penguin.

Ryle, G. (1949) *The Concept of Mind*. London: Heinemann.

Safranski, R. (1998) *Martin Heidegger: Between Good and Evil*. Cambridge, MA: Harvard University Press.

Salomé, L. (2001) *Nietzsche* (trans. S. Mandel). Urbana: University of Illinois Press (First published 1894).

Sartre, J.-P. (1951) *The Chips Are Down* (trans. L. Varése). London: Rider.

Sartre, J.-P. (1955) *Dirty Hands* (trans. L. Abel). New York: Vintage Books (First published 1948).

Sartre, J.-P. (1964) *Words* (trans. B. Frechtman). New York: George Braziller.

Sartre, J.-P (1967) *Baudelaire* (trans. M. Turnell). New York: New Directions.

Sartre, J.-P. (1968) *Search for a Method* (trans. H.E. Barnes). New York: Vintage (First published 1960).
Sartre, J.-P. (1973a) *Existentialism and Humanism* (trans. P. Mairet). London: Methuen (First published 1946).
Sartre, J.-P. (1973b) *Penguin Plays: Altona, Men without Shadows, The Flies* (trans. S. Gilbert). London: Penguin (First published 1943/1959).
Sartre, J.-P. (1977) *Life/Situations. Essays Written and Spoken* (trans. P. Auster and L. Davis). New York: Pantheon Books (First published 1975).
Sartre, J.-P. (1979) Between Existentialism and Marxism. *Situations, 8–9* (trans. J. Mathews). New York: Morrow Quill (First published 1974).
Sartre, J.-P. (1981) *The Family Idiot* (trans. C. Cosman). Chicago, IL: University of Chicago (First published 1971–72).
Sartre, J.-P. (1983) *Saint Genet: Actor and Martyr* (trans. B. Frechtman). New York: Braziller (First published 1952).
Sartre, J.-P. (1985) *The Freud Scenario* (ed. J.-B. Pontalis and trans. Q. Hoare). London: Verso.
Sartre, J.-P. (1990) *In Camera and Other Plays* (trans. S. Gilbert). London: Penguin (First published 1944).
Sartre, J.-P. (1991) *Critique of Dialectical Reason, Vol.2, The Intelligibility of History* (trans. Q. Hoare). London: Verso (First published 1985).
Sartre, J.-P. (1992) *Notebook for an Ethics* (trans. D. Pellauer). Chicago, IL: University of Chicago Press (First published 1983).
Sartre, J.-P. (2000) *Nausea* (trans. R. Baldick). London: Penguin (First published 1938).
Sartre, J.-P. (2002) *The Roads to Freedom (The Age of Reason, The Reprieve, Iron in the Soul)* (trans. E. Sutton and G. Hopkins). London: Penguin (First published 1945–49).
Sartre, J.-P. (2003) *Being and Nothingness: An Essay in Phenomenological Ontology* (trans. H.E. Barnes). London: Routledge (First published 1946).
Sartre, J.-P. (2004) *Critique of Dialectical Reason,* vol. 2 (trans. A. Sheridan-Smith). London: Verso.
Sartre, J.-P. (2013) *We Have Only This Life to Life: Selected Essays of Jean-Paul Sartre 1939–1975* (ed. R. Aronson and A. van den Hoven) New York: New York Review of Books.
Schaie, K.W. (1993) Ageist Language in Psychological Research. *American Psychologist*, 48: 49–51.
Scalzo, C. (2010) *Therapy with Children: An Existential Perspective*. London: Karnac.
Schacht, R. (1994) *Nietzsche*. London: Routledge.
Schaler, J.A. (1999) *Addiction is a Choice*. Chicago, IL: Open Court.
Scheler, M. (1915) *Ressentiment*. Milwaukee, WI: Marquette University Press.
Schopenhauer, A. (2004) *The Essays of Schopenhauer: Counsels and Maxims* (trans. T. Saunders). Dumfries and Galloway: Anodos (First published 1896).
Sears, E. (1986) *The Ages of Man: Medieval Interpretations of the Life Cycle*. Princeton, NJ: Princeton University Press.
Sharr, A. (2006) *Heidegger's Hut*. London. MIT Press.

Sheehy, G. (1976) *Passages*. New York: Bantam.
Silverman, H.J. (1979) Biographical Situations, Cognitive Structures and Human Development: Confronting Sartre and Piaget. *Journal of Phenomenological Psychology* 10.2: 119–137.
Simms, E.M. (2008) *The Child in the World: Embodiment, Time, and Language in Early Childhood*. Detroit, MI: Wayne State University Press.
Singer, J. (2004) Narrative Identity and Meaning Making Across the Adult Lifespan: An Introduction. *Journal of Personality*, 72.3: 437–459.
Slaughter, V. and Griffiths, M. (2007) Death Understanding and Fear of Death in Young Children. *Clinical Child Psychology and Psychiatry*, 12: 525–535.
Sophocles (1947) *The Theban Plays* (trans. E.F. Watling). London: Penguin.
Smith, J., Flowers, P. and Larkin M. (2009) *Interpretative Phenomenological Analysis: Theory, Practice and Method*. London: Sage.
Speece, M.W. and Brent, S.B. (1992) The Acquisition of a Mature Understanding of three Components of the Concept of Death. *Death Studies*, 16: 211–229.
Stadlen, N. (2004) *What Mothers Do Especially When It Looks Like Nothing*. London: Piatkus Books.
Stadlen, N. (2011) *How Mothers Love, and How Relationships are Born*. London: Piatkus.
Steffen, E. (2007) Death and Mid Life: Why an Understanding of Life-Span Development is Essential for the Practice of Counselling Psychology. *Counselling Psychology Review*, 22.3: 21–26.
Stern, D. and Bruschweiler-Stern, N. (1998) *The Birth of a Mother. How the Motherhood Experience Changes You Forever*. London: Basic Books.
Stewart, J. (ed.) (1998) *The Debate between Sartre and Merleau-Ponty*. Evanston, IL: Northwestern University Press.
Stoller, S. (2000) Reflections on Feminist Merleau-Ponty Skepticism. *Hypatia,* 15: 1.
Stoller, S. (ed.) (2014) *Simone de Beauvoir's Philosophy of Age: Gender, Ethics, and Time*. Berlin: de Gruyter.
Stolorow, R. (2007) *Trauma and Human Existence: Autobiographical, Psychoanalytic and Philosophical Reflections*. London: The Analytic Press.
Stolorow, R. (2011) *World, Affectivity and Trauma*. London: The Analytic Press.
Strasser, F. and Strasser, A. (1997) *Existential Time-Limited Therapy*. Chichester: Wiley.
Sugarman, L. (2001) *Life-Span Development: Frameworks, Accounts and Strategies*. Hove: The Psychology Press.
Sugarman, L. (2012) *Counselling and the Life Course*. London: Sage.
Sullivan, S. (1997) Domination and Dialogue in Merleau-Ponty's Phenomenology of Perception. *Hypatia,* 12: 1.
Tallis, R. (2011) *Aping Mankind – Neuromania, Darwinitis and the Misrepresentation of Humanity*. Durham: Acumen.
Thane, P. (ed.) (2005) *The Long History of Old Age*. London: Thames and Hudson.
Thompson, M.G. (2004) Nietzsche and Psychoanalysis. *Existential Analysis,* 15: 203–217.
Tidd, U. (2004) *Simone de Beauvoir*. London: Routledge.
Tougas, K. and Shandel, T. (1989) *Did You Used to be R.D. Laing?* Vancouver: Third Mind Productions.

Tubali, S. (2018) *Hannah Arendt and the Human Duty to Think.* https://philosophynow.org/issues/125/Hannah_Arendt_and_the_Human_Duty_to_Think, Accessed 09/04/2018.
van den Berg, J. H. (1961) *The Changing Nature of Man: Introduction to a Historical Psychology.* New York: W.W. Norton.
Verliefde, E. and Stapert, M. (2008) *Focusing with Children: The Art of Communicating with Children at School and at Home.* Ross-on-Wye: PCCS.
Vogel, L. (1994) *The Fragile 'We': Ethical Implications of Heidegger's Being and Time.* Evanston, IL: MIT.
Warnock, M. (1970) *Existentialism.* Oxford: Oxford University Press.
Weinstein, A. (2003) *A Scream Goes Through the House: What Literature Teaches Us About Life.* New York: Random House.
Weinstein, A. (2011) *Morning, Noon, and Night: Finding the Meaning of Life's Stages Through Books.* London: Random House.
Weiss, G. (2002) The Anonymous Intentions of Transactional Bodies. *Hypatia,* 17: 4.
Welsh, T. (2013) *The Child as Natural Phenomenologist: Primal and Primary Experience in Merleau-Ponty's Psychology.* Evanston, IL: Northwestern University Press.
Whiteside, K.H. (2014) *Merleau-Ponty and the Foundation of Existential Politics.* Princeton, NJ: Princeton University Press.
Whitmire, J.F. (2006) The Double Writing of Les Mots: Sartre's Words as Performative Philosophy. *Sartre Studies International,* 12.2: 61–82.
Winnicott, D.W. (1991) *Playing and Reality.* London: Routledge.
Wong, P.T. (2000) Meaning of Life and Meaning of Death in Successful Aging. In A. Tomer (ed.) *Death Attitudes and the Older Adult: Theories Concepts and Applications.* Hove: Routledge.
Woolfe, R. and Biggs, S. (1997) Counselling Older Adults: Issues and Awareness. *Counselling Psychology Quarterly,* 10.2: 189–194.
Wordsworth, W. (1994) *The Collected Poems of William Wordsworth.* Ware: Wordsworth Editions (First published 1807).
Yalom, I. (1980) *Existential Psychotherapy.* New York: Basic Books.
Yalom, I. (1974) *Every Day Gets A Little Closer: A Twice-Told Therapy.* New York: Basic Books.
Yalom, I. (1992) *When Nietzsche Wept.* London: Harper.
Yalom, I. (2008) *Staring at the Sun.* London: Piatkus.
Yalom, I. (2015) *Creatures of a Day.* London: Piatkus.
Yates, P. (2011) The Three Metamorphoses and Philosophy. In J. Luchte (ed.) *Nietzsche's Thus Spoke Zarathustra: Before Sunrise* London: Continuum.
Young, I. (1985) Pregnant Subjectivity and the Limits of Existential Phenomenology. In D. Ihde and H.J. Silverman (eds) *Descriptions.* New York: SUNY Press.
Young, I. (2005) *On Female Body Experience: 'Throwing Like a Girl' and Other Essays.* Oxford: Oxford University Press.
Young, J. (2002) *Heidegger's Later Philosophy.* Cambridge: Cambridge University Press.

Index

Druck:
Canon Deutschland Business Services GmbH
im Auftrag der KNV-Gruppe
Ferdinand-Jühlke-Str. 7
99095 Erfurt